IMAGES of America

OSSINING REMEMBERED

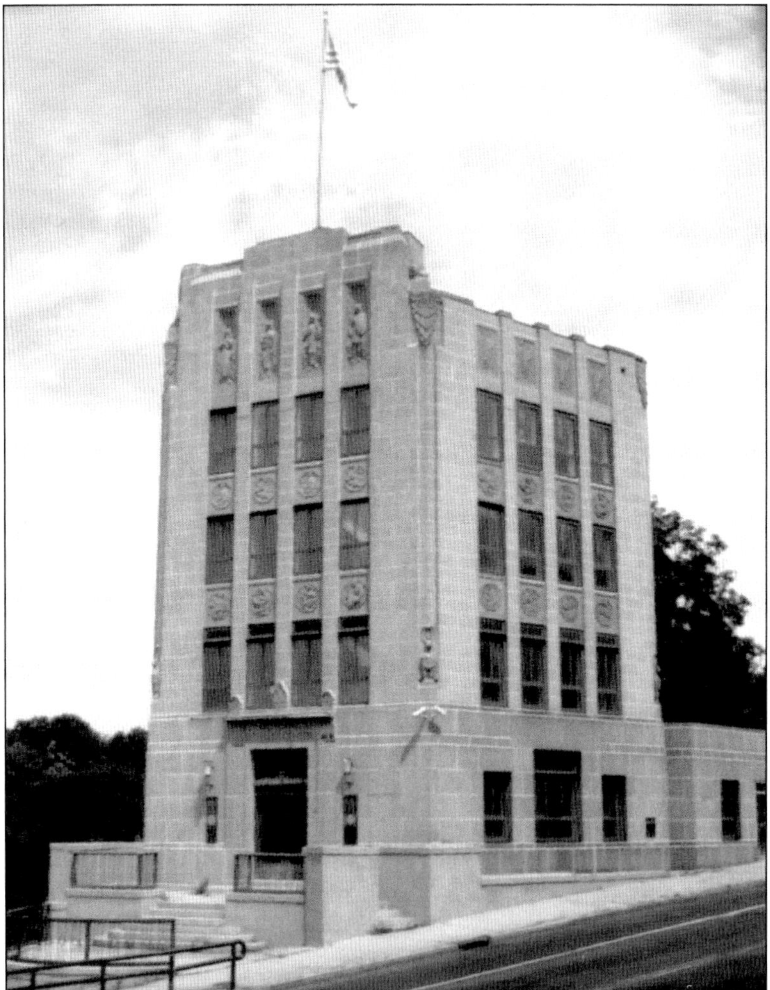

This reprint of *Ossining Remembered* has been made possible by the generosity of the Emigrant Bank, located at 13 Croton Avenue.

IMAGES
of America

OSSINING REMEMBERED

The Ossining Historical Society

ARCADIA
PUBLISHING

ISBN 978-0-7385-4948-4

Published by Arcadia Publishing
Charleston, South Carolina

Printed in the United States of America

Library of Congress Catalog Card Number: 2006933262

For all general information contact Arcadia Publishing at:
Telephone 843-853-2070
Fax 843-853-0044
E-mail sales@arcadiapublishing.com
For customer service and orders:
Toll-Free 1-888-313-2665

Visit us on the Internet at www.arcadiapublishing.com

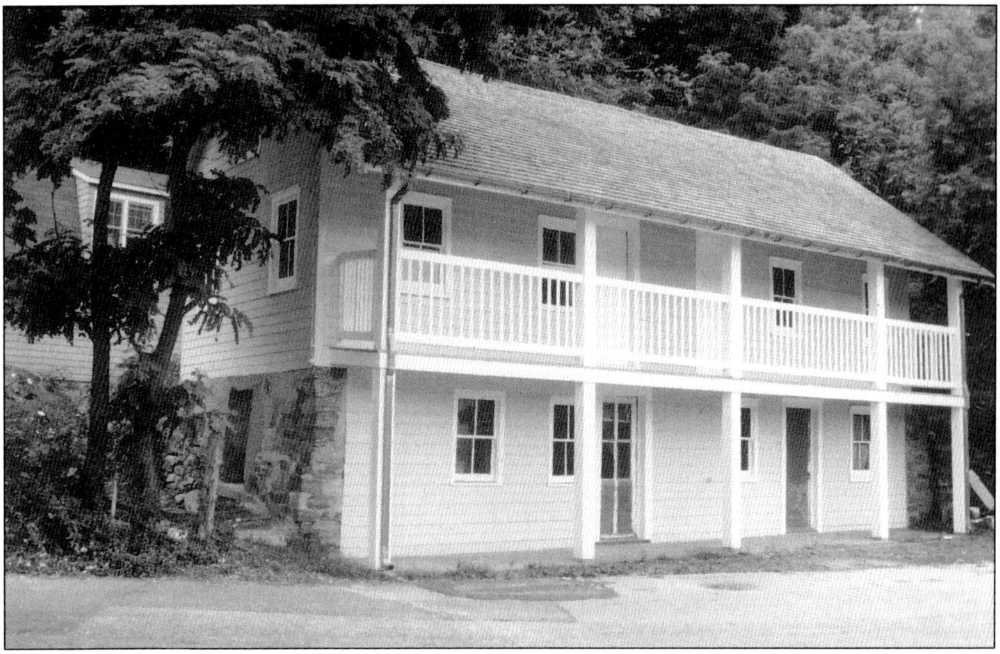

Standing at the gateway to Sparta, where Rockledge Avenue intersects Revolutionary Road (once a part of the historic Albany Post Road), is the Jug Tavern, probably constructed about 1760. To protect Sparta against change in the future, the neighborhood was designated as a Historical Architectural Review District by the local government. The Ossining Restoration Committee acquired the property in 1970 and has fully restored the structure.

Contents

Acknowledgments

This was truly a unique and memorable experience that centered on the Ossining community, which each of us cares so deeply about. The energy, sensitivity, time, and effort that was given by Jerry Campbell, Cathy Crisfield, Jack Hoye, Eileen O'Connor, and Deborah Van Steen was totally incredible. Each of these remarkable people is owed enormous thanks for bringing this view of Ossining to life as we enter the 21st century. This compilation of photographs and thoughts represents Ossining as we knew it until 1950. The sole exception to going beyond that time is the inclusion of photographs from the extensive archives of the Ossining Historical Society Museum to illustrate the result of urban renewal. Those images of present day downtown were taken by George Potanovic Jr. A special affection for their supreme support and direction goes to Robert Globerman and Roberta Arminio, who is the director of our museum.

— Carl Oechsner

INTRODUCTION

Just before the new millennium, a small handful of friends got together to reminisce about "the good old days." A couple of us were teenagers in the 1940s, and a few were teenagers in the 1950s. In view of the extreme changes in the town over the past few decades (after the effects of urban renewal but before the focus on historic preservation), the ensuing discussions revolved around the group's special memories of the town as we knew it. Meeting week after week, month after month, at each other's homes, we pored over old photographs with the goal of producing a collection of photographs and captions that would present a general picture of Ossining over the past century.

However, something happened that made the endeavor more than a clinical collection of data. We recalled our halcyon days of Americana as we knew them in Ossining. We realized that we are likely to be the last generation available to portray our town as it was in the middle of the 20th century, as some of the following photographs illustrate. We realized that if we did not share our pictures and memories, they were not likely to survive. Countless meetings and untold hours of remembering and reliving brought us great joy, which we present here now.

One

BROADWAY AND 42ND STREET

The intersection of Main Street at Spring Street was practically one word: Mainandspring. Main Street began at the railroad tracks of the New York Central, just inland from the waterfront of the Hudson. For three blocks, it wound uphill, lined with houses but no businesses. For a block afterward, "lower Main Street," packed with stores, stretched to Main and Spring Streets (the busiest spot in town) where, at some point, you met everyone you knew. A policeman who you knew stood at the intersection directing traffic, the bus stopped at Ankerson's corner, and people criss-crossed from corner to corner all day long. As Main Street continued upward for another very long block, the sidewalks were always crowded with Ossiningites shopping in the somewhat limited area. There were, after all, no more than four blocks of this activity, three blocks of Main Street and little more than one block on Spring Street. But store after store lined these streets, and rarely was one ever unoccupied.

A person could go to the store for a single item and take two hours to get home because everyone you knew was somewhere on the sidewalk, and it was a social affair to meet these friends. In the warm weather, awnings were rolled out over storefronts, and merchants sat outside in those days before air conditioning. As you passed each store, you shared greetings with the owners because everyone knew each other over many generations.

The Victoria Theater, almost at the top of the hill before the Albany Post Road, was another Mecca where everyone's paths crossed. Even from Croton, the next town to the north, people came to the Victoria. Every movie eventually had a showing there, since the fare changed two and three times a week. Every weeknight, the double feature began at seven. On weekends, shows were continuous all day, and (of course) the Saturday matinee included the current cliff-hanging serial.

With grocery stores, clothing stores, candy stores, drug stores, and jewelry stores, it was rare that what you wanted was not in one of the town's stores. Sometimes you took the train in to Manhattan, but for the most part, all shopping was done on Main and Spring Streets (before the days of supermarkets and malls). Narrow storefronts were similar in width, usually with a display window on each side of a center entrance, and the interiors ran very deep. Hardwood floors often creaked. Two levels of apartments were usually above the stores, and their names were painted on wood or metal signs (Who knew what plastic was?).

Clothiers and shoe stores supplied outfits as people grew from child to adult since merchants and customers lived their whole lives in Ossining.

The varsity boys from Ossining High could be seen in their maroon cardigans with the white stripes on the sleeve, designating their years on the team. Pretty cheerleaders wore their short maroon skirts with the white lining. Everybody sported saddle shoes or white bucks.

It was the war years, when women wore lipstick, rouge, and knee-length dresses, and blouses with padded shoulders were in style. Hair was worn in a pompadour, and no one used eye makeup or hair spray. Men wore fedoras, while women wore hats with veils. It was rare that someone in high school had a car because you walked to most places, and when you did not, you usually took a bus.

Main Street was Times Square, and the thoroughfare was peopled by the entire town. The *Citizen Register*, the local daily paper, had a regular feature known as "Town Talk," which kept you up to date on who was going where on vacation, who was having a birthday party (and who attended), and who was in the hospital on Spring Street.

Although the town had a few restaurants, people did not eat out the way they do today. Soda fountains did okay, though. Cherry Cokes at Kipp's were a nickel, hot dogs were a dime, and everyone enjoyed hot chocolate at Ankerson's. Food was not frozen, and whipped cream was real. Main and Spring Streets each had a pool hall, and there was a bowling alley farther down Spring Street (over the Grand Union). There was even a roller skating rink at one time. Beyond these things, entertainment was self-made.

Everyone rooted for the high school's football team, known as the Indians. The recreation center, near the movies, was a popular spot for the non-school sponsored games and meeting friends. Abelon, the one music store in town, sold 78s for 52 ¢ (there was no tax back then) in a tan paper sleeve. The records were sold as singles with RCA Victor, Columbia, Decca, Bluebird, and Capitol labels. You played them so many times, the black turned gray, and the sound became scratchy (Who knew it could get better? Who even knew the word television? Not even Martin Block on the *Make Believe Ballroom*.). But those songs of the war years are memorable still. As busy as our "Times Square" was, the saying in those days went, "They rolled up the sidewalks early."

Today, most of Spring Street and a good deal of Main Street are no more. If a friend of our youth who had moved away were to return now, not having seen the town in a couple of decades, he or she would be dumbstruck, for our old Ossining is gone with the wind.

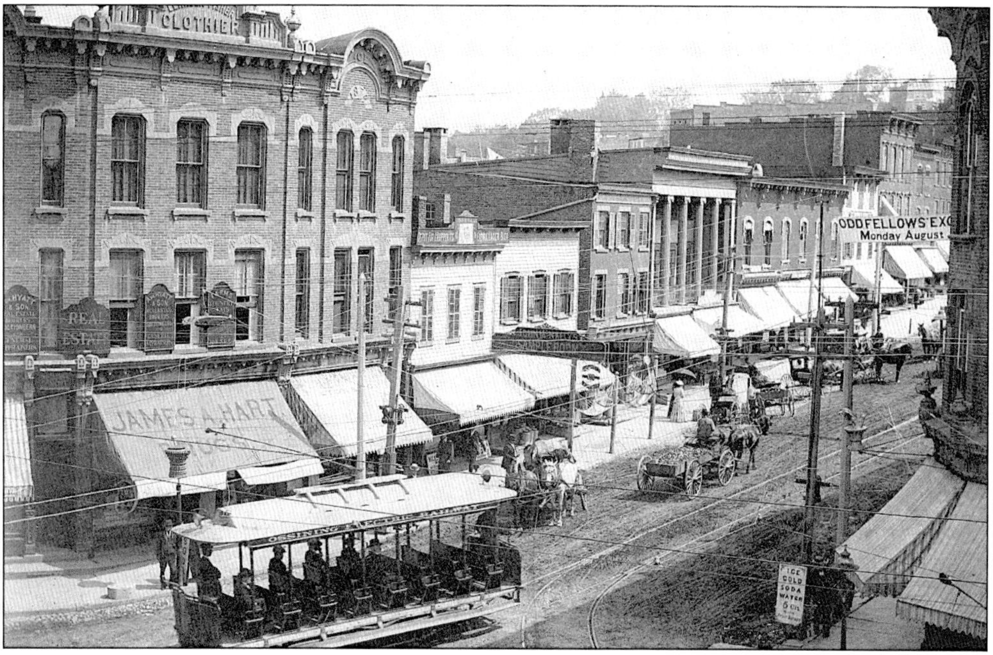

The Crescent, a long curving block on Main Street, is seen here in 1905. A series of fires around 1870 caused major rebuilding from wood to brownstone with elaborate cornices of sheet metal and prominent brackets. Pediments contained the year of construction and building name. Trolleys began running in 1893, and shopping was concentrated downtown. The area developed in the 1800s to serve travelers on the Albany Post Road (now Route 9), and farmers delivered produce to the Sing Sing docks.

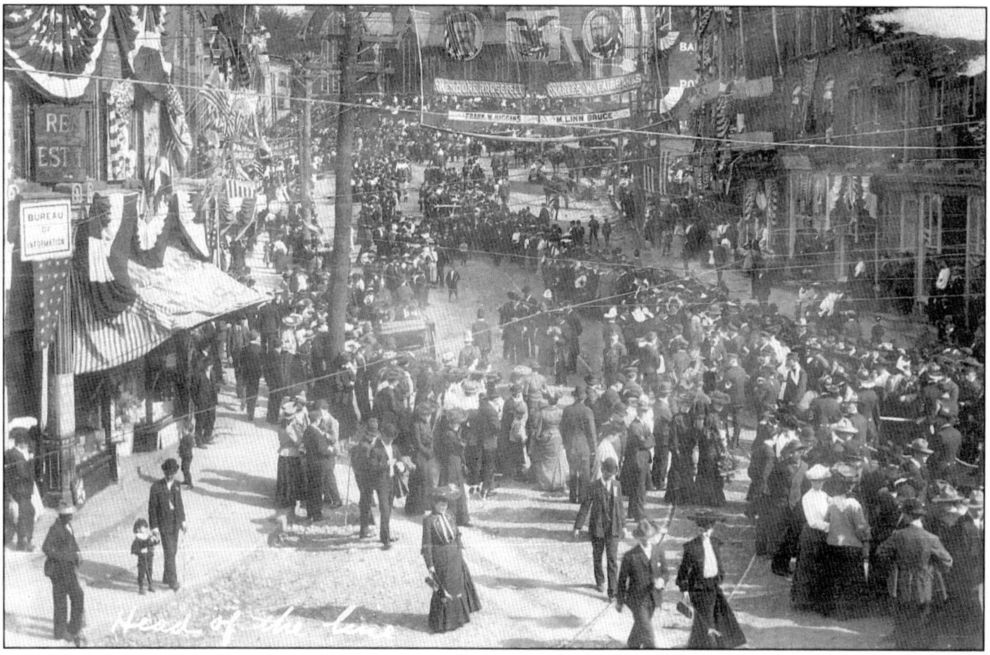

In 1904, President Theodore Roosevelt was running for re-election, and a political rally and parade brought local citizens to Main Street.

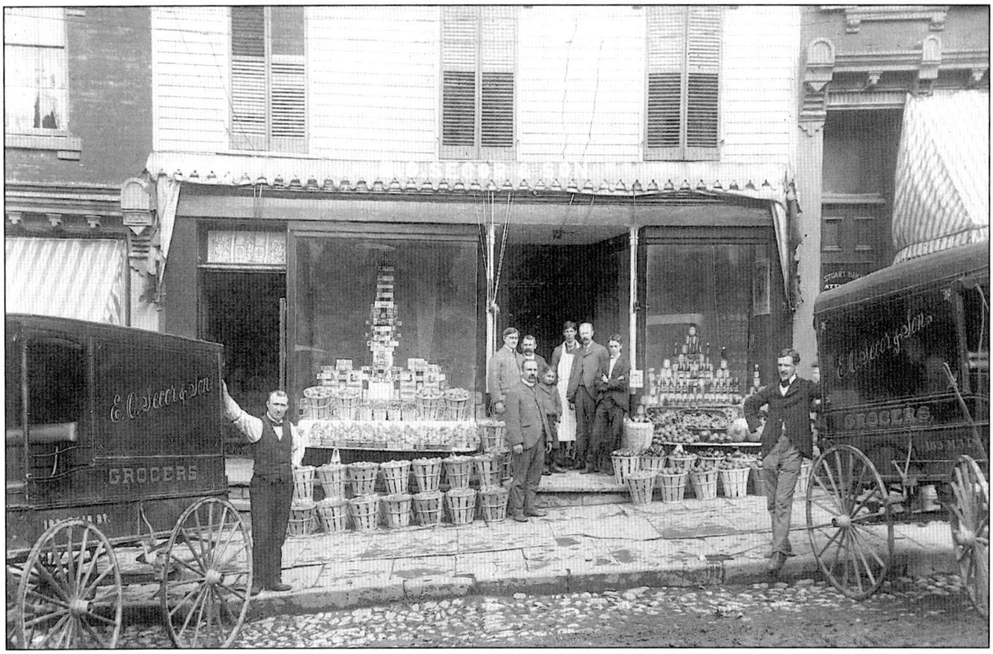

Leonard Secor operated this store at 163 Main Street (seen here about 1900). The store featured wagon delivery service, fancy and staple groceries and provisions, as well as imported and domestic delicacies. Mr. Secor was known as "a most agreeable man with hosts of friends who like him for his geniality and integrity of character."

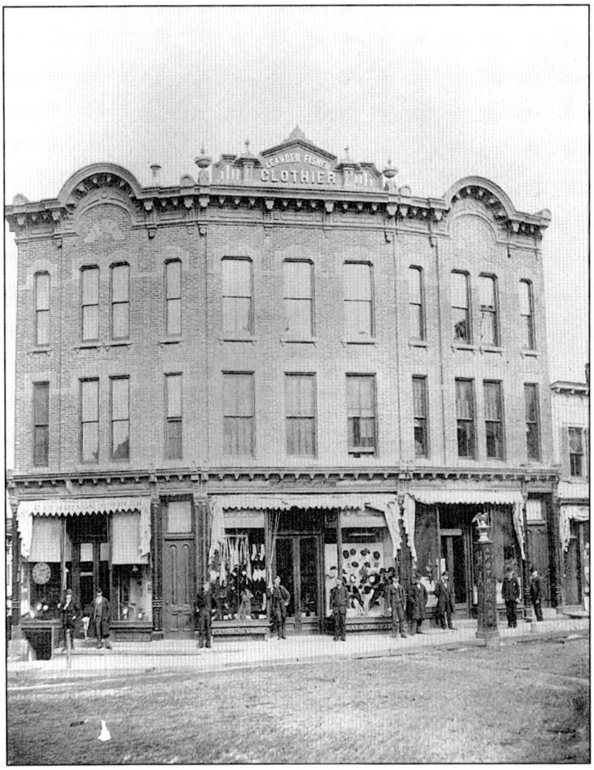

Constructed in 1874 as a multi-use structure, this unique brownstone, at 141–145 Main Street, housed a number of owners in the early 1900s. One owner was Leander Fisher (clothier), and another was James A. Hart (druggist). Tenants upstairs included a dentist, a real estate agency, an insurance agency, and an attorney.

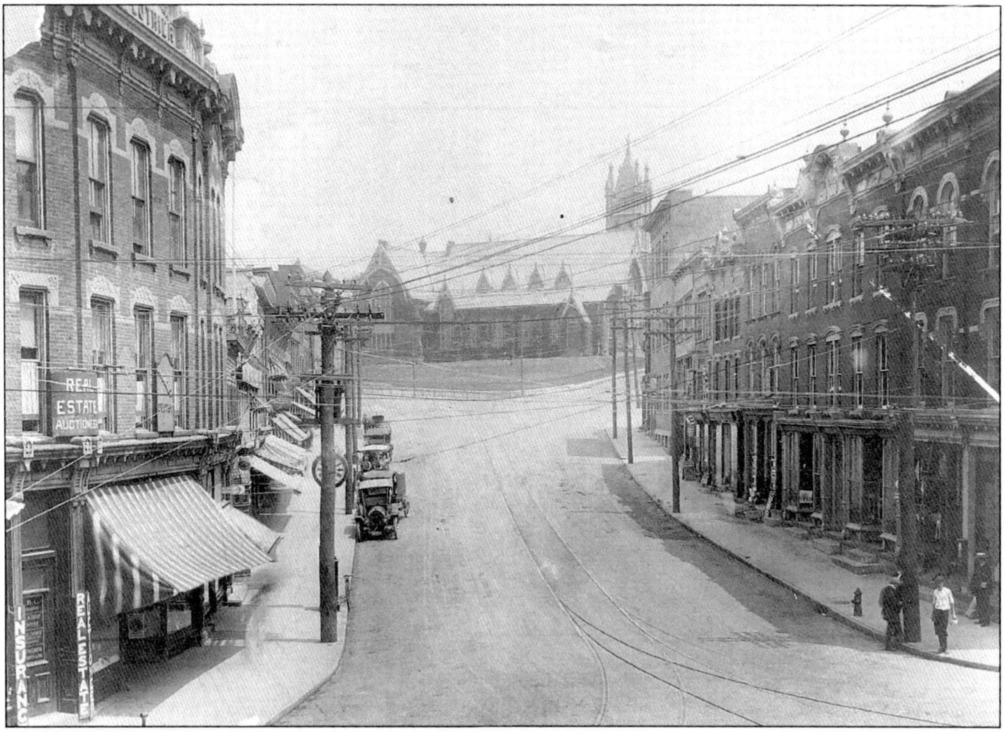

Shown here is a quiet Sunday in 1913 in Ossining. The First Baptist Church is standing in the distance with the Crescent to the left. Trolley tracks are coming down to the corner of Spring Street as telephone lines criss-cross the thoroughfare.

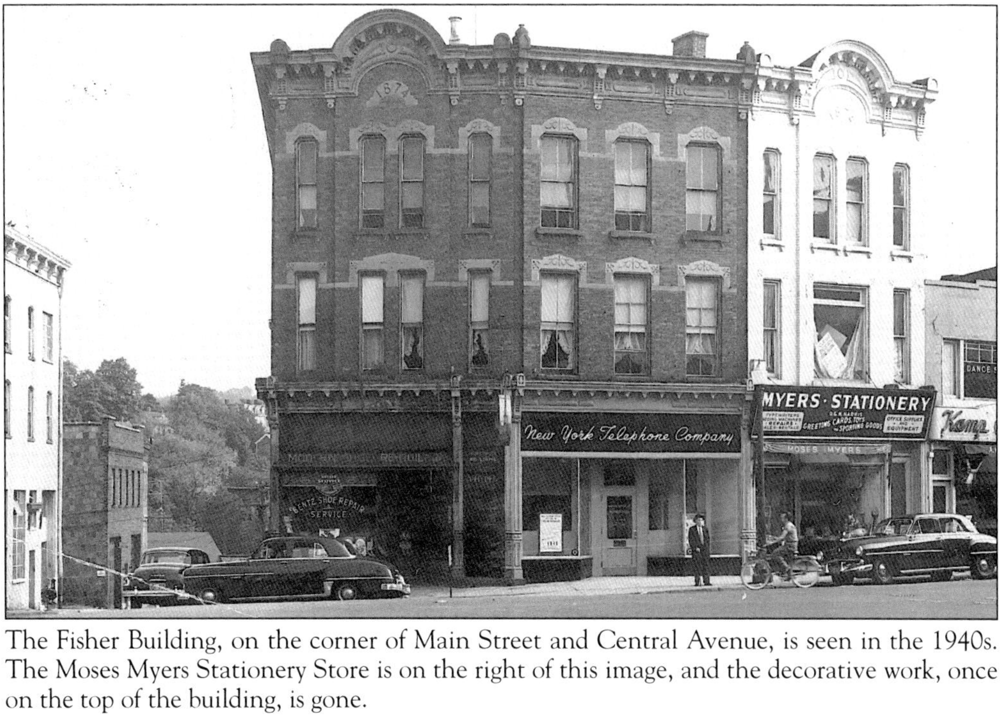

The Fisher Building, on the corner of Main Street and Central Avenue, is seen in the 1940s. The Moses Myers Stationery Store is on the right of this image, and the decorative work, once on the top of the building, is gone.

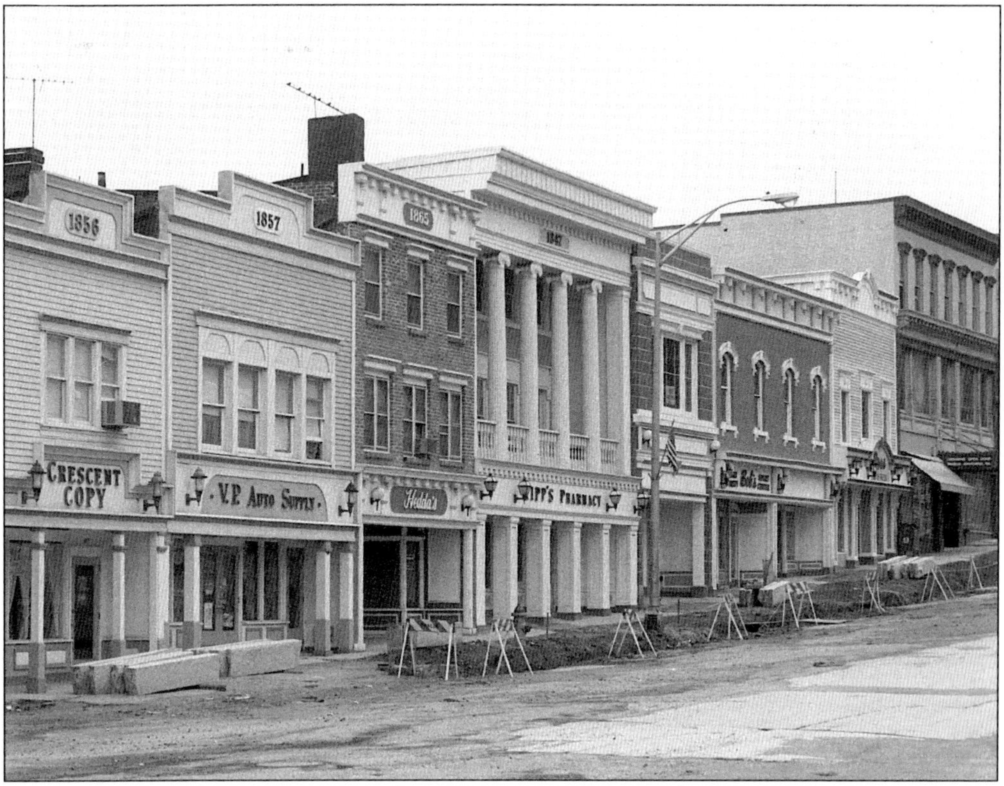

The north side of Main Street, east of Spring Street, is shown here as it appeared during urban renewal in the 1970s. The oldest structure on the street, dated 1847, is Kipp's Pharmacy, featuring its prominent Classical-Doric colonnade.

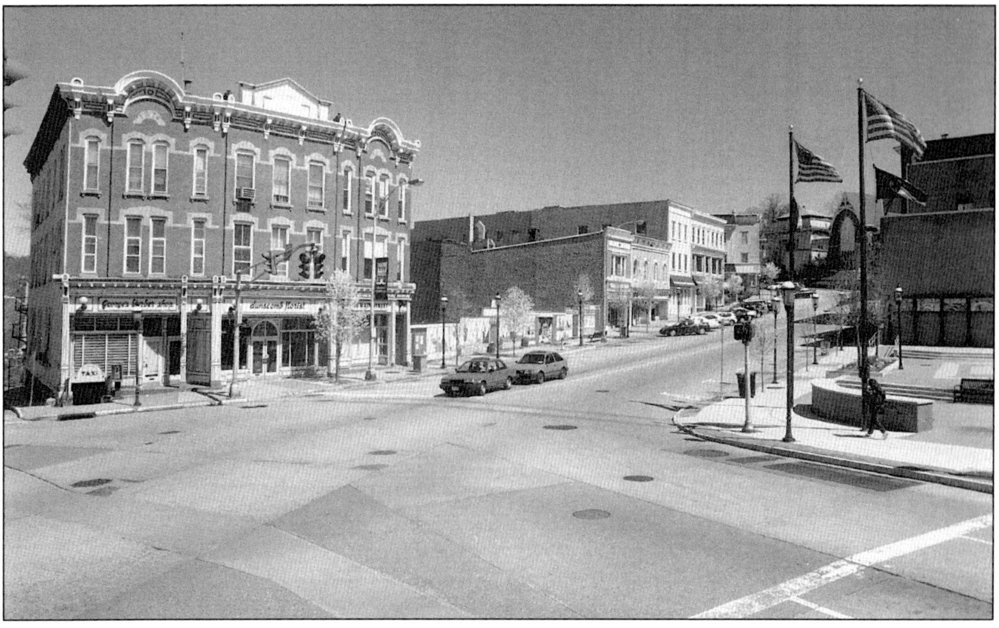

This image of Main and Spring Streets was taken in 1999.

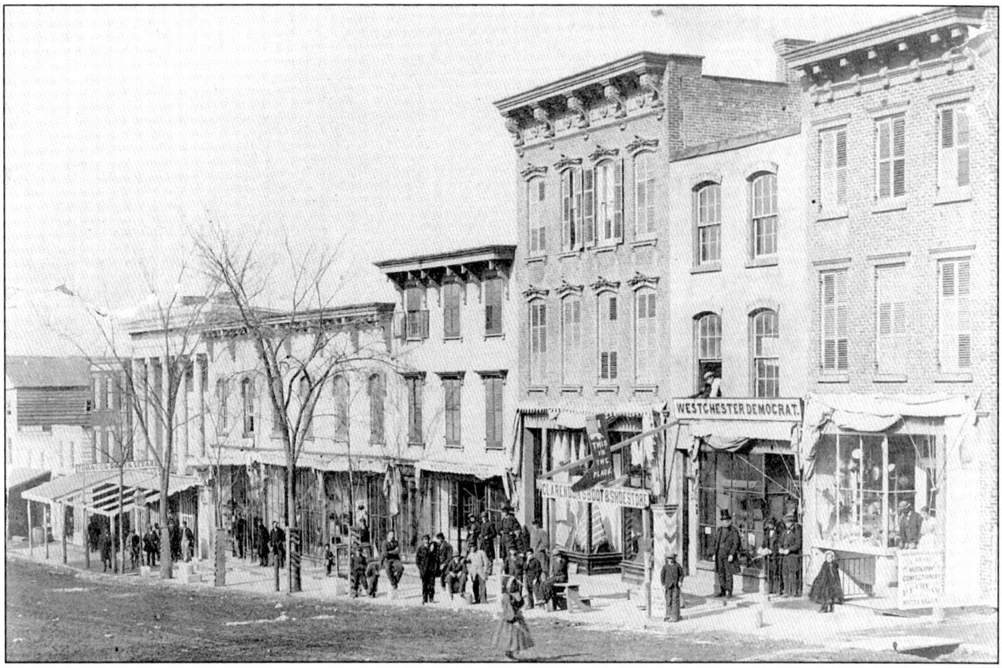

Main Street is shown here in 1856, looking west towards Spring Street. Retailers seen here include the *Westchester Democrat* newspaper; Oyster Saloon Restaurant; Clarendon's Boot & Shoe Store; and Tobacco, Snuff & Segars.

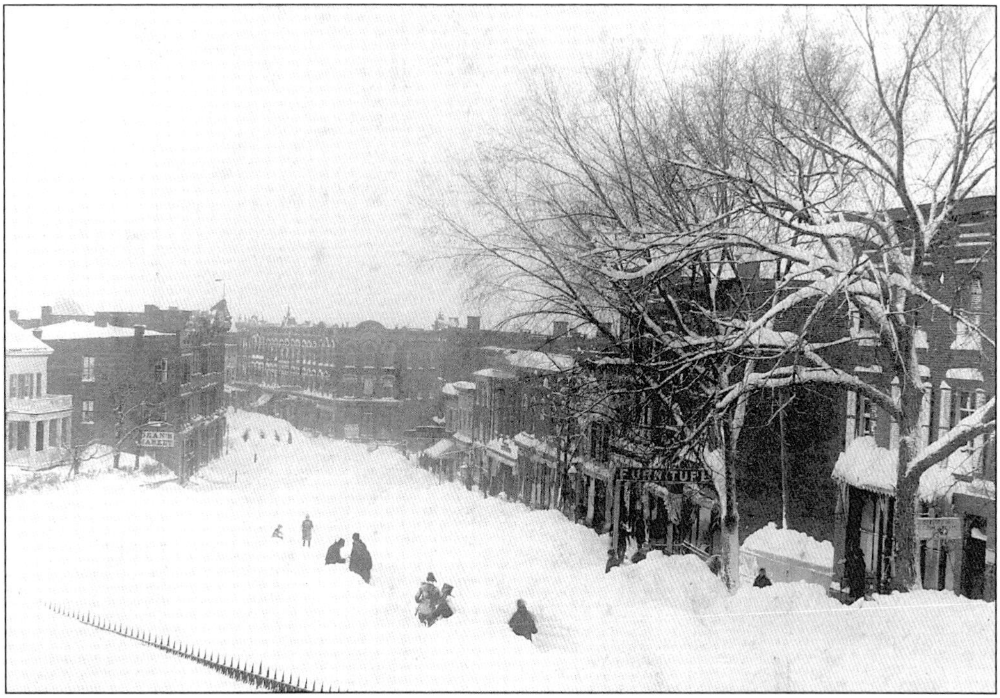

This image looks down Main Street from the First Baptist Church on March 12, 1888. The blizzard, which blew in from the Midwest, isolated Sing Sing with snowdrifts up to 20 feet high. Business downtown was suspended for days.

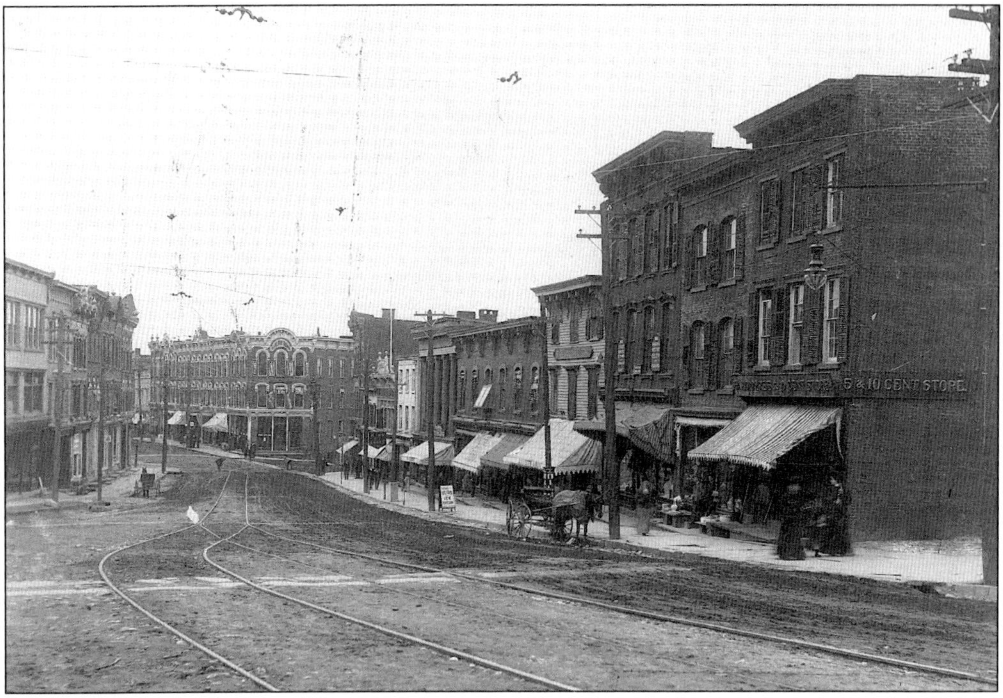

Main Street is seen here in the 1890s. Awnings afforded shade for shoppers. Stores located on Main Street at this time included Frederick Hopper's 5 & 10 Cent Store, Griffin & Hilliker Bee Hive Department Store, and E.O. Secor and Son Grocers. Professional offices were located on most of the upper levels. The Barlow Block, in the distance, housed the local post office.

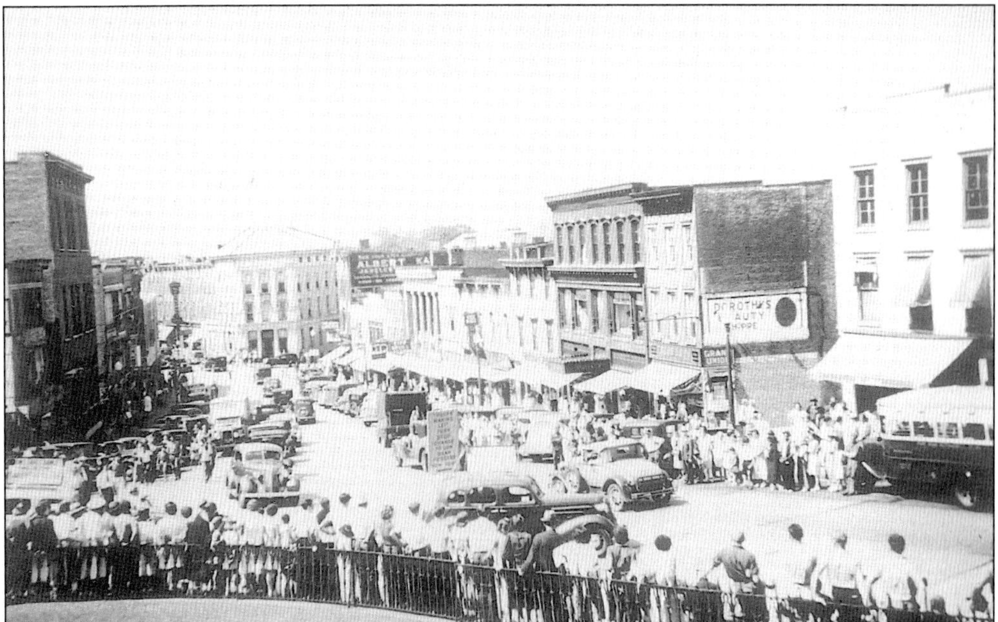

The community gathered for a parade on Main Street in the 1940s. Retailers on the right included the Grand Union, Hilliker's Department Store, Albert Kamp Jewelers, and Dorothy's Beauty Shoppe.

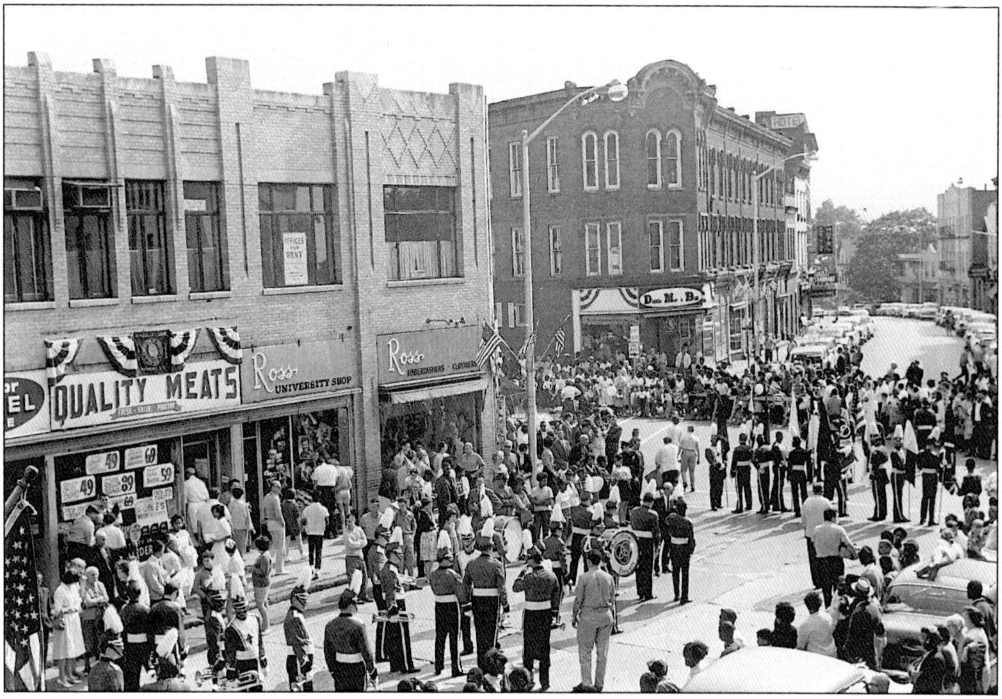

Another celebration is shown here gathering on the corner of Main and Spring Streets around 1953. The Starling Building is shown to the left, along with the Quality Meat Market (featuring fresh-killed poultry) and Marvin Ross Haberdashers. Located across the street, on lower Main Street, was Diddie Mae & Bills Clothing as well as the Ossining Hotel.

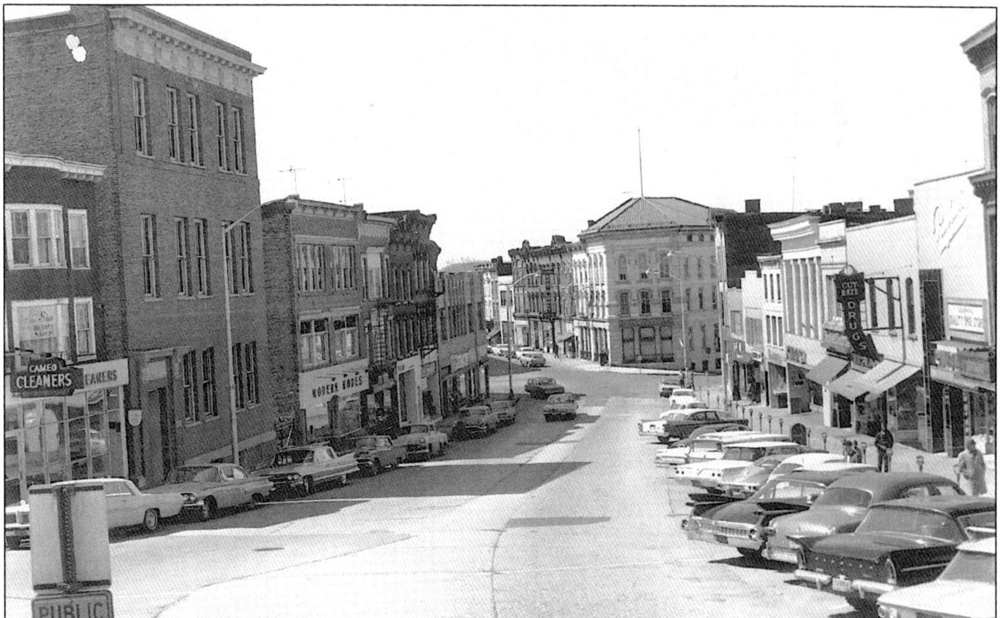

Downtown was still active in this 1963 view. To the right of this image are Raybin's Bootery, Cut Rate Drugs, and Kipp's Pharmacy, while to the left, Cameo Cleaners, New York Telephone Company, Modern Modes, and the Pilat Florist can be seen.

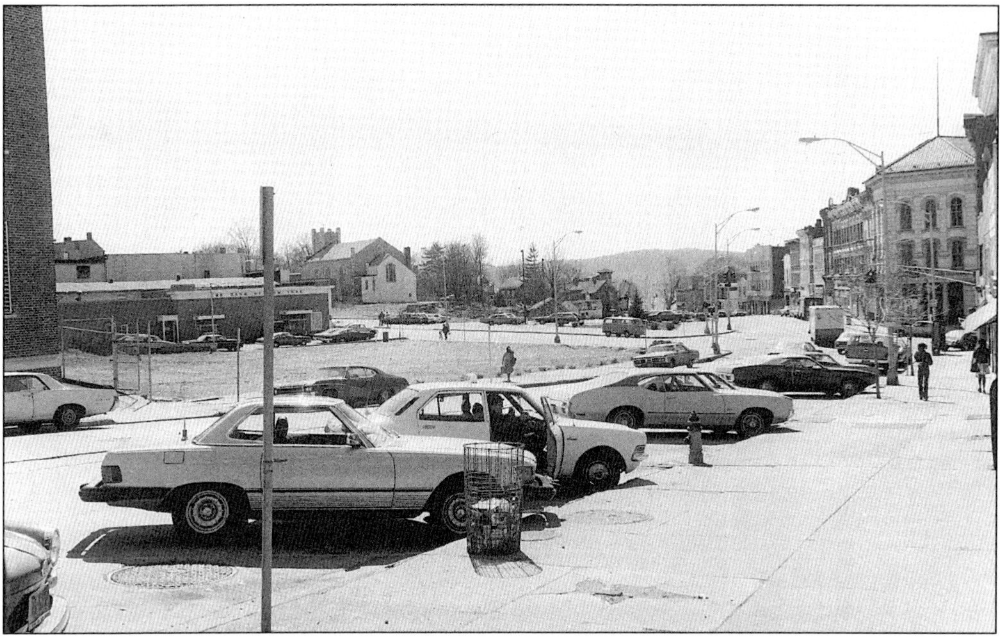

Urban renewal had claimed numerous Italianate brownstones from the 19th century. Many of the Victorian structures and closely spaced stores, which were easily accessible to one another on foot, were sacrificed due to the development of vehicular transportation. Gas stations and shopping strips with ample parking, like the Arcadian on South Highland Avenue, began to spring up on undeveloped land outside the village center. This photograph was taken in 1977.

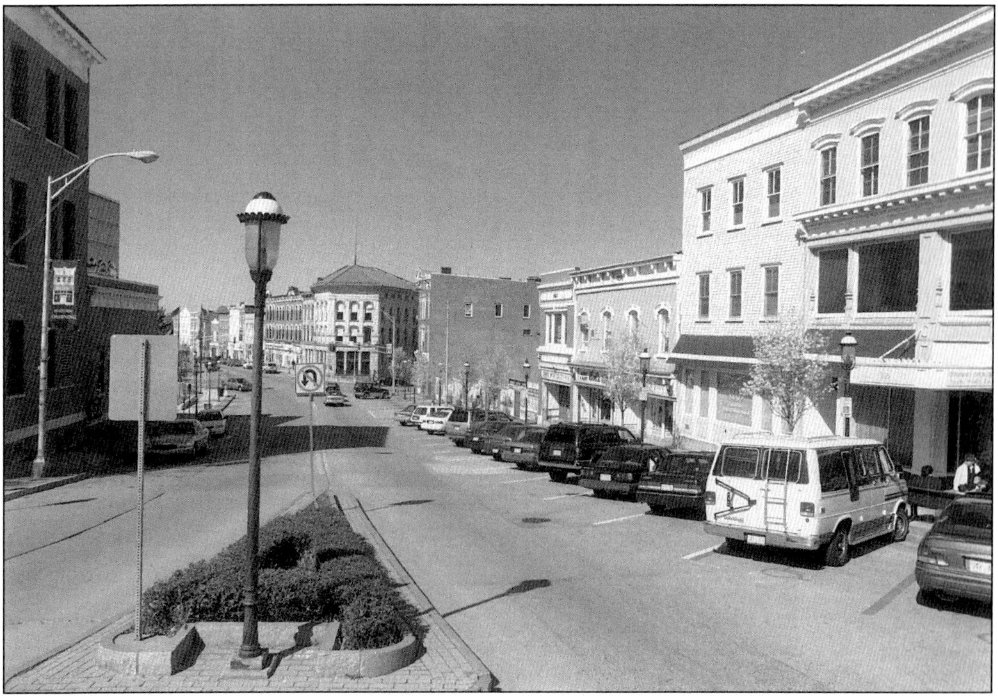

This photograph presents a view from the First Baptist Church looking down Main Street to Spring Street in 1999.

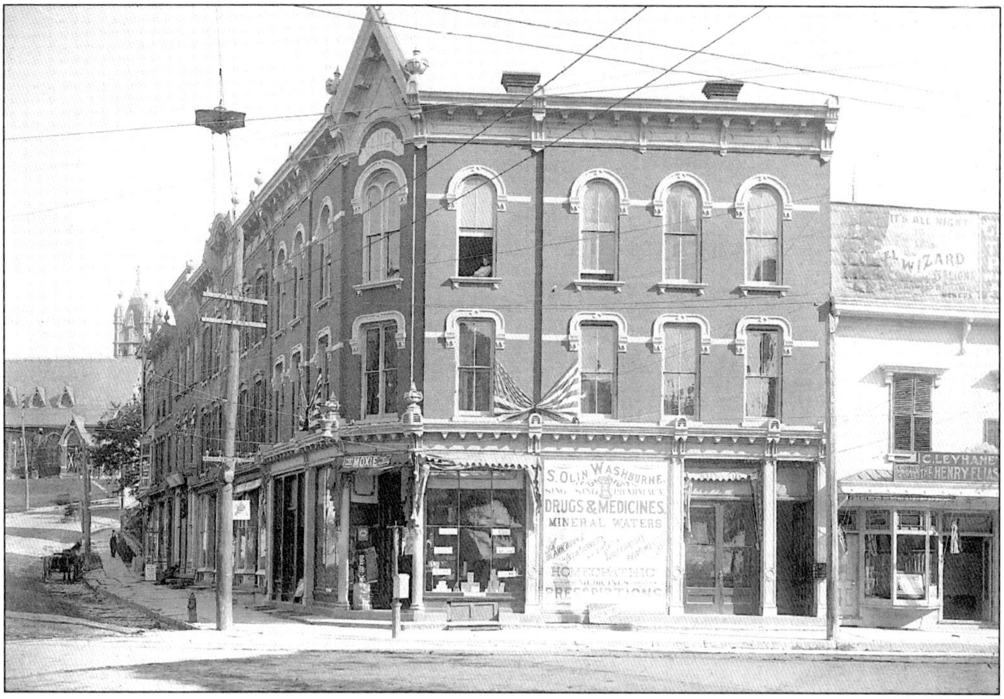

The southeast corner of Main and Spring Streets is shown here in the 1890s. The Vance Building contained the S. Olin Washburne's Sing Sing Pharmacy downstairs and offices above. It was a brick edifice with attention given to architectural detail. C. Leyhane's Liquor & Cigar Store can be seen next door, while the First Baptist Church is in the distance.

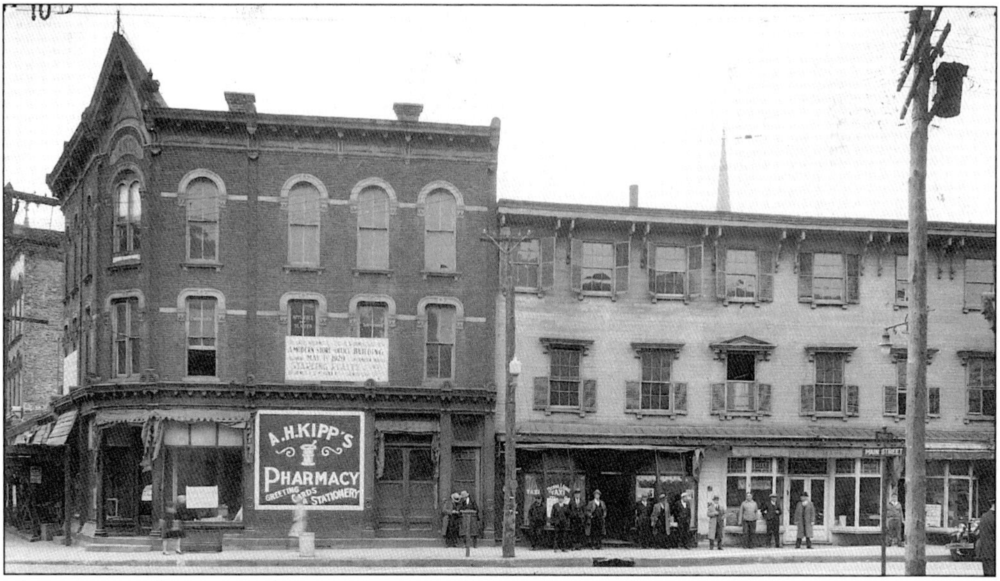

The corner of Main and Spring Streets is seen here in 1929. A.H. Kipp's Pharmacy was located on the corner, while a taxi service and meat market followed down Spring Street. The spire of the First Presbyterian Church is seen in the background. The sign on the Vance Building announced, "Starling Realty Company a Modern store-office building to open on May 1st 1929."

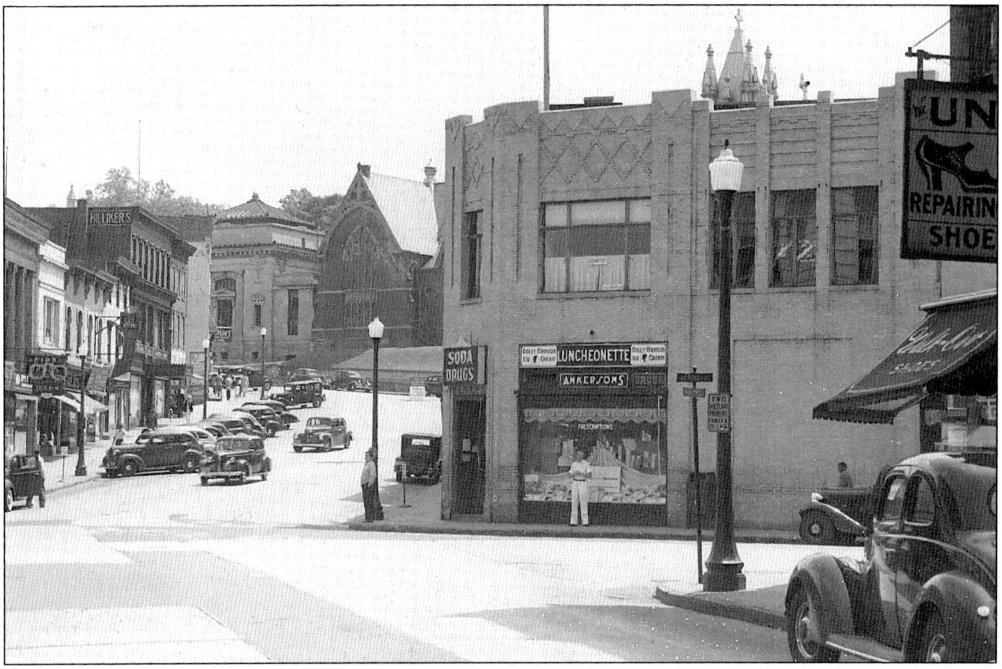

The new Starling Building, a fine example of the art deco style, occupies the corner of Main and Spring Streets in 1940. Ankerson's Soda Drug Store Luncheonette, which featured Dolly Madison Ice Cream, had moved in at this time. To the left of the image, on Main Street, Falk's Clothing, Kipps Drugs, and Hilliker's Department Store can all be seen.

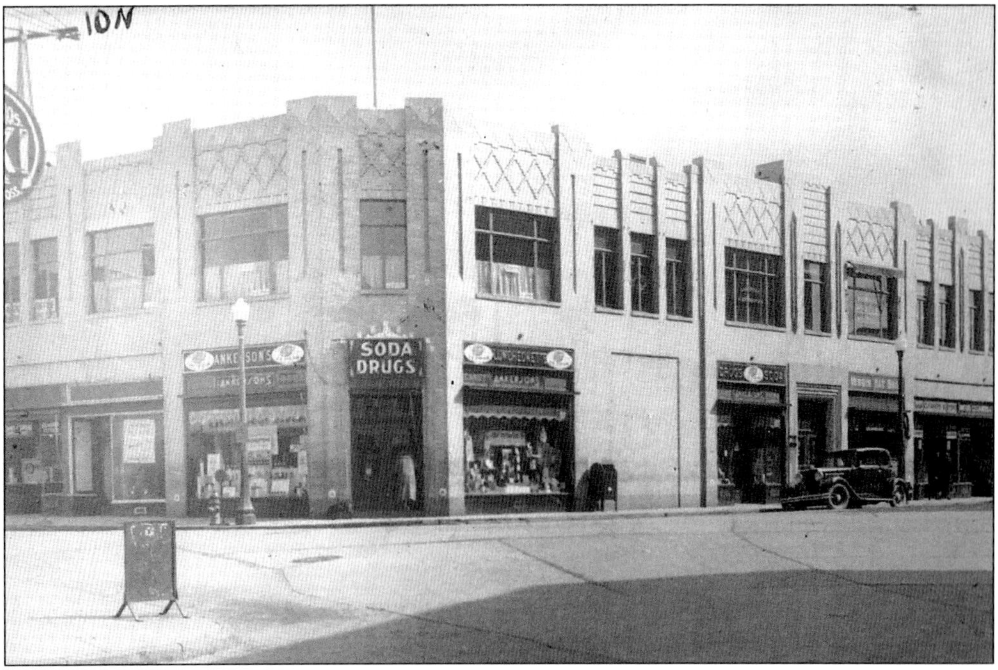

In the 1940s, the Starling Building emphasized art deco motifs including chevron moldings; stepped edges; and flat, intersecting, curved designs. The verticality of the facade gave it an elegant touch.

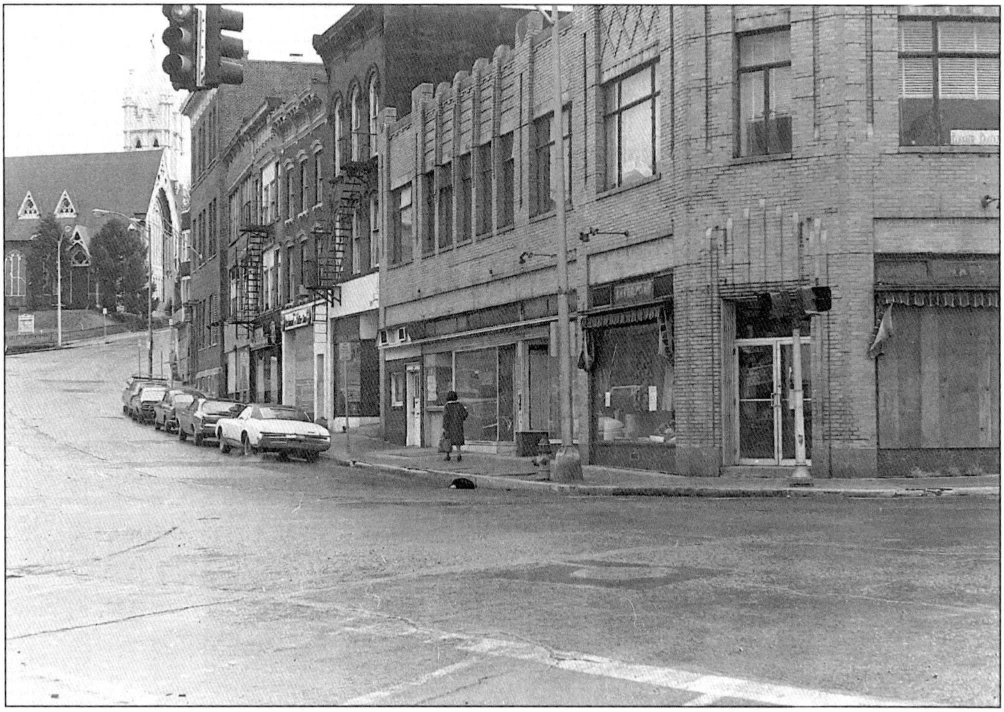

The corner of Main and Spring Streets is shown here about 1970.

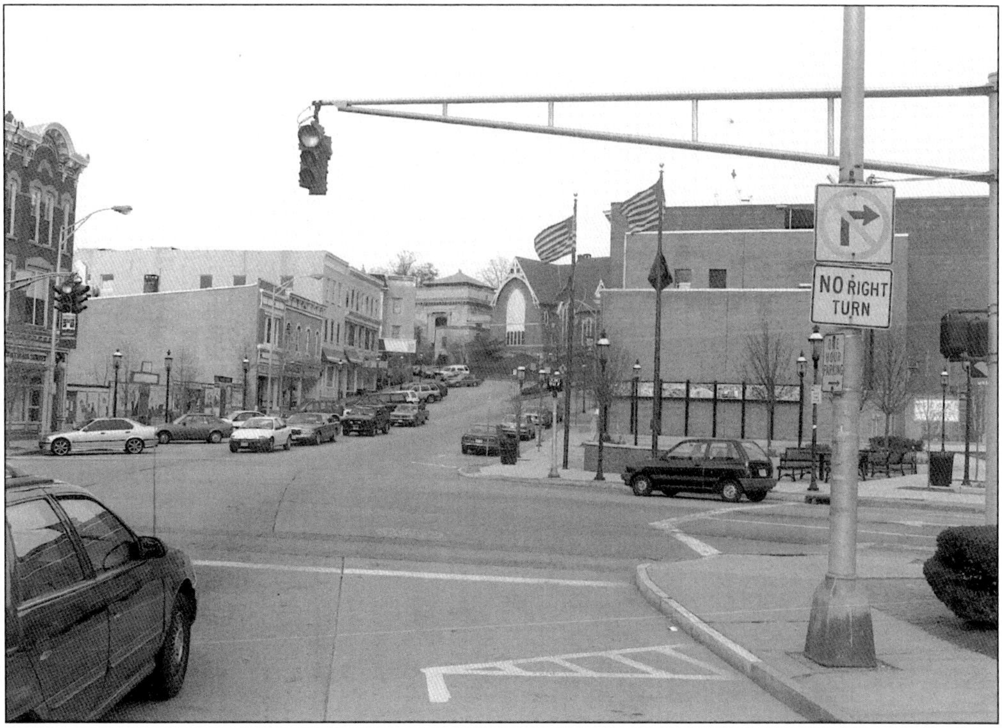

The same view is shown again in 1999. Spring Street is shown to the right of the image with the Crescent to the left.

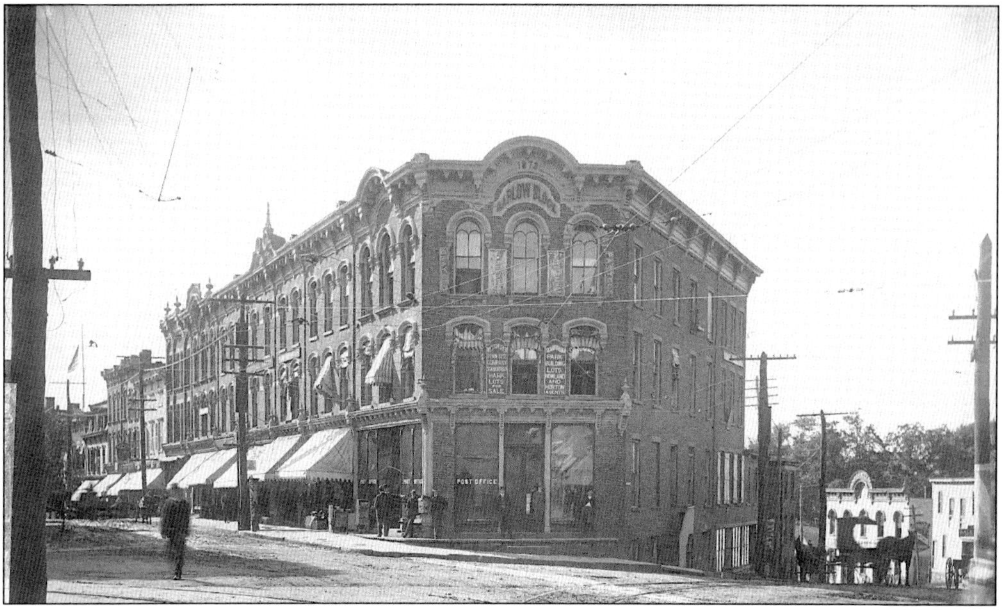

The Barlow Block, on the north side of Main Street at the junction of Central Avenue, was built in 1873 after a fire leveled the earlier wooden structures. It was done in the High Victorian Italianate style. The post office was located here for many years. To the left of the post office was the Central Hotel, and on the second floor, signs advertised the following: "Westchester Town Site Company—Scarborough Park Building Lots."

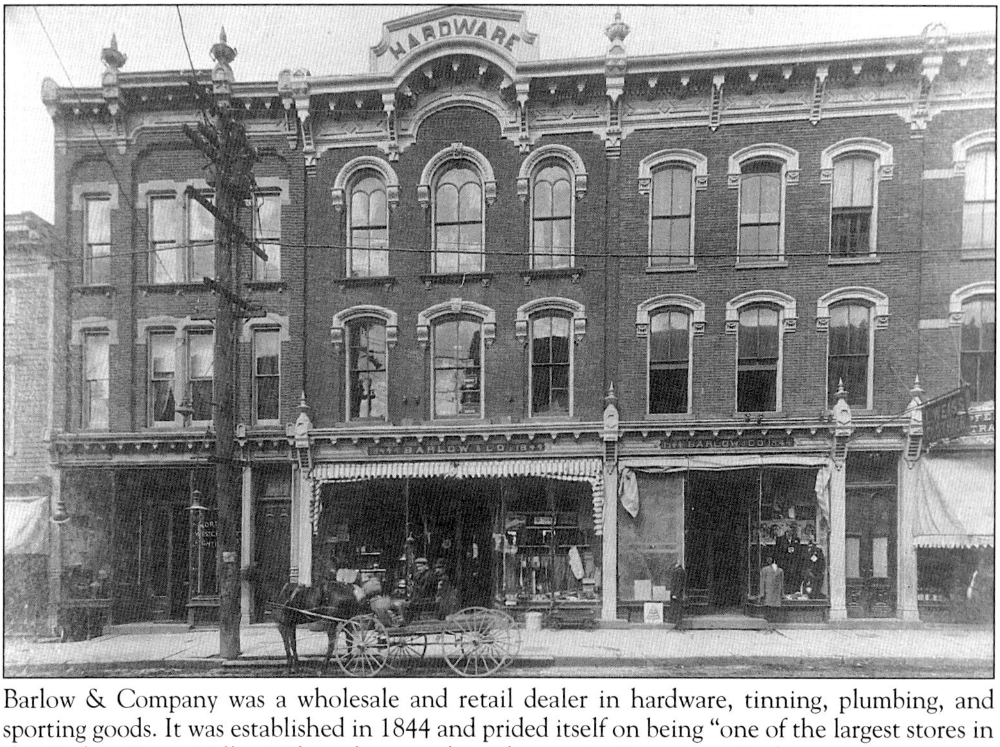

Barlow & Company was a wholesale and retail dealer in hardware, tinning, plumbing, and sporting goods. It was established in 1844 and prided itself on being "one of the largest stores in the Hudson River Valley." They also ran a branch store in Croton-on-Hudson.

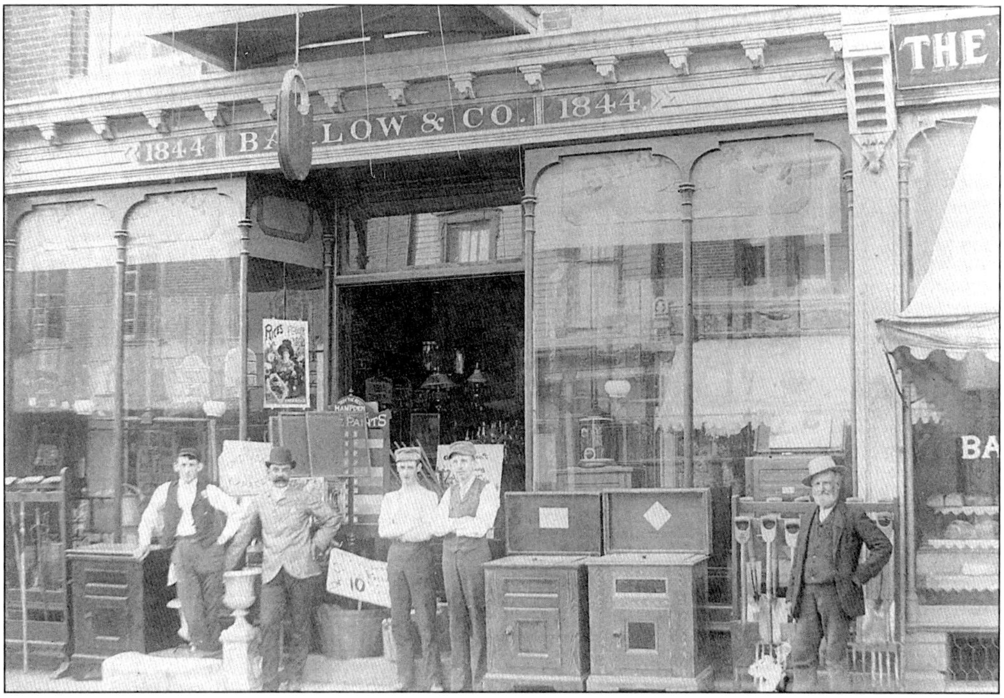

Owner George Barlow and employees are shown in front of their store in the 1890s. Advertisements around the entrance included American Express, Hampden House Paints, and Rice's Flower Seeds. A bakery was located next door.

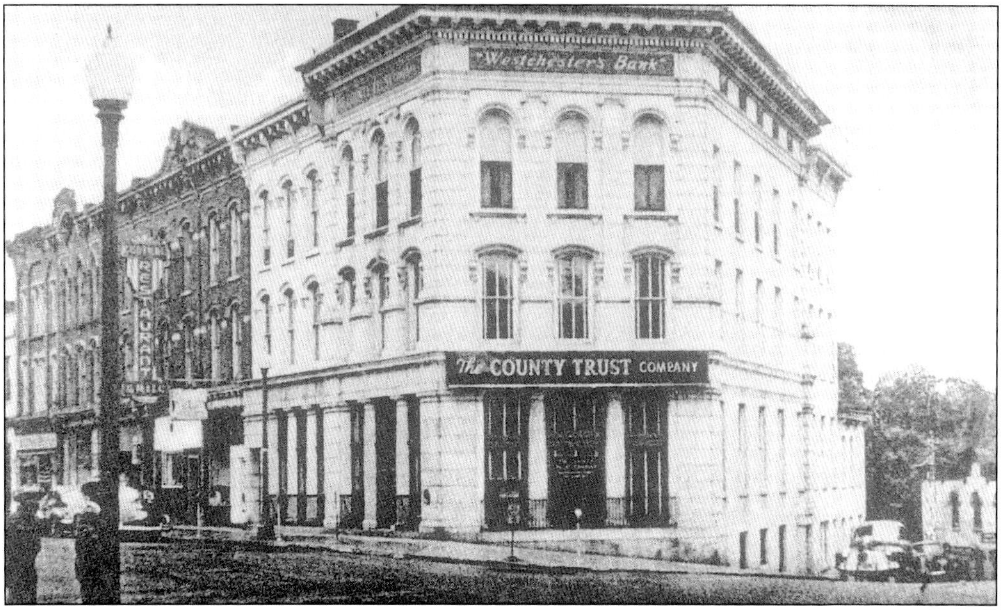

When the Ossining Post Office moved further up Main Street in 1906, part of the Barlow Block became the Ossining National Bank. The architectural design of the facade was patterned after the famous library of St. Mark in Venice, Italy. The first story was pink granite in the Doric order. The second and third stories were creamy white terra cotta in the Ionic order with a steep pitched Spanish tile roof. In 1945, the County Trust Company moved into the same building.

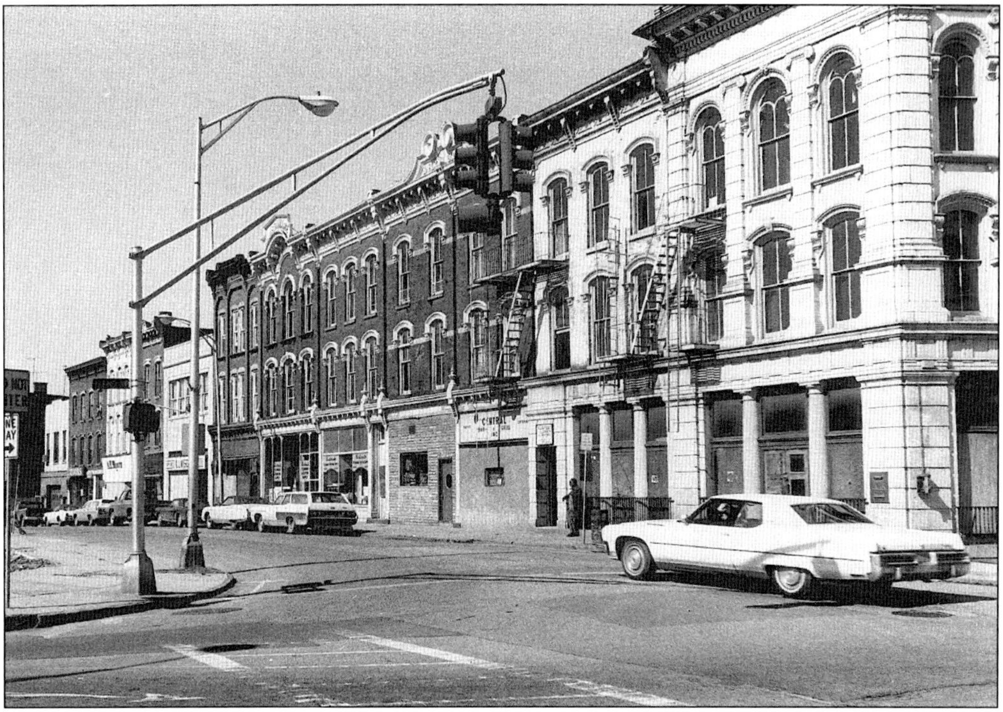

The Barlow Block on lower Main Street is shown here in 1975.

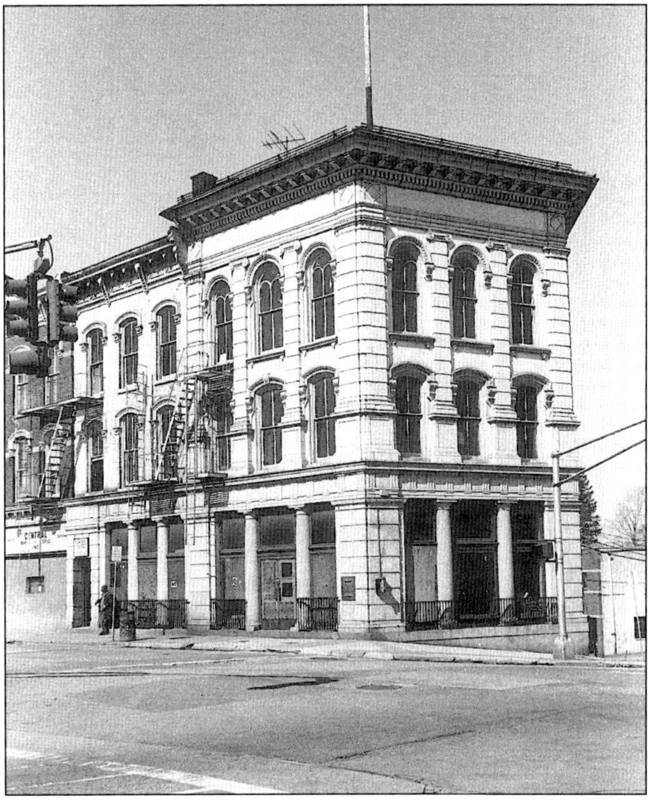

This close-up of the former County Trust Company Bank Building, in the Barlow Block, was taken in 1975.

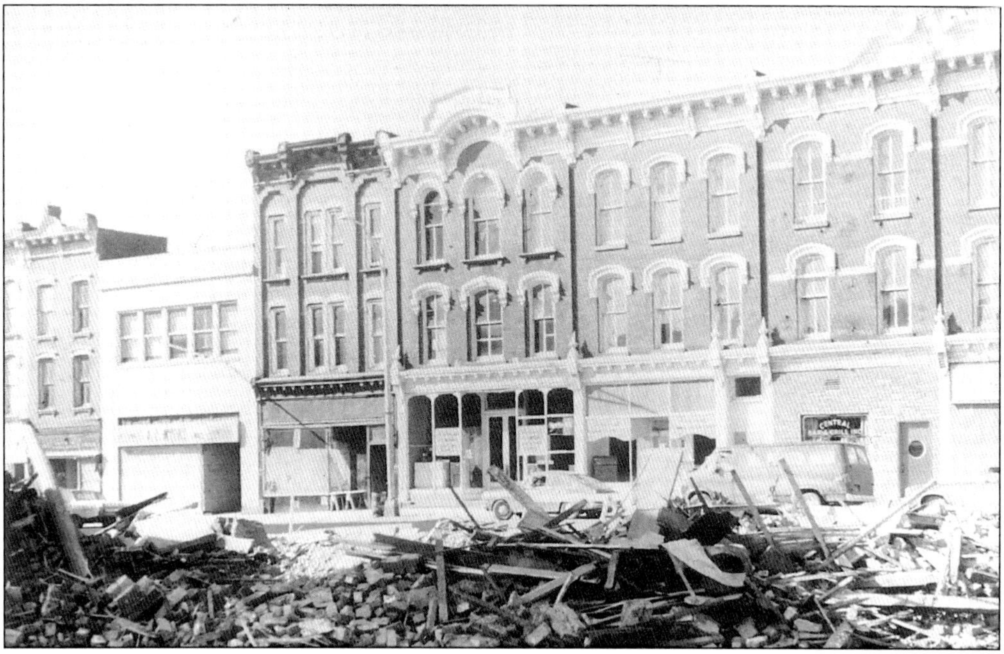

The Barlow Block is shown here after the east side of lower Main Street had been demolished in the 1970s.

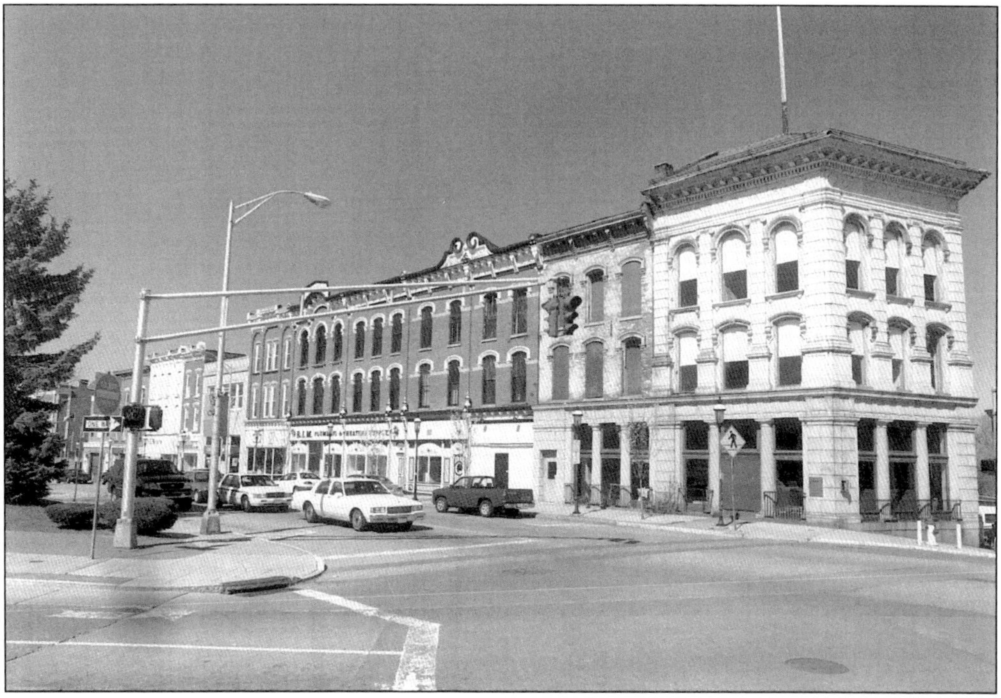

This photograph depicts the Barlow Block as it looks in 1999. Spring Street is to the left of the image, Main Street is in the center, and Central Avenue can be seen to the extreme right.

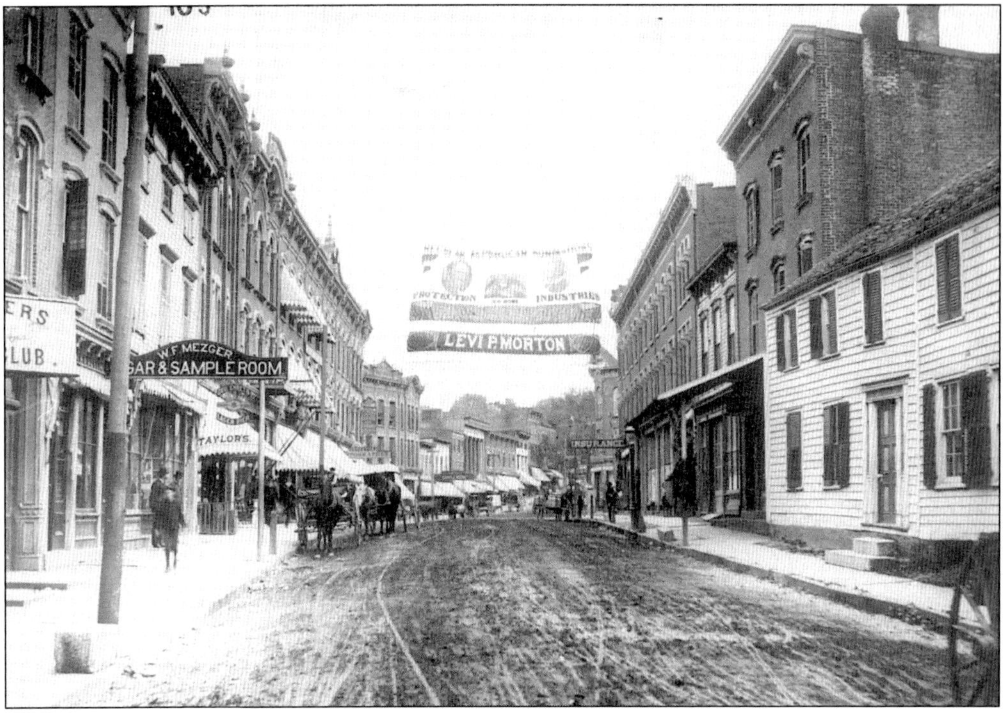

Main Street is represented in this image west of Spring Street looking east in 1888. The Barlow Block is to the left of the photograph, while wooden houses are to the right. Business signs displayed in the image include ones for W.F. Mesger Cigars & Sample Room, George Ehret's Lager Beer, an insurance office, and Vanderbilt Photographer. A political campaign banner hangs over the street with the names of Benjamin Harrison of Indiana and Levi P. Morton of New York, both of whom were Republicans elected to the White House in 1888.

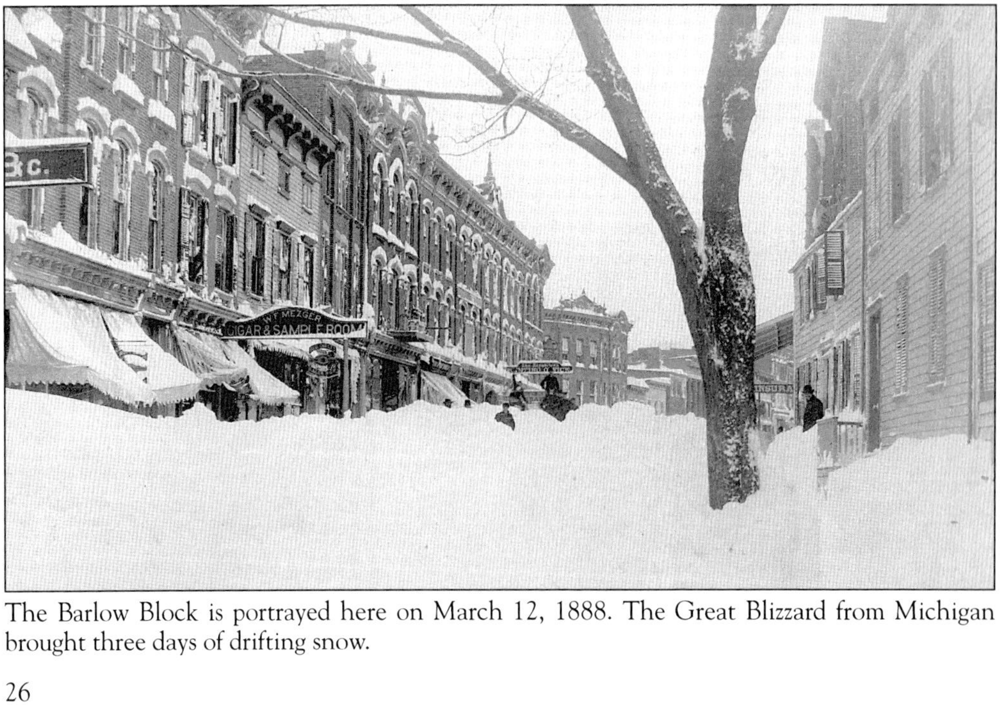

The Barlow Block is portrayed here on March 12, 1888. The Great Blizzard from Michigan brought three days of drifting snow.

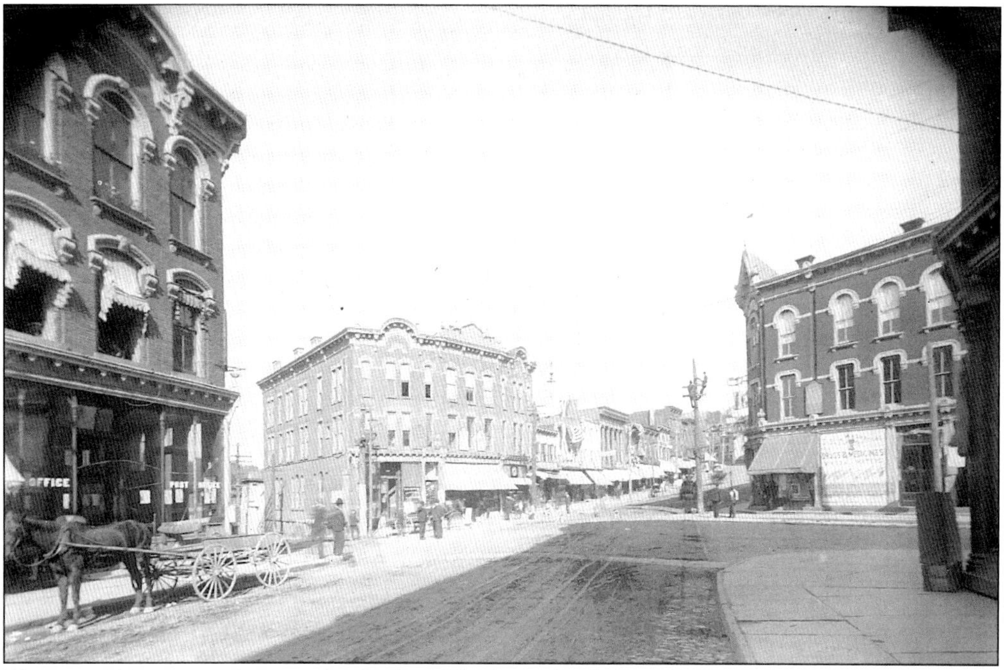

This *c.* 1890s image depicts the Barlow Block to the left and Foshay Building to the right. Across the square, to the left, is the Leander Fisher-Hart Building, while to the right is the Vance Building.

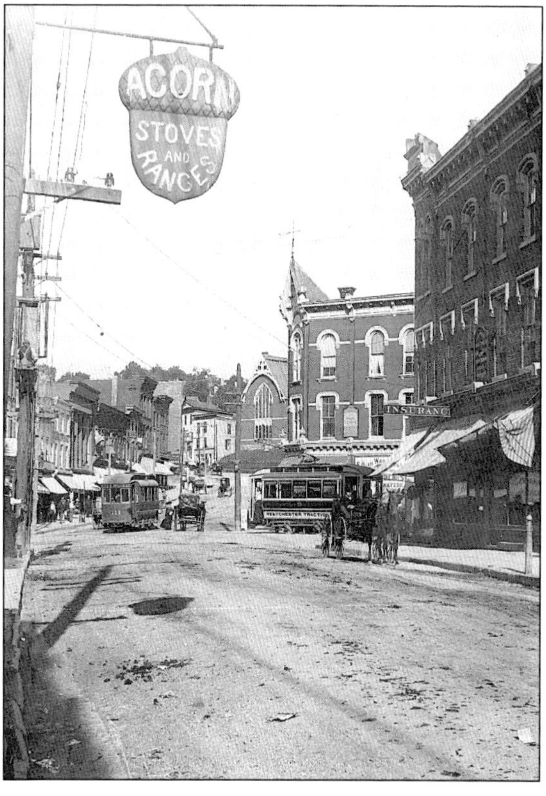

This photograph looks east from the Barlow Block in the 1890s. The Sing Sing Trolley Company began operation in 1893 and was the first of three businesses to service the village until 1924.

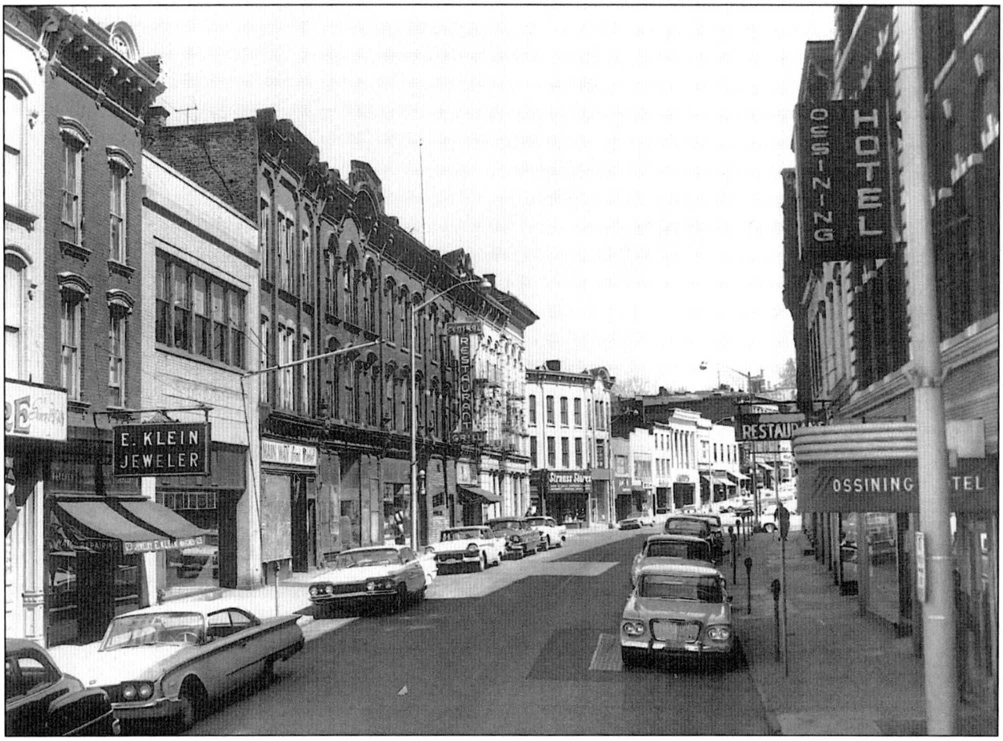

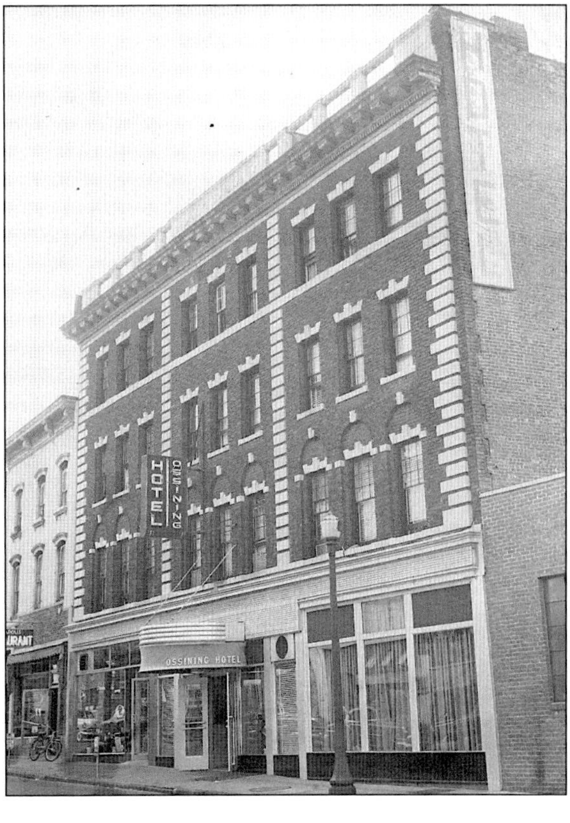

Shown here is a view looking east on lower Main Street from State Street taken in 1963.

The Acker Building was constructed about 1900 on the east side of lower Main Street, opposite the Barlow Block. The building contained three stores on the street level and nine apartments upstairs. All were equipped with "fine ventilation, running water, gas ranges, finely appointed baths and toilets and other modern improvements." Later, it became the Ossining Hotel.

The Acker Building is presented here around 1973, and the Starling Building is seen in the background.

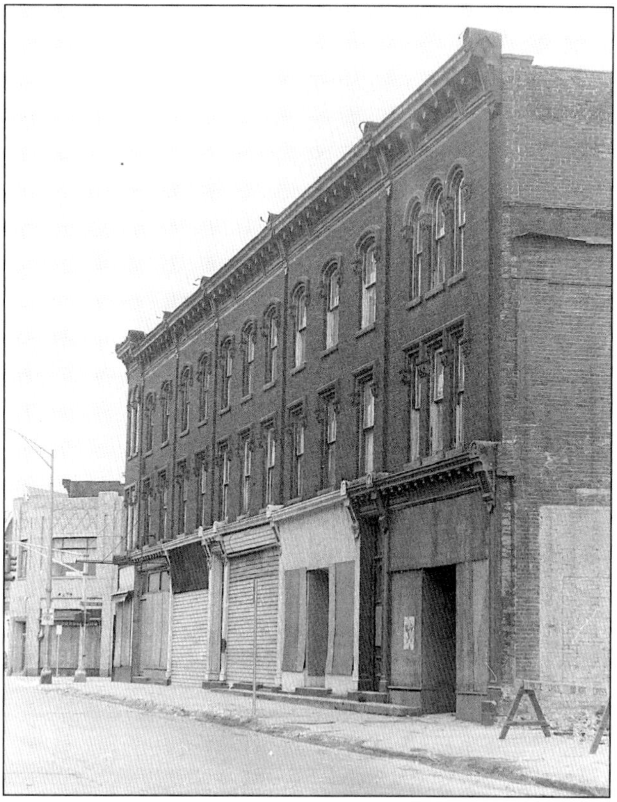

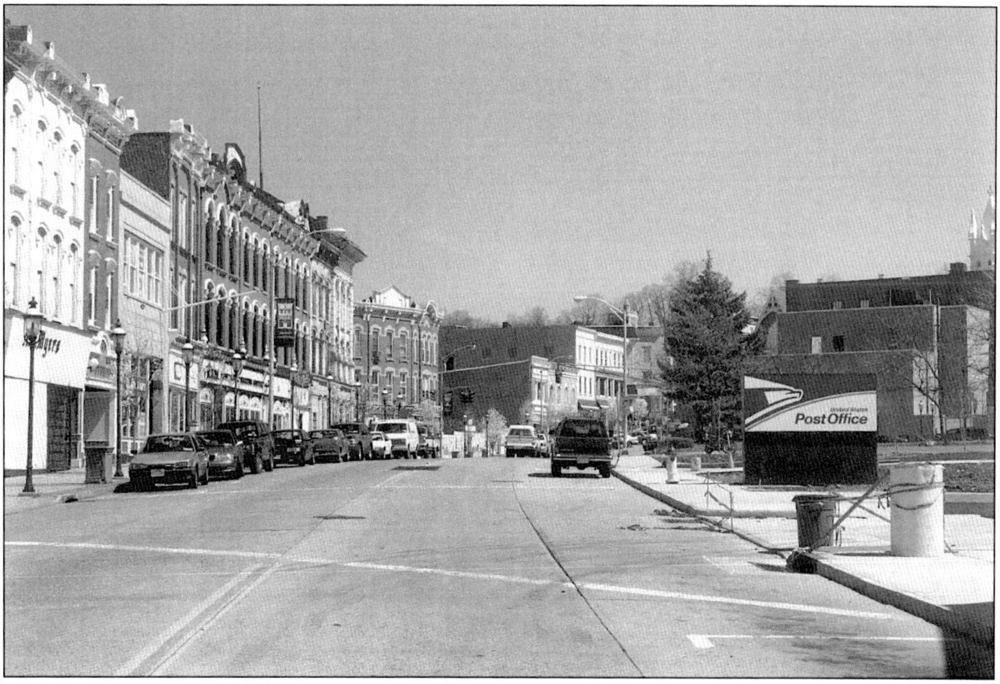

Lower Main Street is portrayed here in 1999, looking toward Spring Street and the Crescent. The new post office entrance sign can be seen on the right.

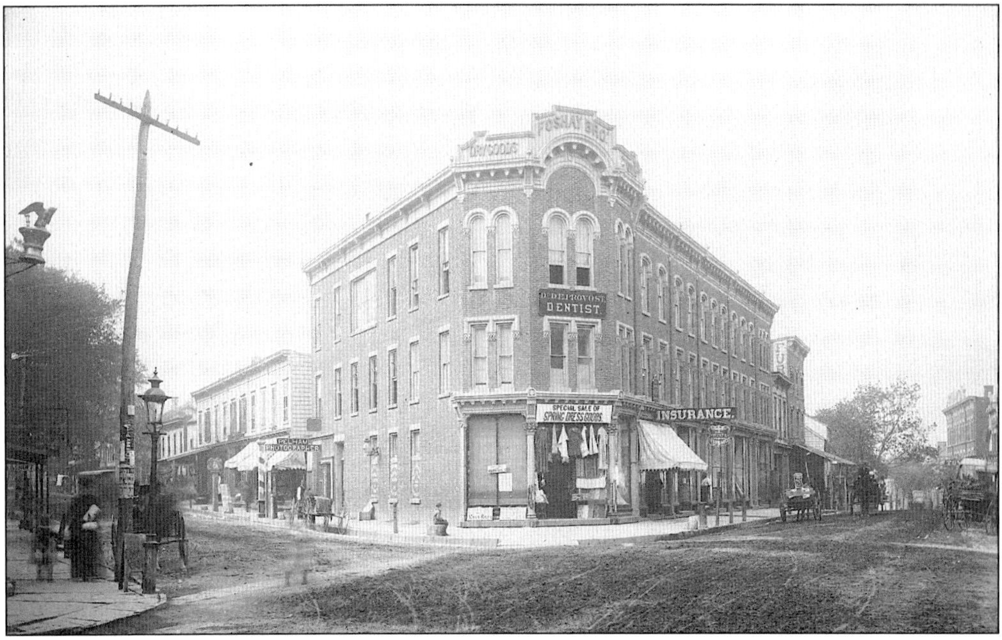

The southwest corner of Spring and Main Street is seen here about 1890. The Foshay brothers owned the business block, which housed their dry goods firm from 1868 to 1898. Dr. D.E. Provost, dentist, was on the second floor. Dirt roads, gas street lamps, and hitching posts can be seen in front of the stores.

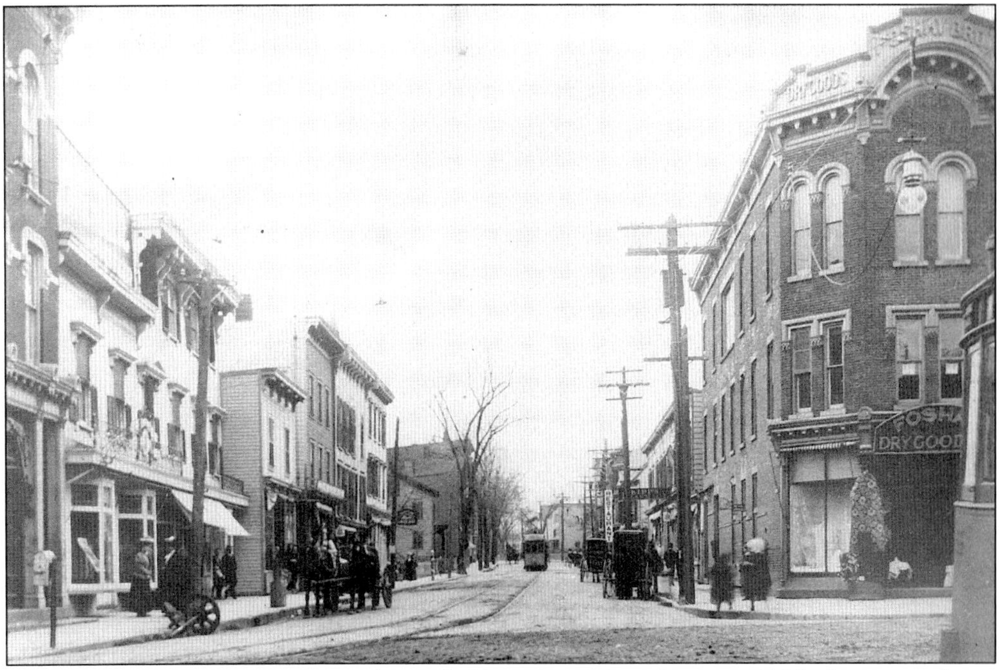

Looking down Spring Street towards Maple Place from Main Street in 1895, this image shows Foshay Dry Goods to the right, with an active row of businesses on both sides of Spring Street. Note the two trolleys, one coming down Spring Street and the other making its way up from the railroad station.

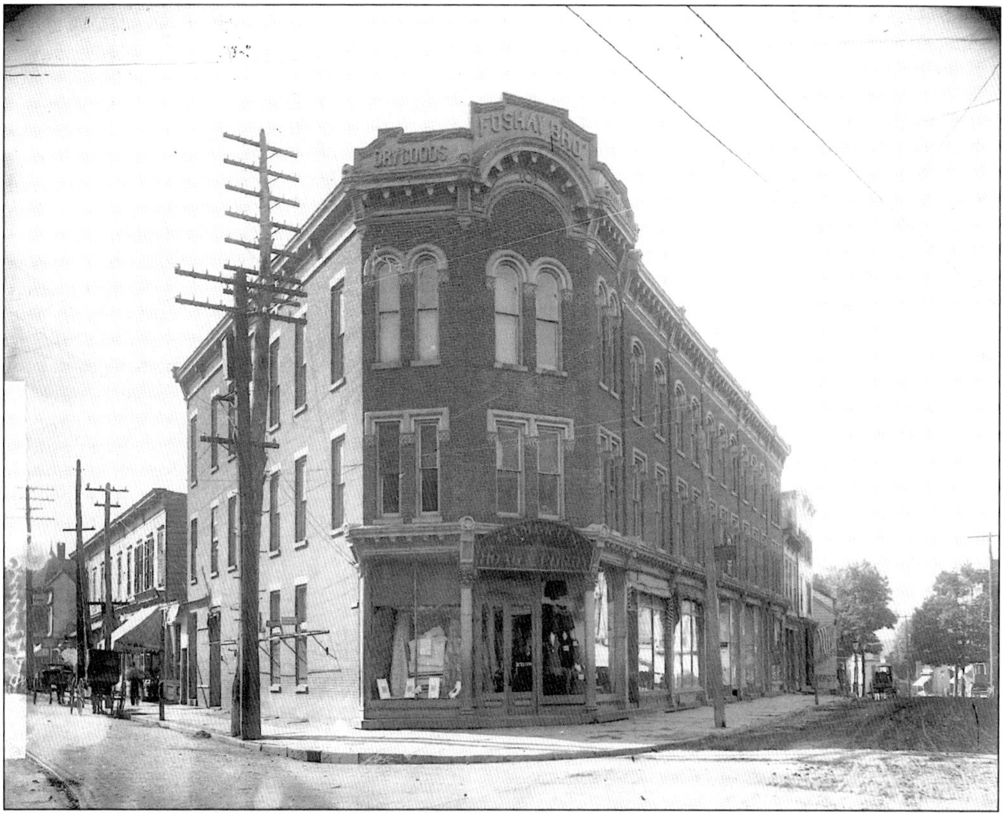

In 1898, the Foshay family pursuit was succeeded by Cameron, Hoag, & Purdy. The store featured "colored dress goods, embroideries, hosiery, patterns, notions, umbrellas, flannel underwear, cloaks, suits, carpets, rugs, upholstery, sheetings and comfortables."

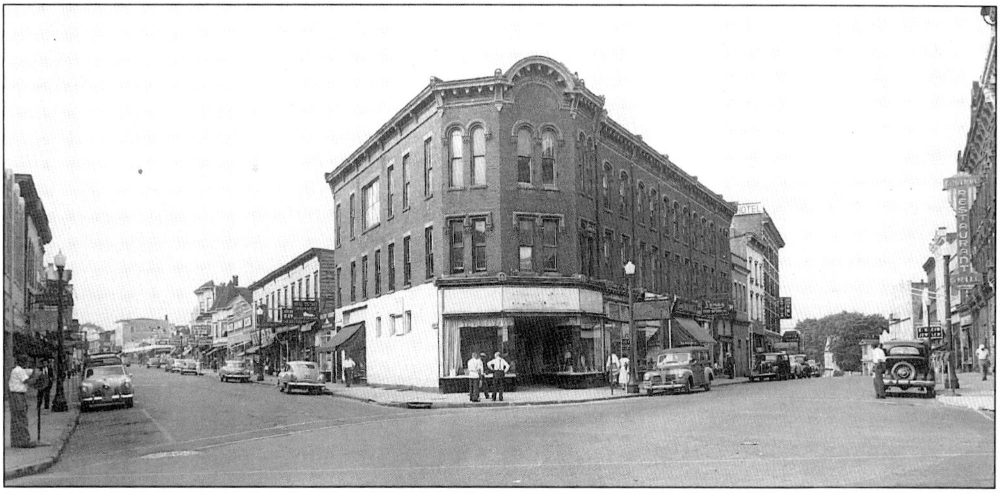

The year 1951 found an economically sound Spring Street. Retailers located on Spring Street included the following: (on the right) Diddie Mae Clothing, Ascherman's Bakery, Crystal Restaurant, Whelan's Drugs, and the Ossining Food Center; (on the left) Verdi's Hats, Abelon Book and Music, Royal Grill, B&J Delicatessen, Ossining Restaurant, Cartoon's Furniture, and Spring Street Bar & Grill.

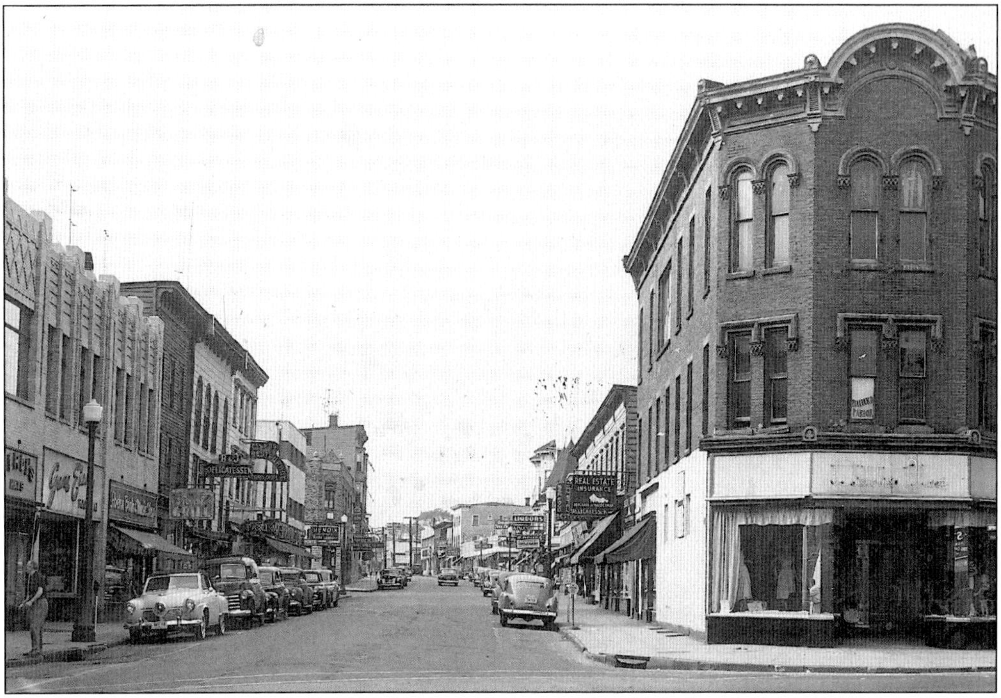

The southwest corner of Spring and Main Streets is seen here in 1951. The unique arched cornice at the top of the Foshay Building was gone by this time. The cornice was stamped metal that protruded beyond the surface of the facade.

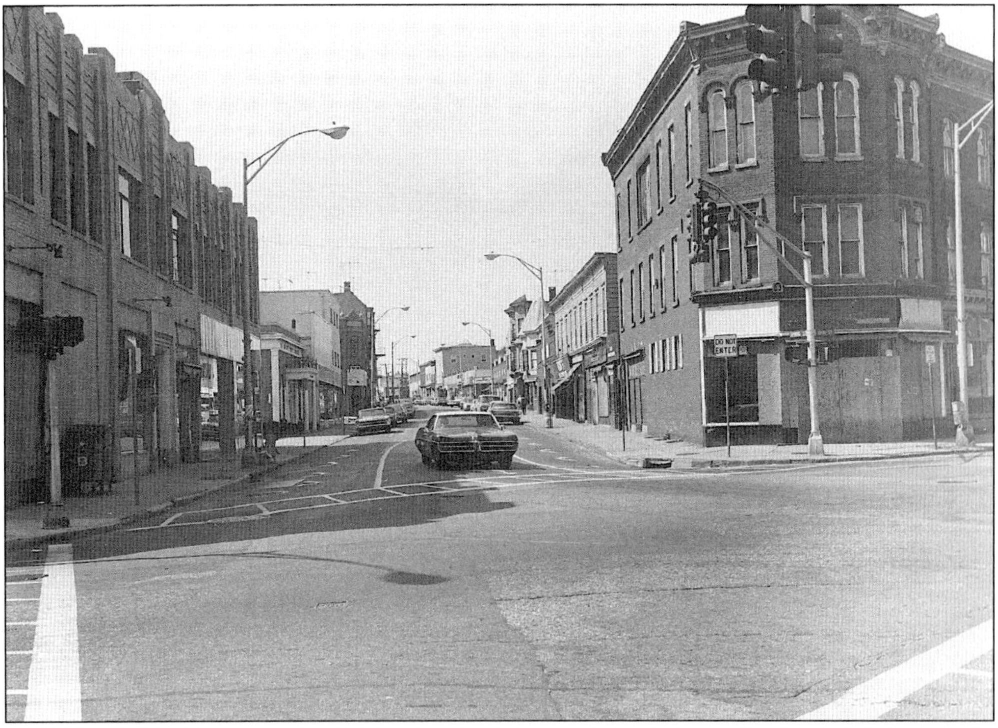

Urban renewal had started by the early 1970s as evidenced by this image.

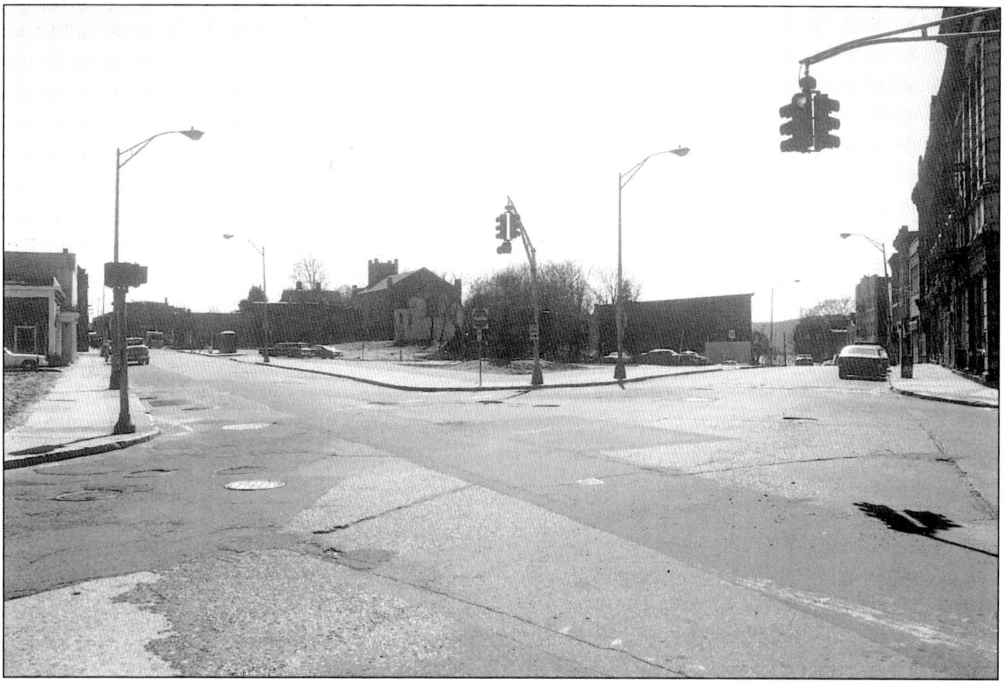

The corner of Main and Spring Streets is shown here as it appeared in August 1974.

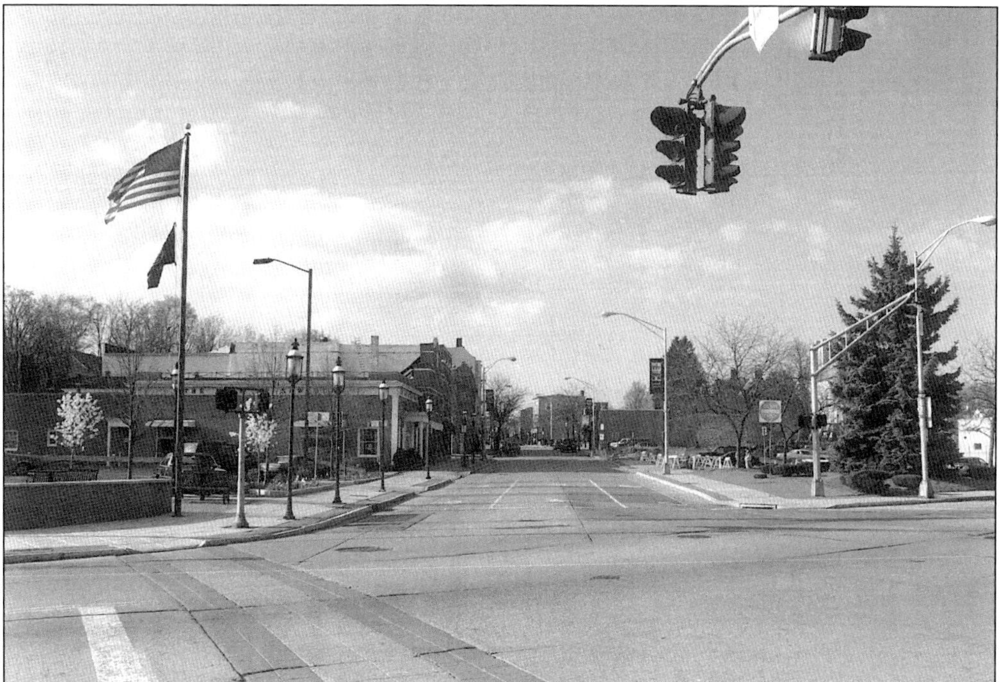

This photograph looks down Spring Street from the corner of Main Street in 1999.

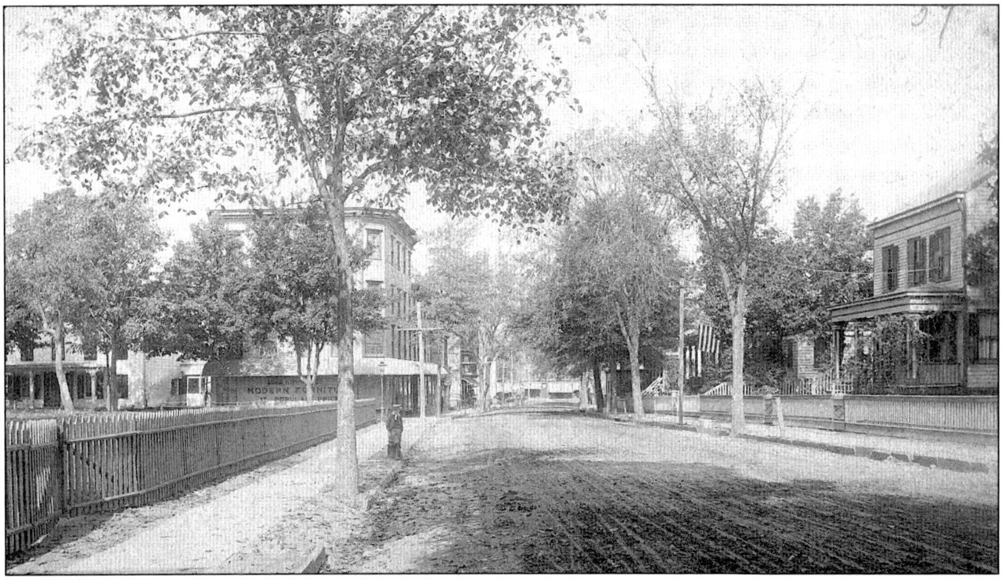

This image of Spring Street looking north from Waller Avenue in the 1890s represents the G.W. & S.C. Kipp Jr. Furniture Store, which was to the left, on the corner of St. Paul's Place.

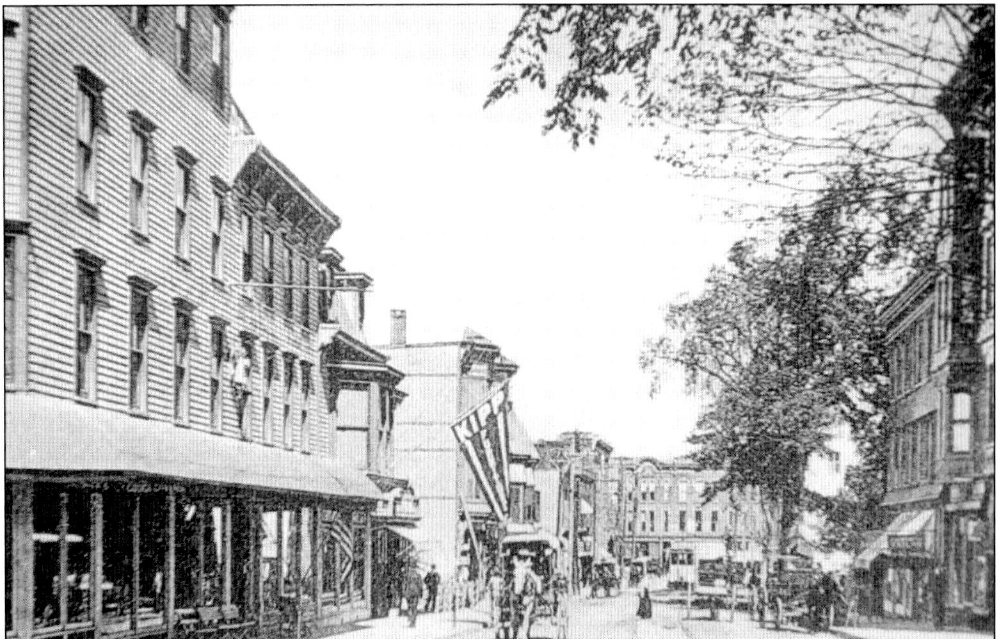

In 1900, Spring Street was busy and prosperous. Twelve doctors and surgeons, four dentists, and two veterinarians were located downtown.

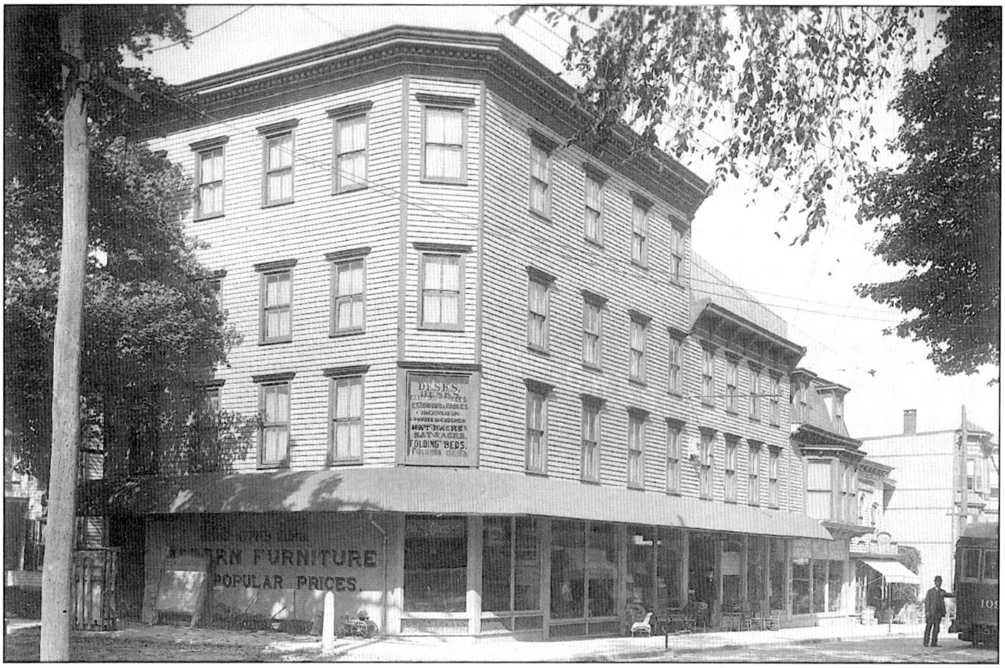

St. Paul's Place and Spring Street are shown here in 1901. Kipp's Furniture Store was established in 1852 and included four stories and 25,000 feet of floor space. They specialized in mattresses, spring beds, mirrors, picture framing, mattings, extension tables, hat racks, folding chairs, and draperies. They were also funeral directors, "prepared to give prompt attention to calls at any hour and their service is always first class."

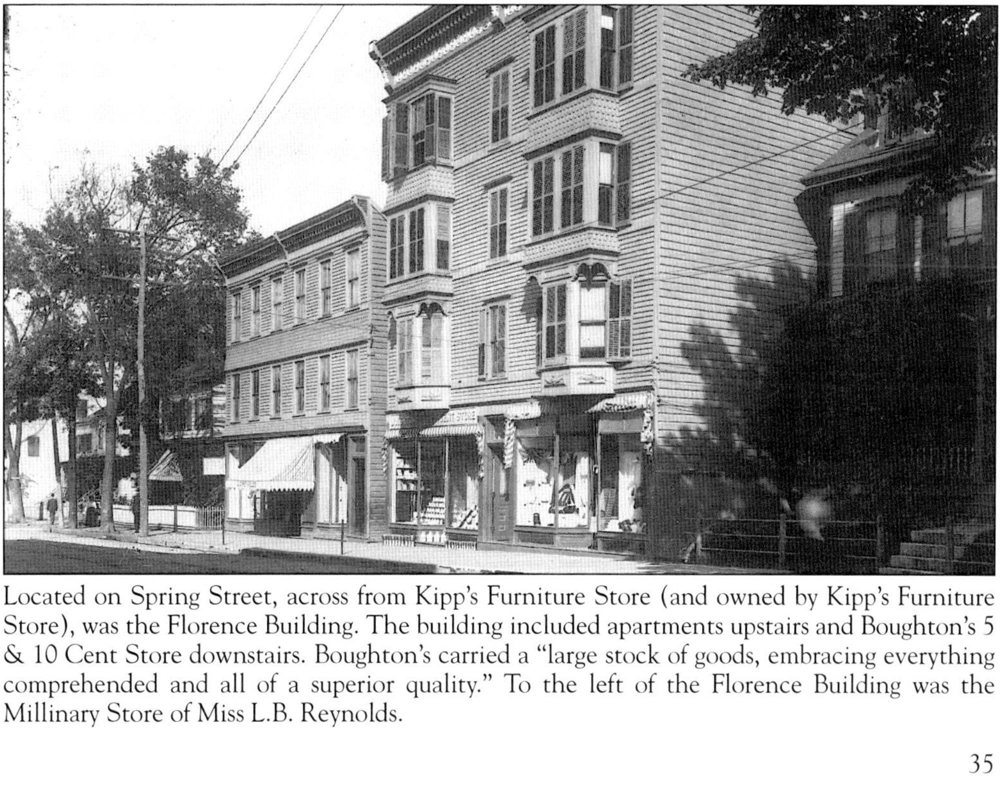

Located on Spring Street, across from Kipp's Furniture Store (and owned by Kipp's Furniture Store), was the Florence Building. The building included apartments upstairs and Boughton's 5 & 10 Cent Store downstairs. Boughton's carried a "large stock of goods, embracing everything comprehended and all of a superior quality." To the left of the Florence Building was the Millinary Store of Miss L.B. Reynolds.

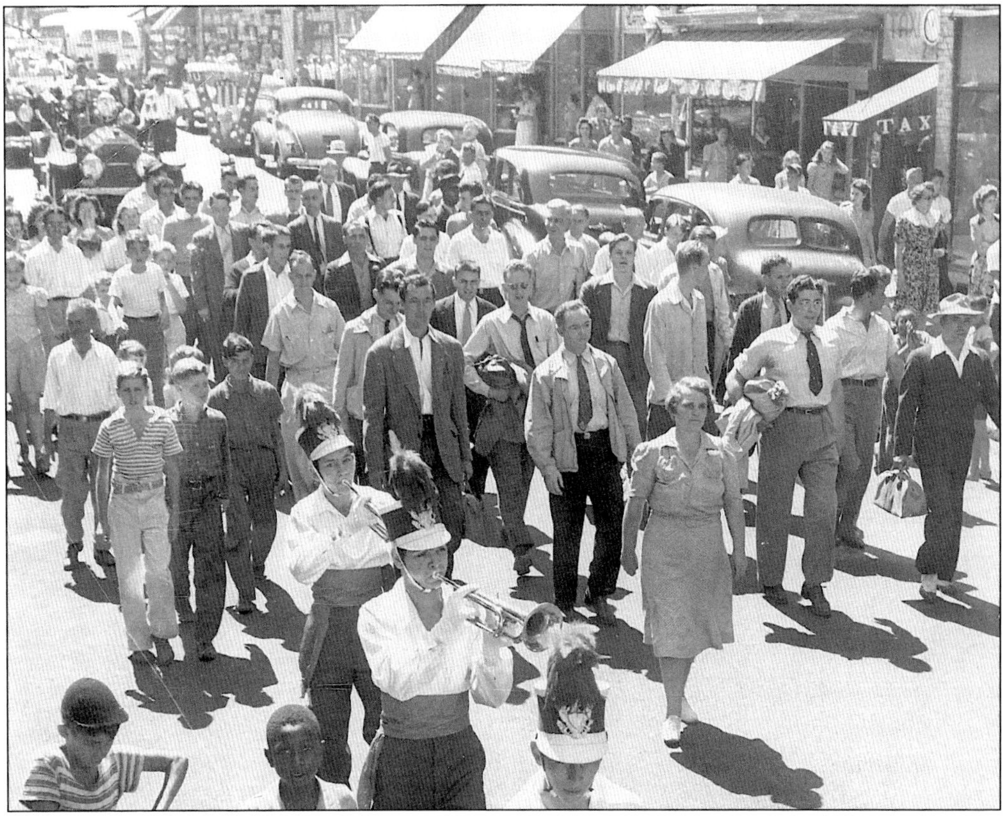

At the time this picture was taken, World War II (WWII) had started, and the nation was mobilizing. This scene, of Ossining Selective Service inductees marching down Spring Street towards the train station, was repeated on a monthly basis depending on government quotas. The local VFW Drum Corps led the way with spirited music as the Ossining Fire Department brought up the rear. It was both a proud and somber moment for the community.

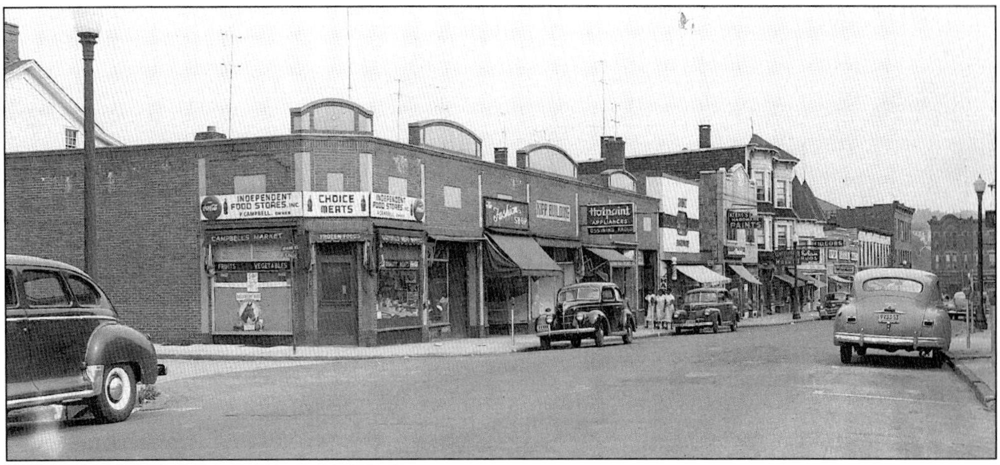

The new, brick Kipp Building, which occupied the corner of Spring Street and St. Paul's Place, included Campbell's Market, the Fashion Shop, and Hotpoint Appliances. Further along Spring Street, Keene's Hardware Store and Abraham Cohen's Kosher Market can be seen in 1951.

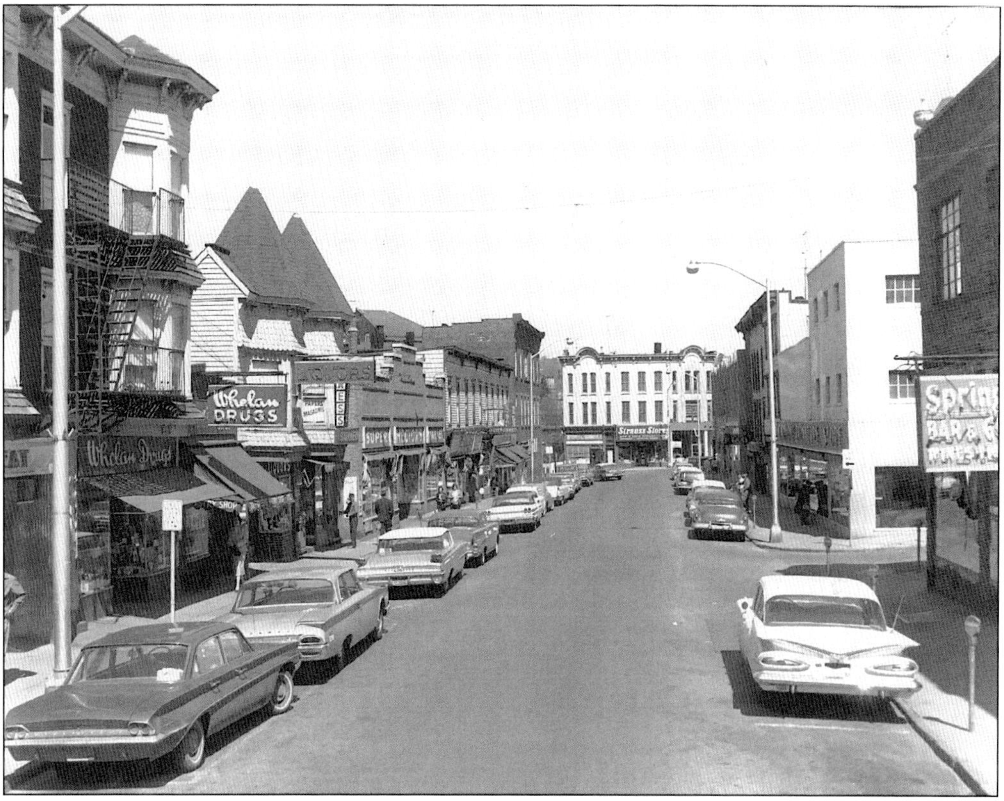

This *c.* 1963 photograph looks north on Spring Street towards Main Street. Maple Place is represented on the right, while the Leander Fisher Building stands at the far end.

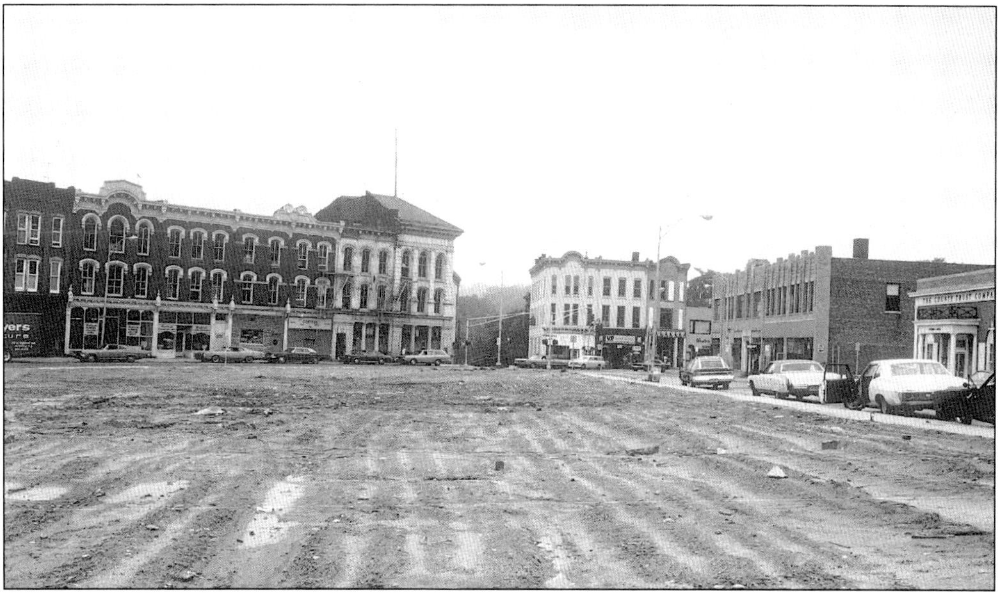

The 1970s brought more demolition. This view is looking north, with Spring Street to the right and Main Street to the left. Buildings represented in the image are, from left to right, as follows: the Barlow Block, Leander Fisher Building, and the Starling Building.

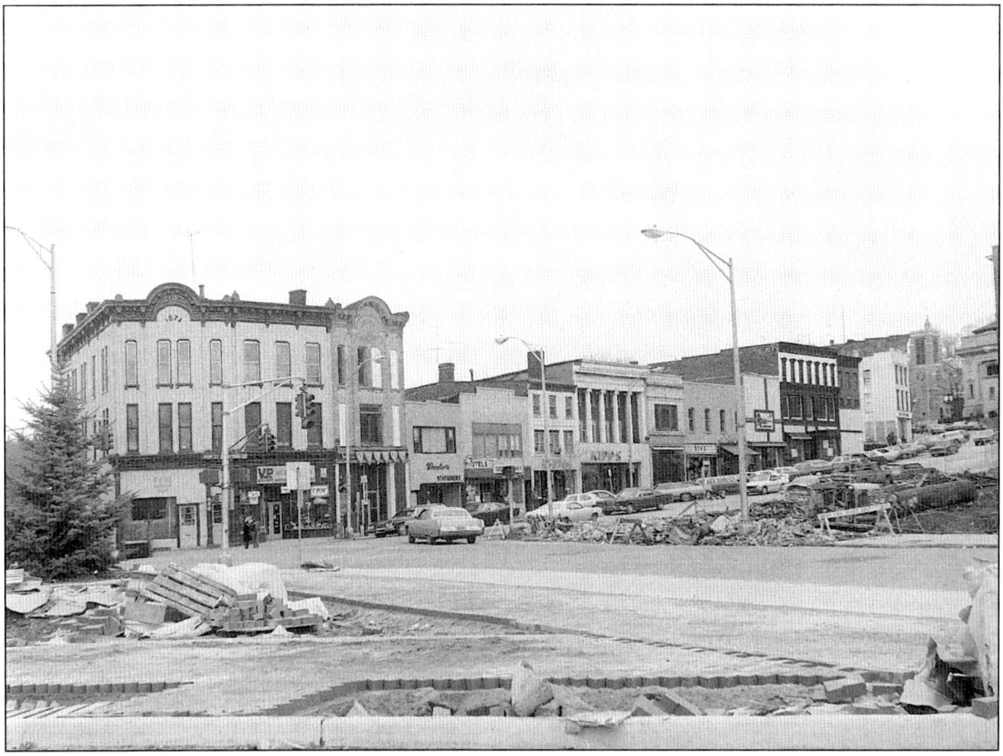

Looking along the Crescent in 1976, the corner of Spring and Main Streets can be seen here.

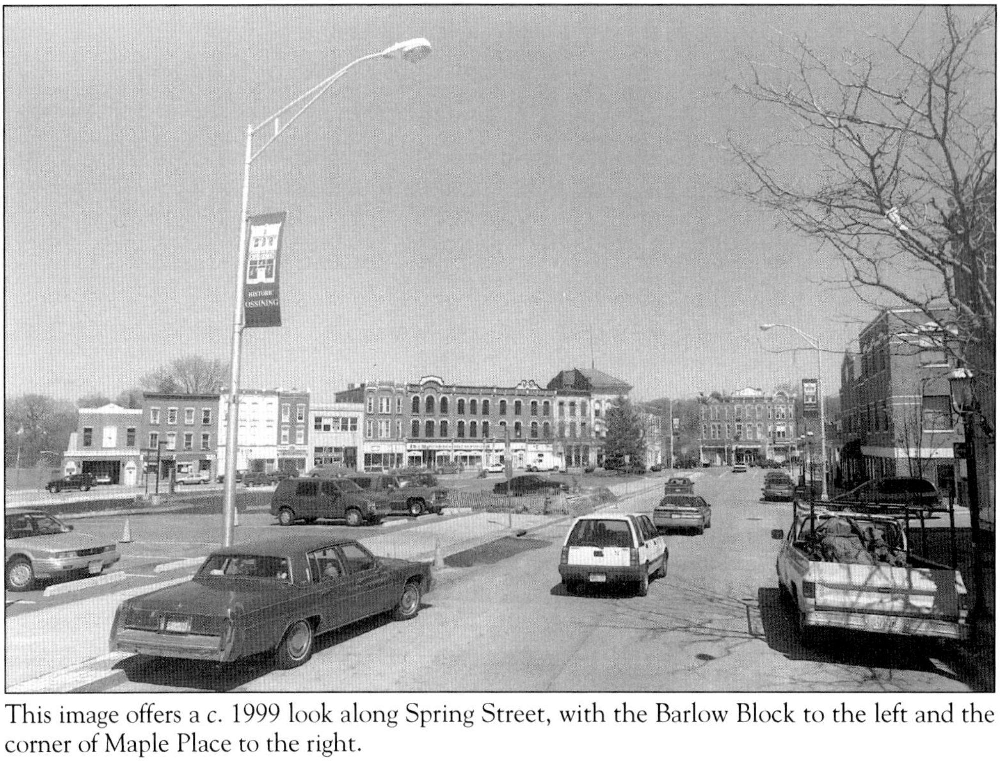

This image offers a *c.* 1999 look along Spring Street, with the Barlow Block to the left and the corner of Maple Place to the right.

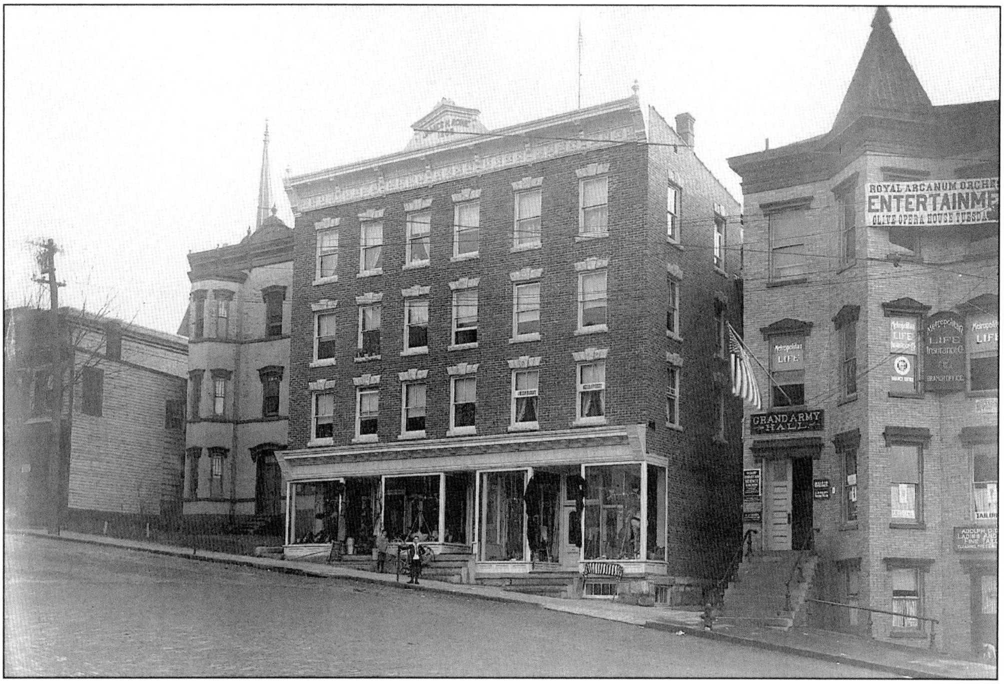

The James H. Rowe Building on Church Street was built in 1908. Mr. Rowe, who owned two businesses on North Highland Avenue specializing in carriages, wagons, sleighs and harnesses, opened two new stores in this building with apartments upstairs. This image shows the Secor Flats apartment house to the left. The Twiggar Building can be seen to the right. It was owned by dentist Dr. Albert W. Twiggar, who was president of the Village of Ossining.

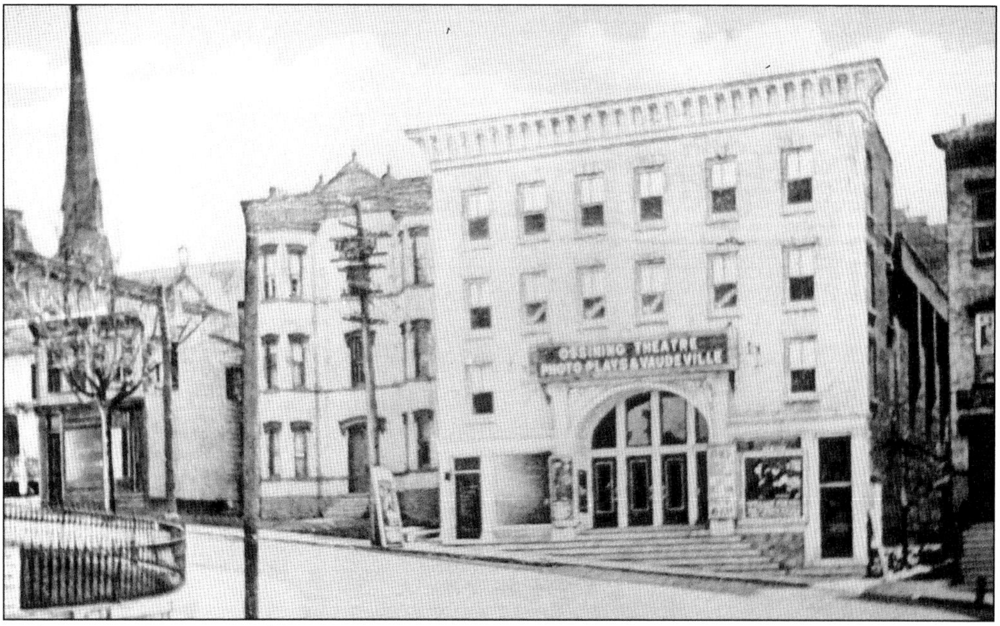

In the 1920s, the Rowe Building was converted into the Ossining Theatre, which featured photoplays and vaudeville. The spire of the First Presbyterian Church can be seen in the background.

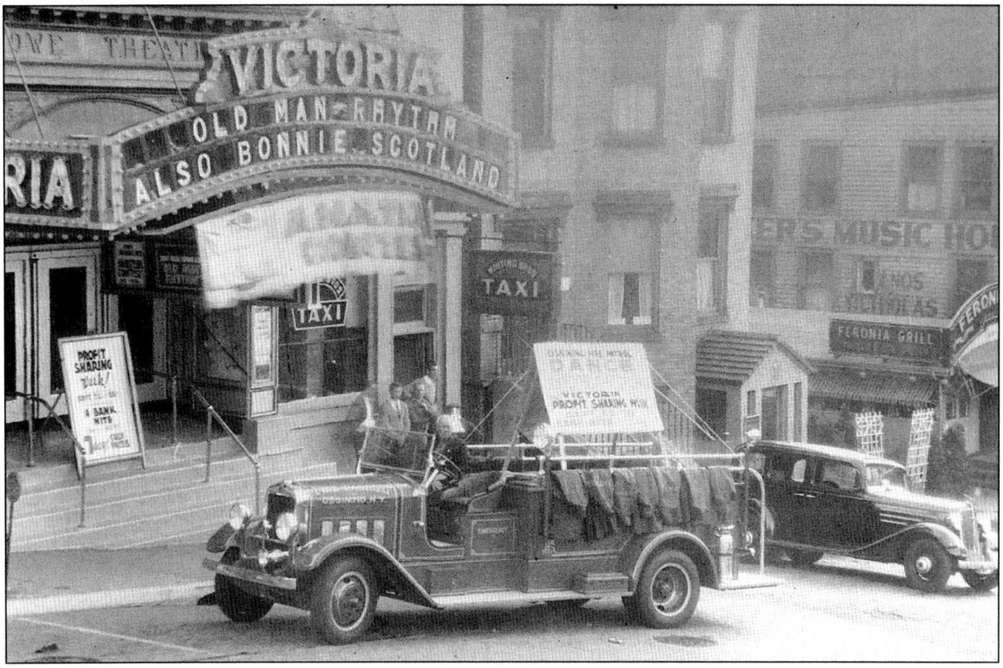

The Ossining Fire Patrol advertised Profit Sharing Week at the new Victoria Theater in 1935. The banner hanging from the marquee announced an amateur contest.

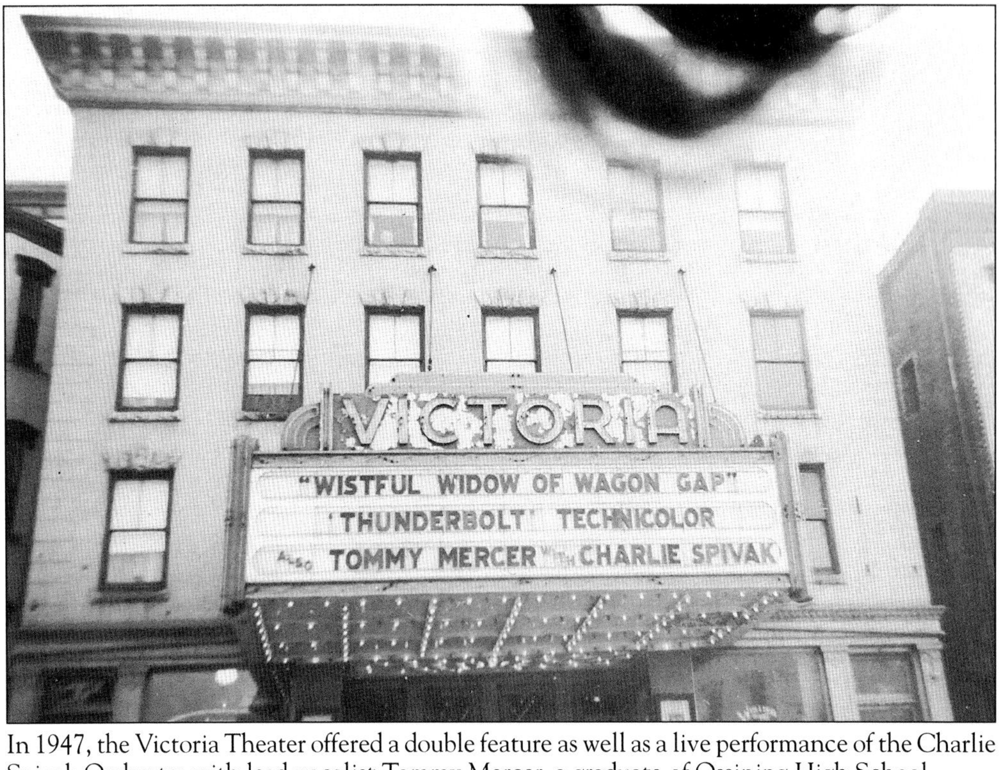

In 1947, the Victoria Theater offered a double feature as well as a live performance of the Charlie Spivak Orchestra with lead vocalist Tommy Mercer, a graduate of Ossining High School.

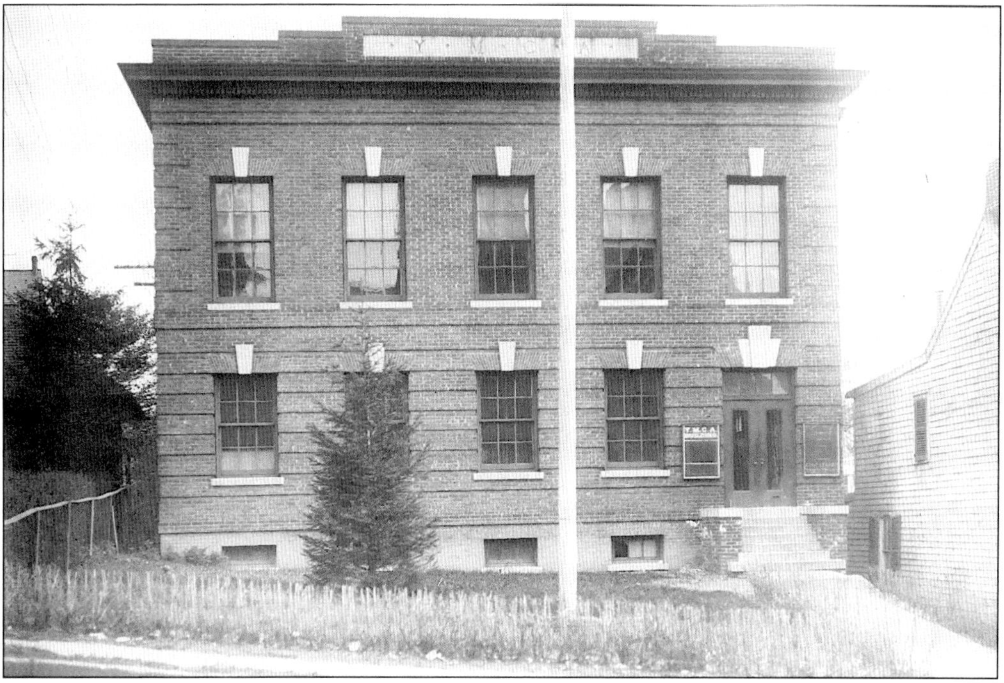

Located just above the Victoria Theater on Church Street, the YMCA building was erected in 1907. Over the years, it was also used as a public school and as the home of the Ossining Recreation Department.

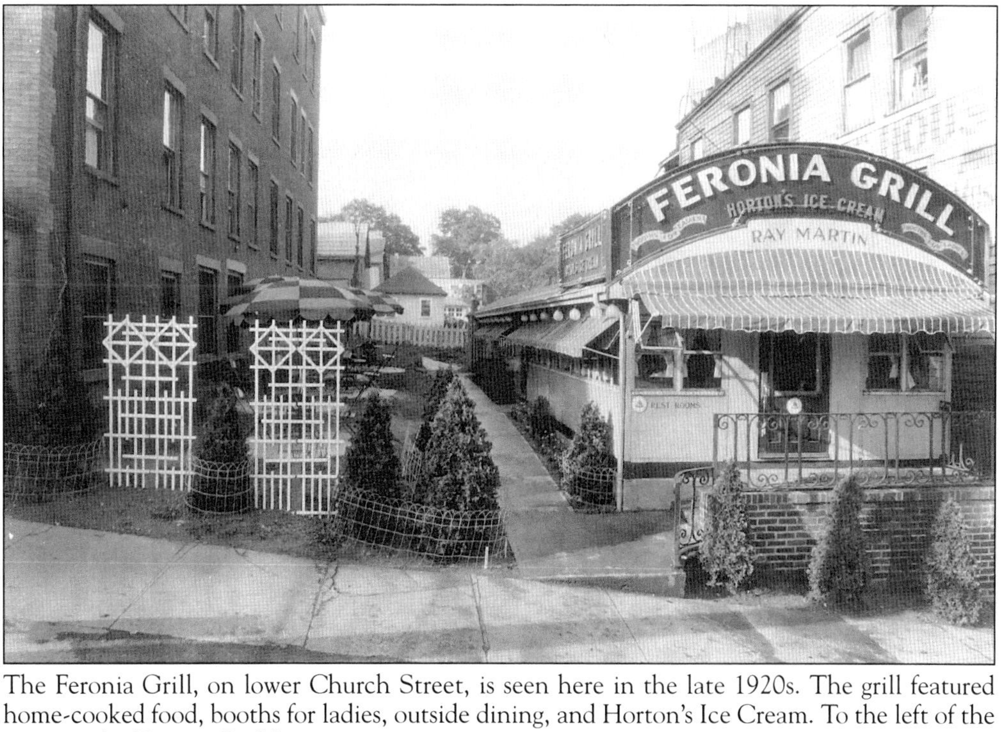

The Feronia Grill, on lower Church Street, is seen here in the late 1920s. The grill featured home-cooked food, booths for ladies, outside dining, and Horton's Ice Cream. To the left of the image is the Twiggar Building.

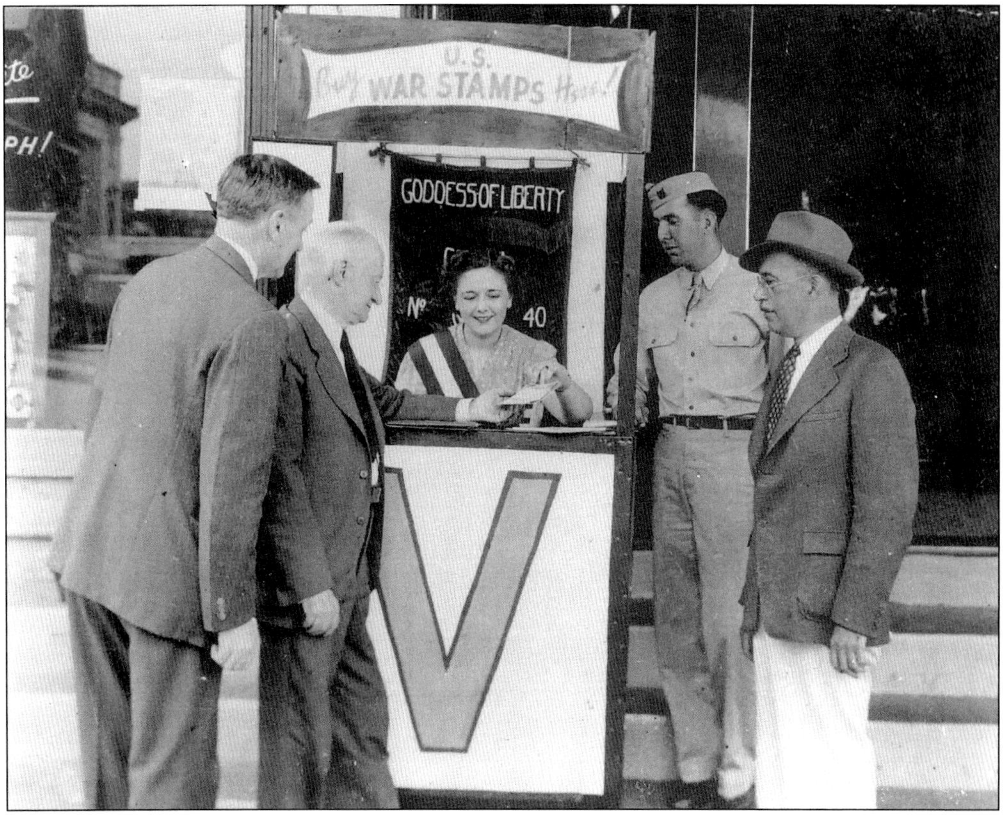

Patriotism was seen on the local level as residents stopped by to purchase U.S. War Stamps to help the WW II effort. The booth stood in front of the Victoria Theater in the early 1940s.

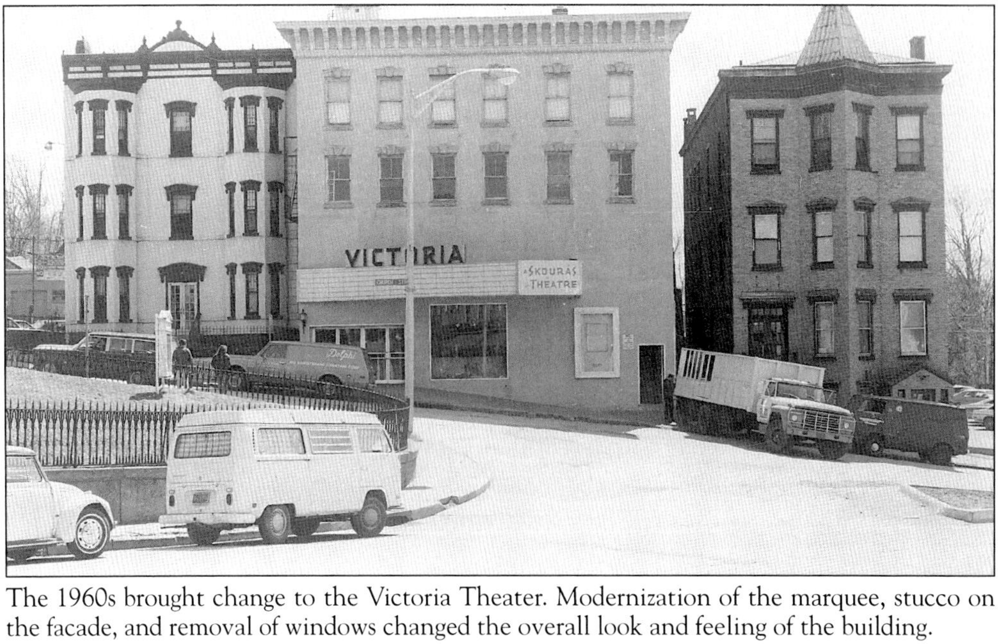

The 1960s brought change to the Victoria Theater. Modernization of the marquee, stucco on the facade, and removal of windows changed the overall look and feeling of the building.

Workers are seen here tearing down the Rowe Building around 1973.

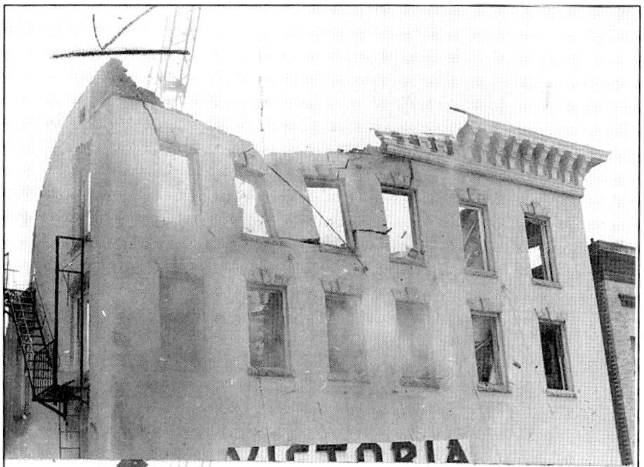

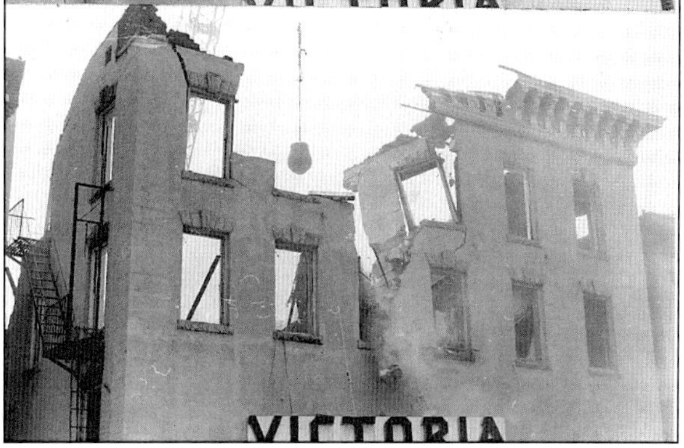

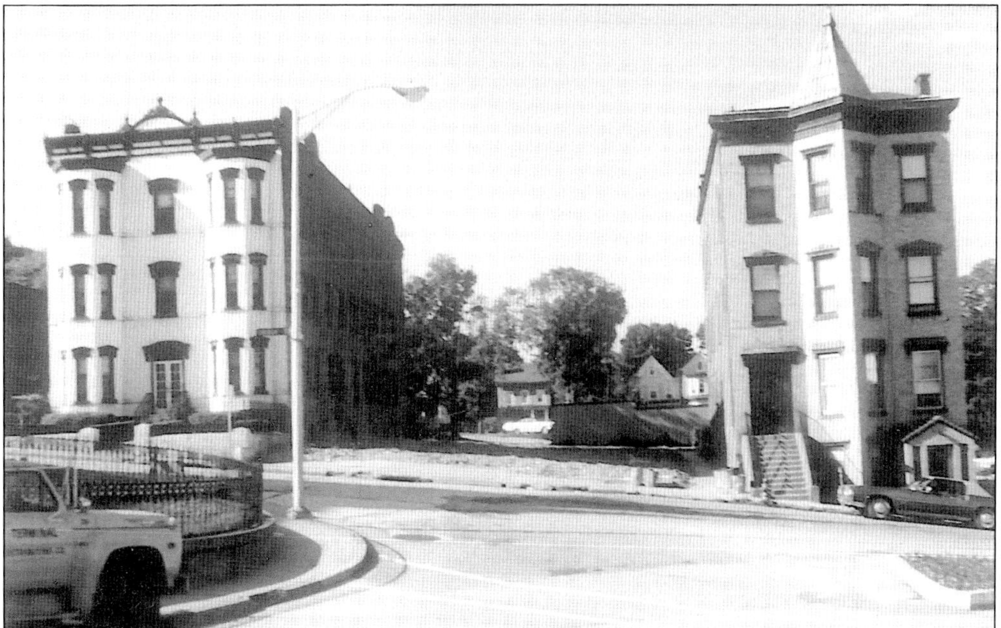

Urban renewal continued through Ossining's downtown. The wrecker's ball would soon arrive to take many precious landmarks including the Twiggar Building (to the right) and the Secor Flats Apartments (to the left).

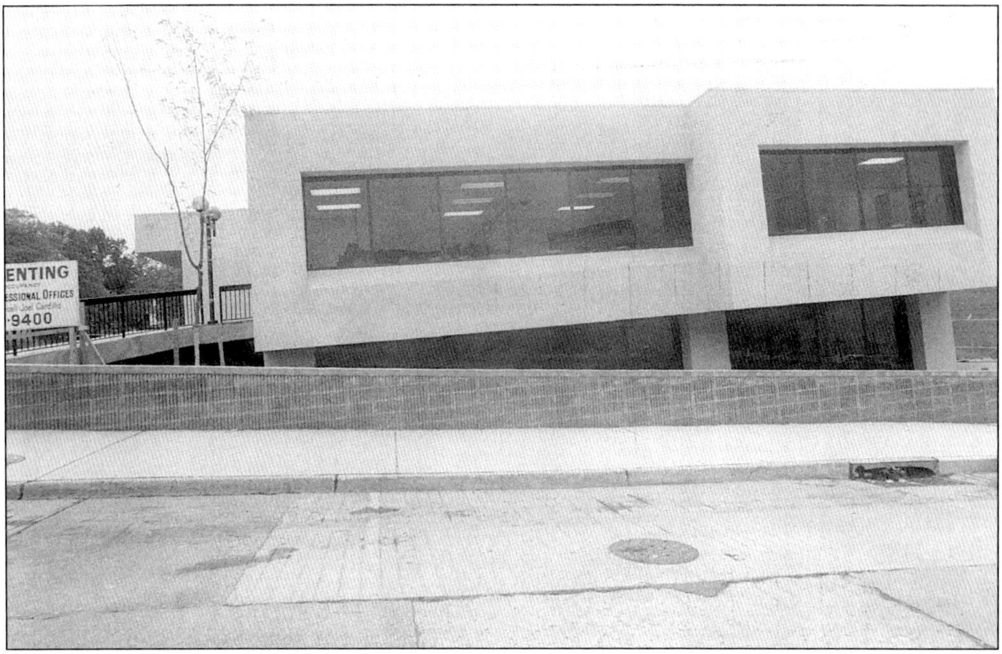

In 1977, the new Halpern Building, a commercial venture on Church Street, replaced the Twiggar, Secor Flats, and YMCA buildings.

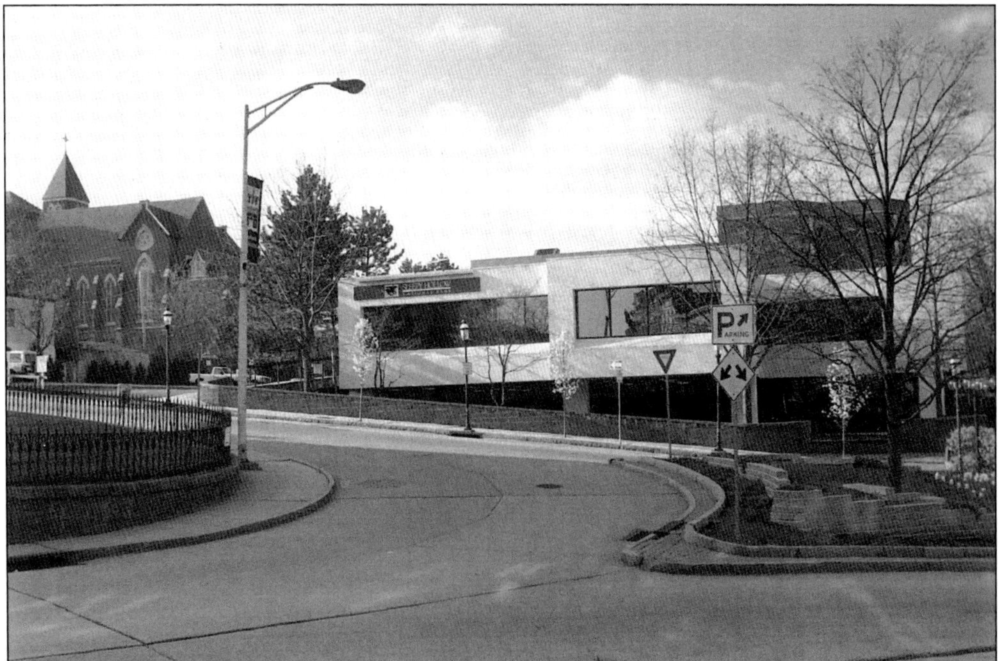

This image presents a view looking across Main Street towards Church Street in 1999. The lawn of the First Baptist Church is to the left of the photo.

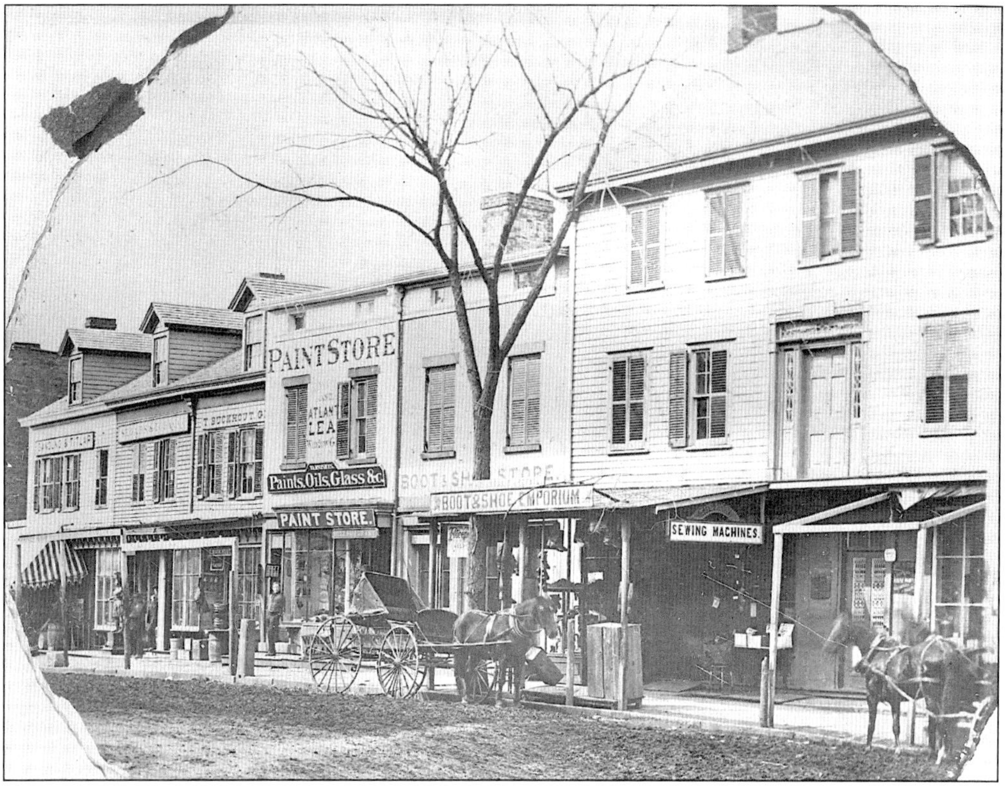

The west side of upper Main Street is shown here in 1871. Most of the structures here were made of wood, and a fire in 1873 resulted in the construction of many brick Italianate brownstone buildings.

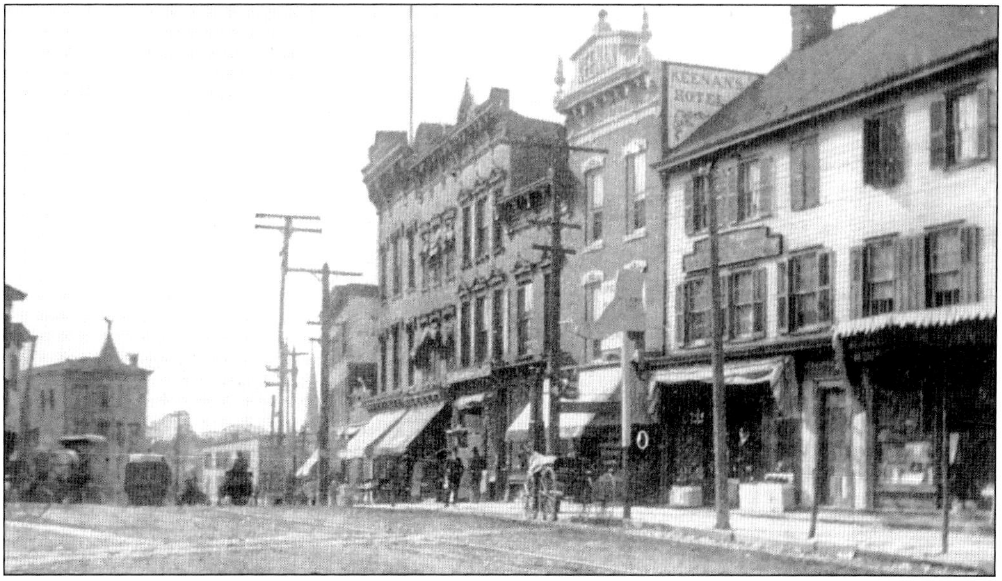

The west side of upper Main Street is shown here as it appeared in 1901. The Keenan Hotel, built in 1878, stands in the middle of the photograph, while the Twiggar Building is seen to the left (in the background).

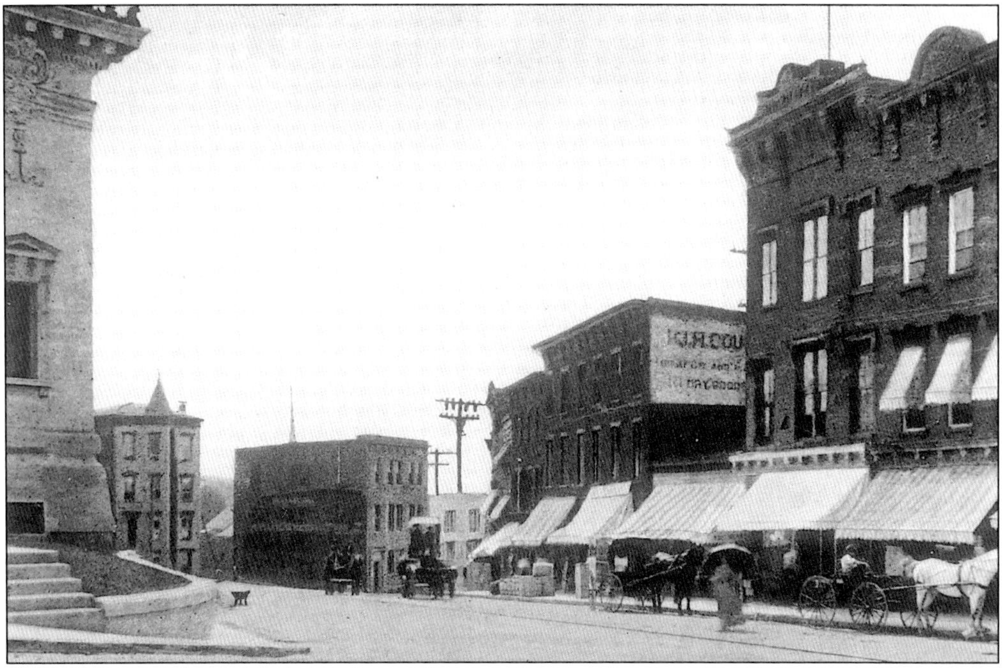

This is a view of upper Main Street looking towards Church Street in 1901. The Bank for Savings is to the left of the photograph, while the Twiggar Building and the spire of St. Paul's Episcopal Church, on St. Paul's Place, can be seen in the distance.

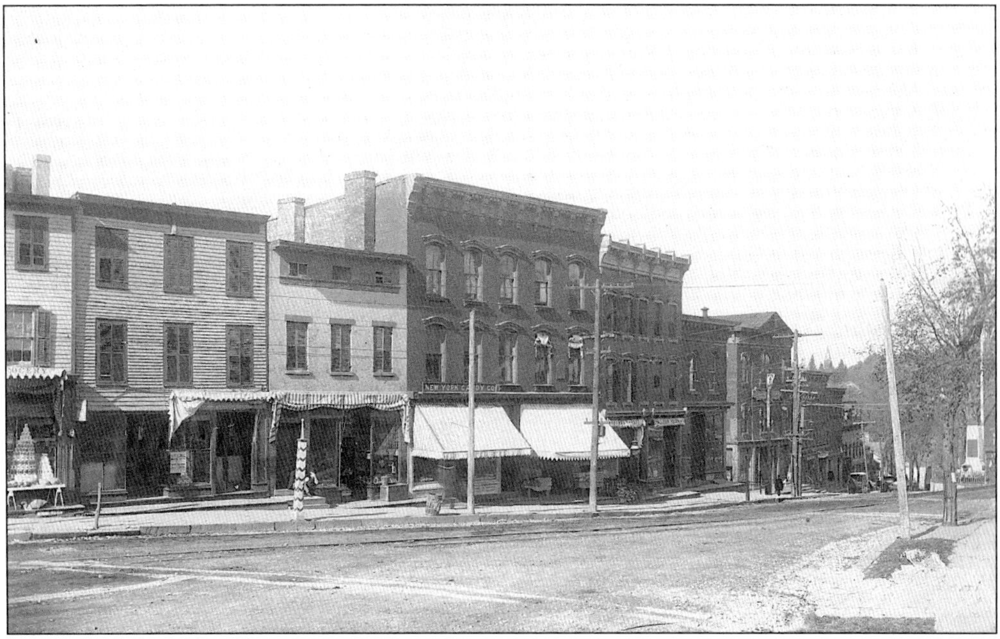

The west side of upper Main Street is shown here looking north towards North Highland Avenue. The Civil War Soldier's Monument and First National Bank are located near the corner of Croton Avenue (to the extreme right). Some of the retail stores include the New York Candy Company, Brown's Market, and the Ossining Pharmacy. This photograph was taken from the front of Trinity Episcopal Church.

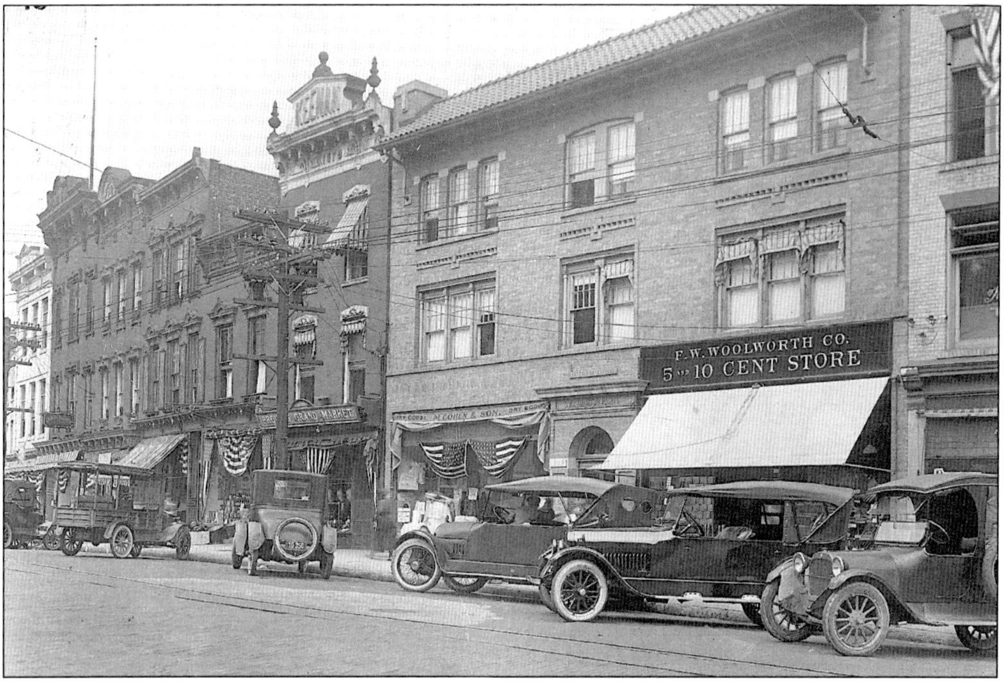

The west side of upper Main Street is represented here in 1921. Businesses located here included Brown Grand Market (in the Keenan Building), M. Cohen & Son Dry Goods, and a barbershop. The F.W. Woolworth Co. 5 & 10 Cent Store was located in the Cartwright Building, which was done in the Mediterranean style with a tiled roof. It was converted from a dwelling to a commercial edifice, with offices on the upper floors.

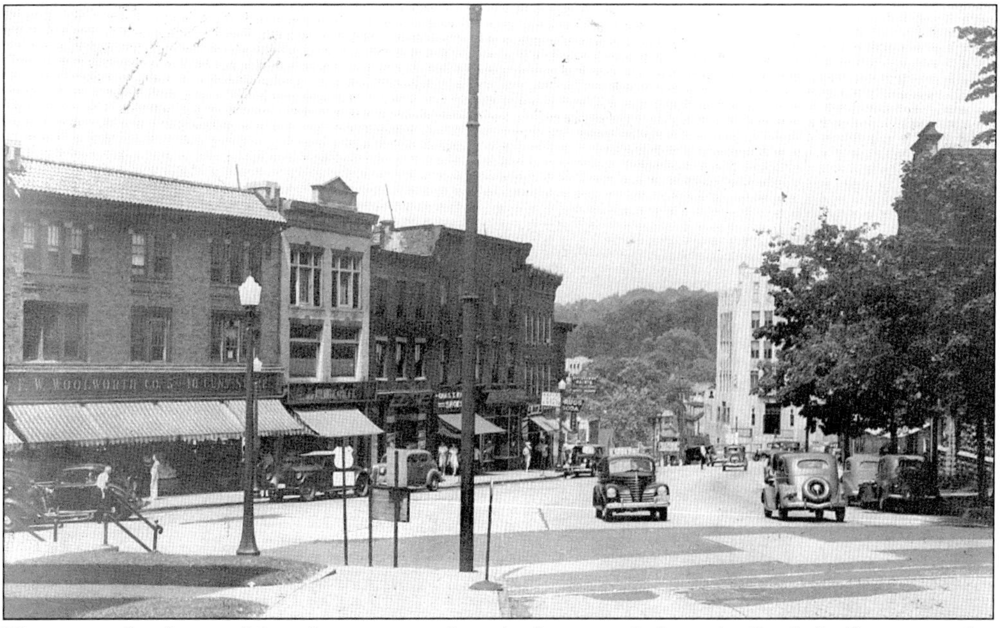

The west side of upper Main Street is seen here looking north from the Bank for Savings in the 1940s. The First National Bank is in the background, while the Trinity Episcopal Church stands to the right of the image.

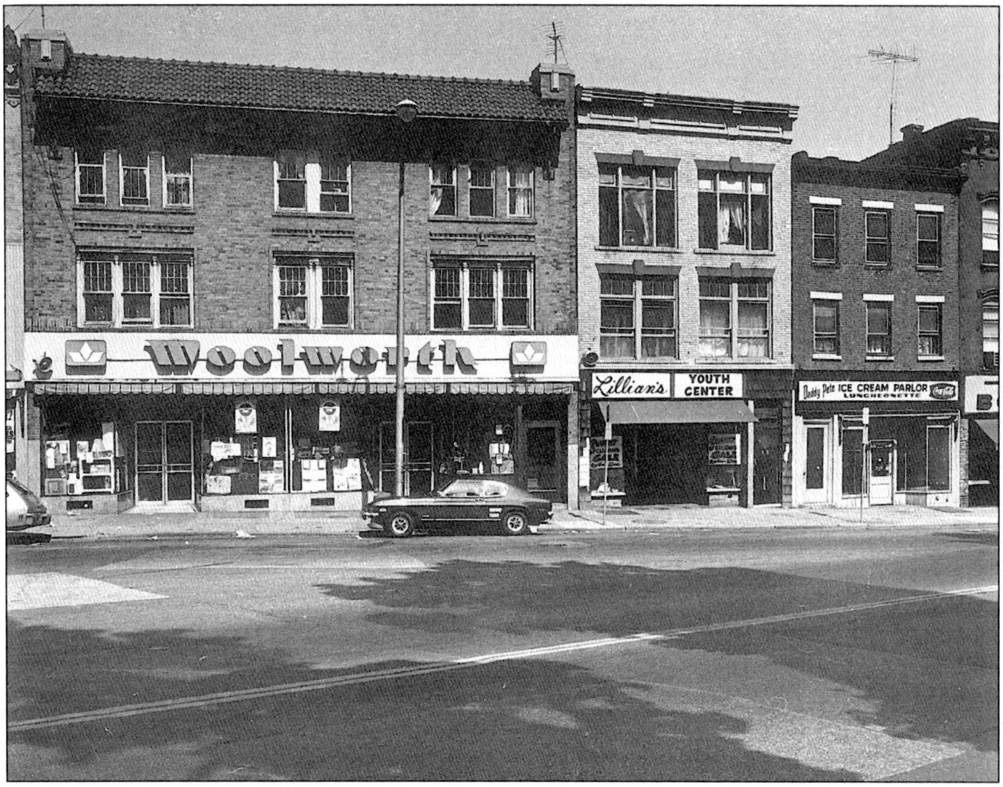

Upper Main Street is seen here in 1974.

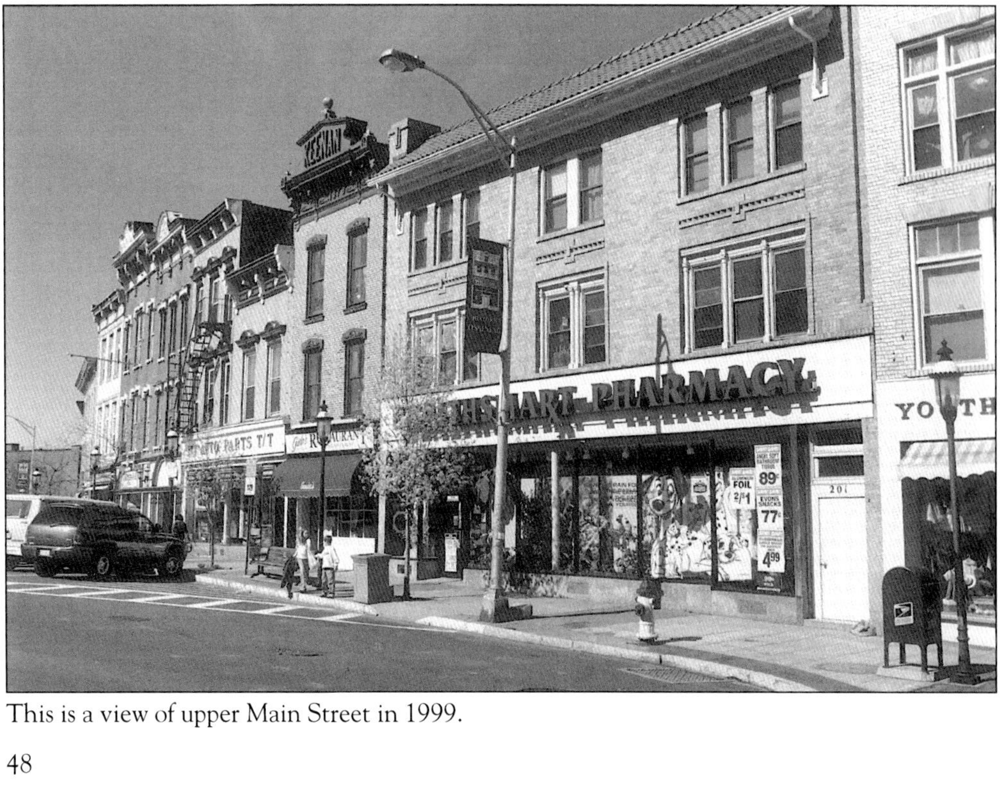

This is a view of upper Main Street in 1999.

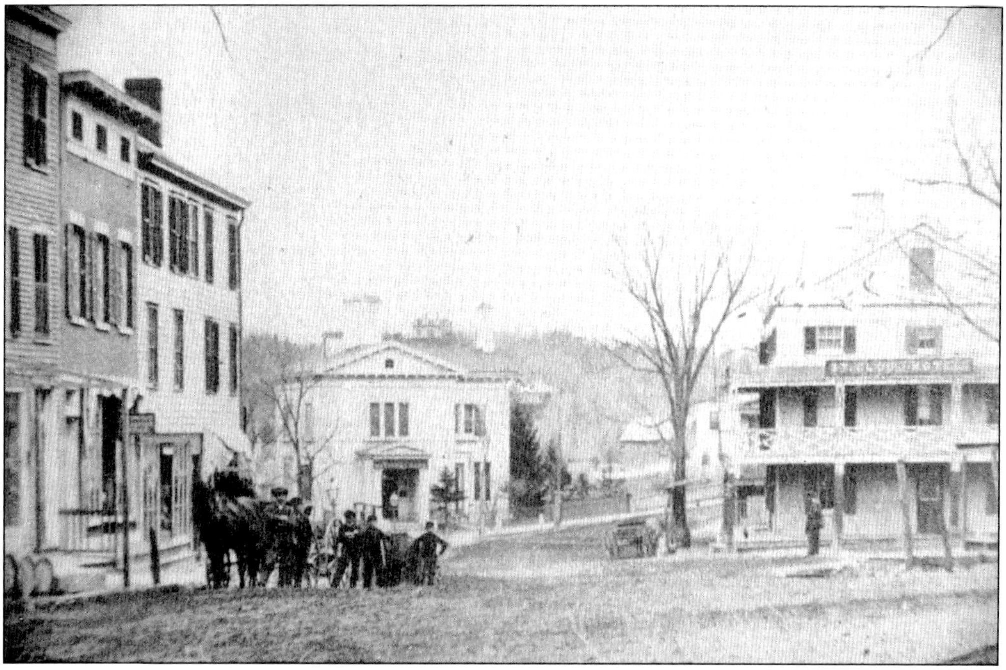

This image presents a view of upper Main Street looking north from the Savings Bank Building around 1891. The St. Cloud Hotel is to the right of the image, on the corner of Eastern Avenue. The National Bank in the background, on the corner of North Highland Avenue and Croton Avenue, was built in 1864.

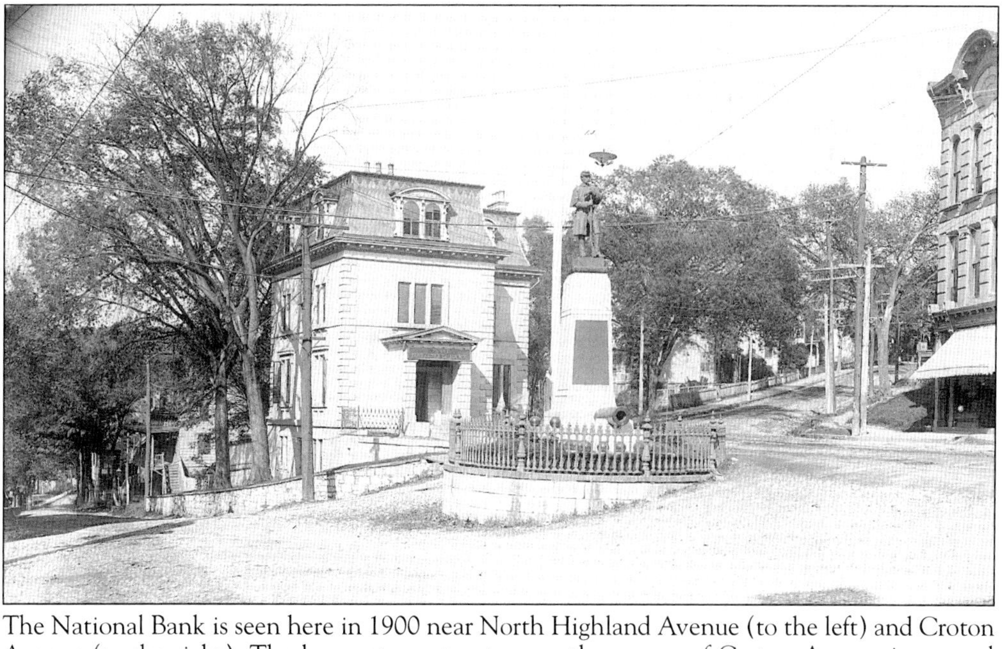

The National Bank is seen here in 1900 near North Highland Avenue (to the left) and Croton Avenue (to the right). The brownstone structure on the corner of Croton Avenue is unusual because it features a rusticated facade with deep V-shaped grooves emphasizing the stone joints. The Soldier's Monument was the highlight of Pleasant Square and was later moved to the corner of Pleasantville Road and Brookville Avenue.

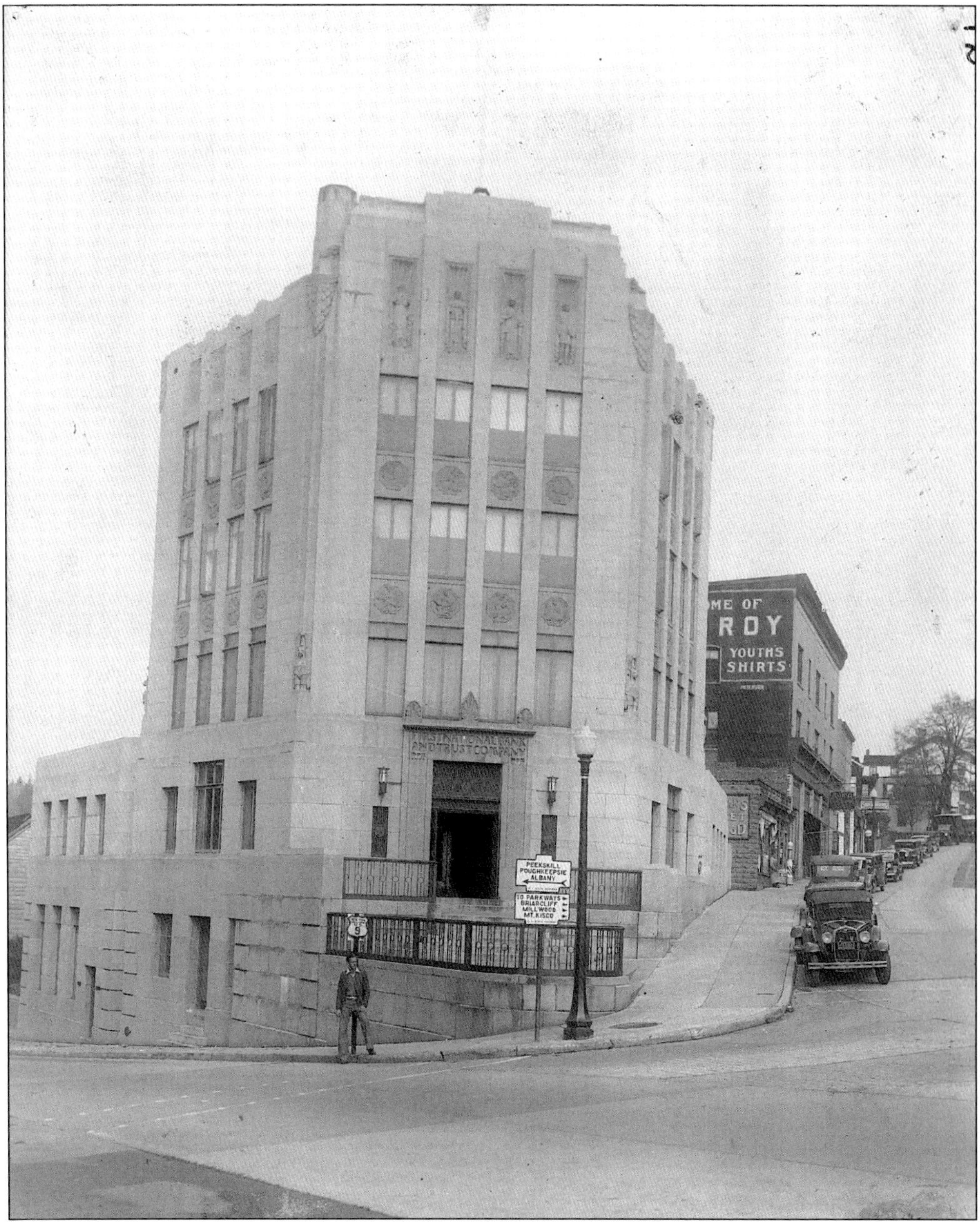

The First National Bank and Trust Company was located on the corner of North Highland and Croton Avenue. It was constructed in the 1930s, during the peak of the art deco style, and featured ornate elements at the top of the facade, gargoyles on the corners, and a Classical entrance with fluted columns. In 2005, the Emigrant Bank opened a banking branch in the building after completing a comprehensive restoration inside and out.

In 1942, during WW II, the community flew this banner at Pleasant Square, also known as the "Crossroads." The banner represented the 1,650 service men and women from the greater Ossining area who were involved in the nation's war effort.

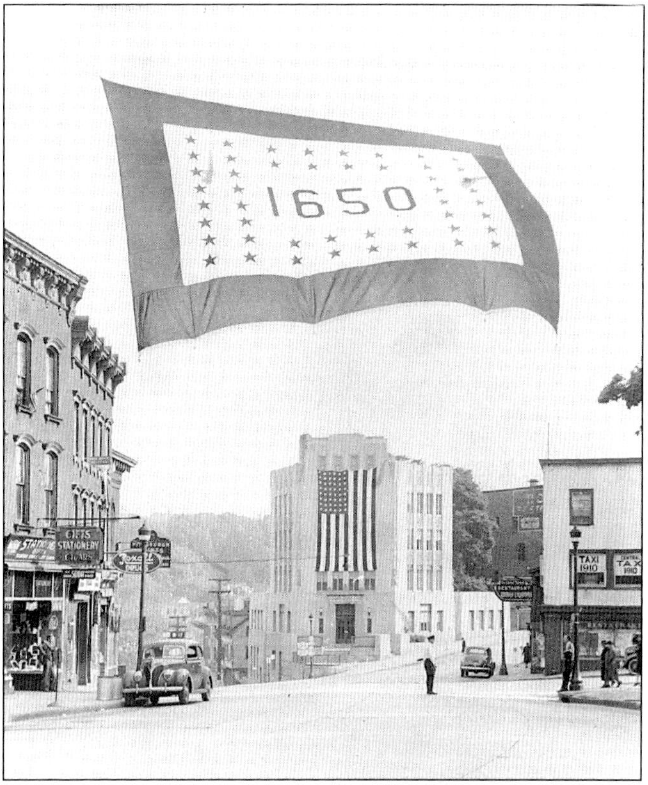

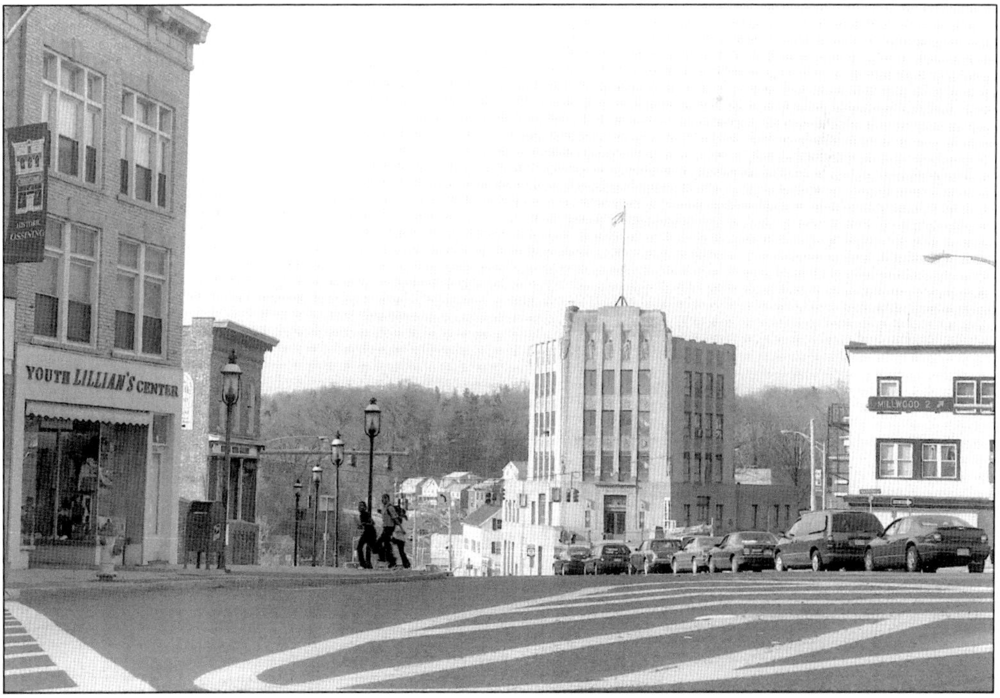

Pleasant Square is seen here in 1999, looking towards the corner of North Highland and Croton Avenues. The photograph was taken from the front of the old Bank for Savings.

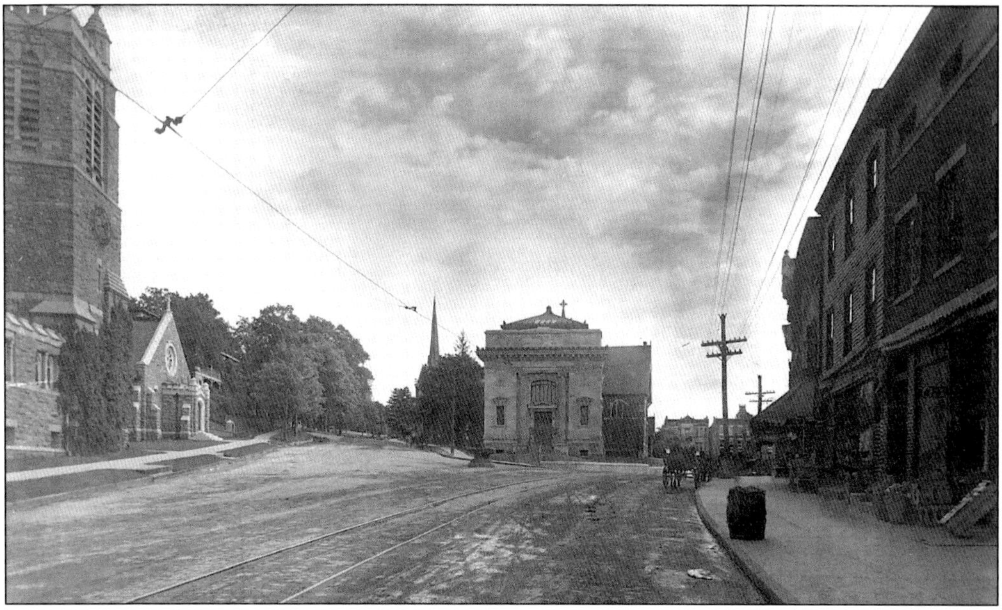

Main Street and South Highland Avenue are seen in this image, looking south toward the Bank for Savings, around 1910. The spire of the First Presbyterian Church can be seen in the background, trolley wires overhead, and trolley tracks below. A stone trough, erected in 1891 by the Sing Sing SPCA in memory of Henry Bergh, "A Friend of the Animals," stood in front of the bank in the square.

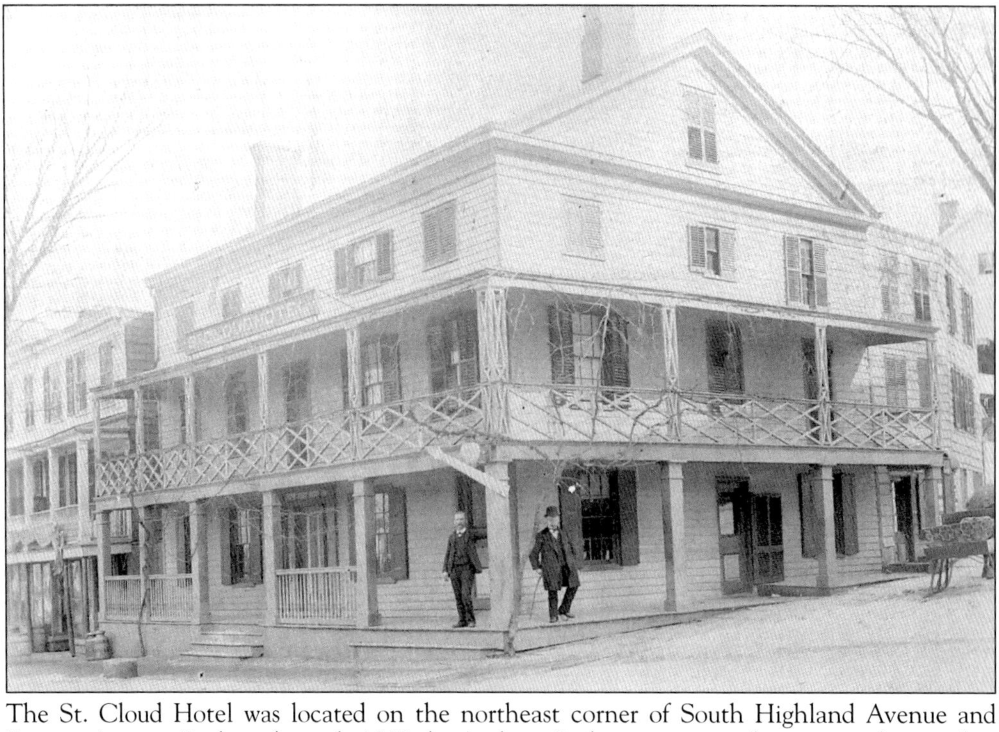

The St. Cloud Hotel was located on the northeast corner of South Highland Avenue and Eastern Avenue. Built in the early 1800s by Andrew Graham, its original name is unknown, but at one point, it was called the Ossining House.

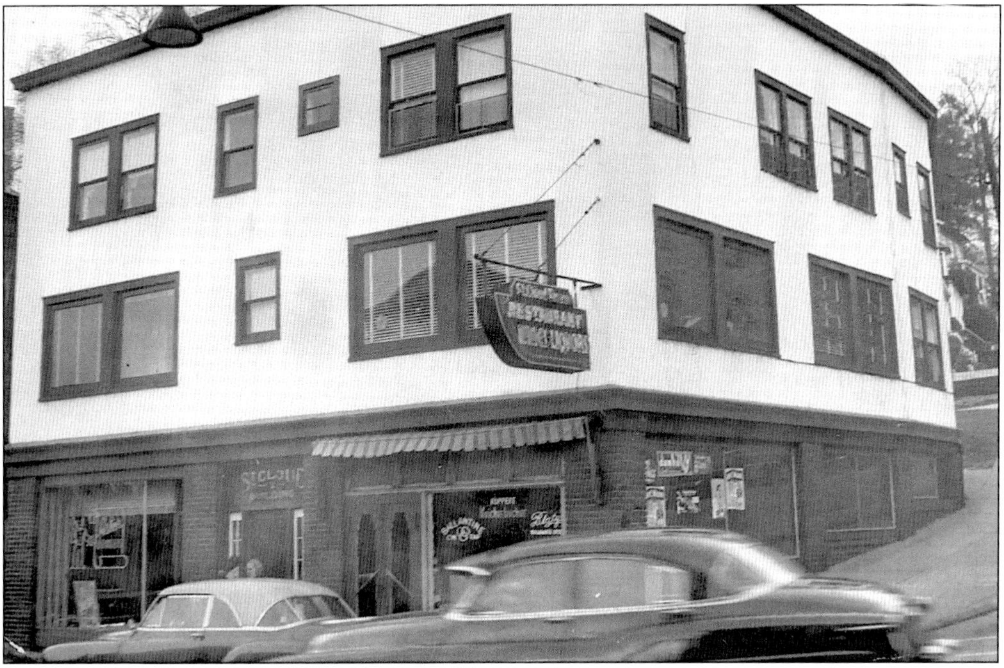

The St. Cloud Hotel was replaced by the St. Cloud Building and Tavern, on the same corner of South Highland Avenue and Eastern Avenue, in 1952.

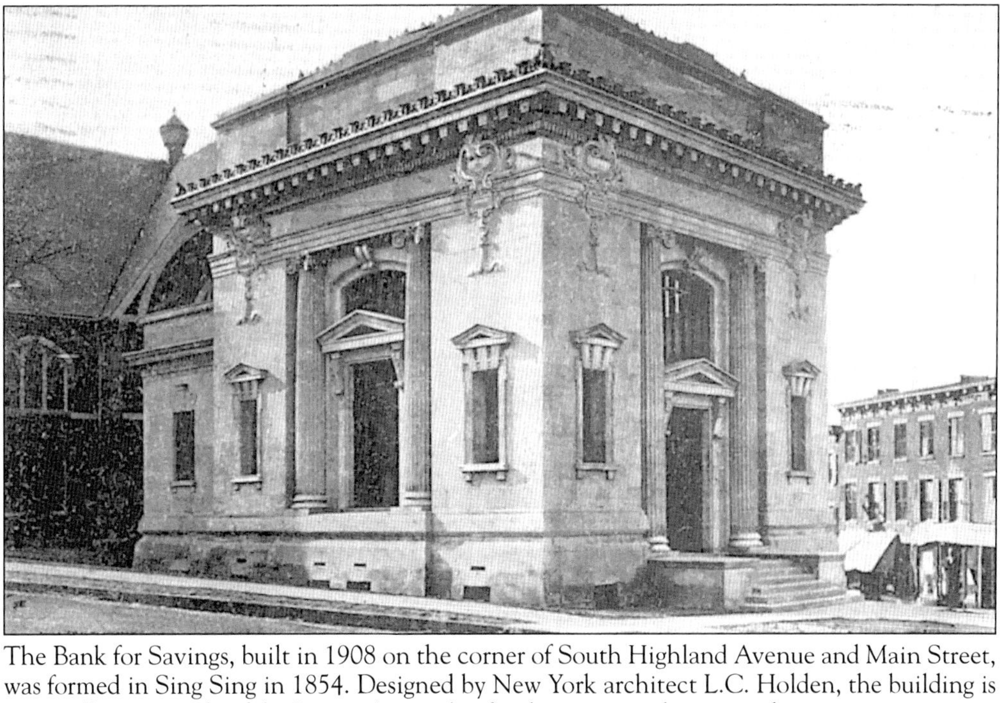

The Bank for Savings, built in 1908 on the corner of South Highland Avenue and Main Street, was formed in Sing Sing in 1854. Designed by New York architect L.C. Holden, the building is an excellent example of the Beaux-Arts style of architecture and commands a major intersection of the village. Features of the building include strong geometric forms, Classical details, Ionic columns, and excellent cartouches (oval decorations). It is one of the best examples of this style in Westchester County.

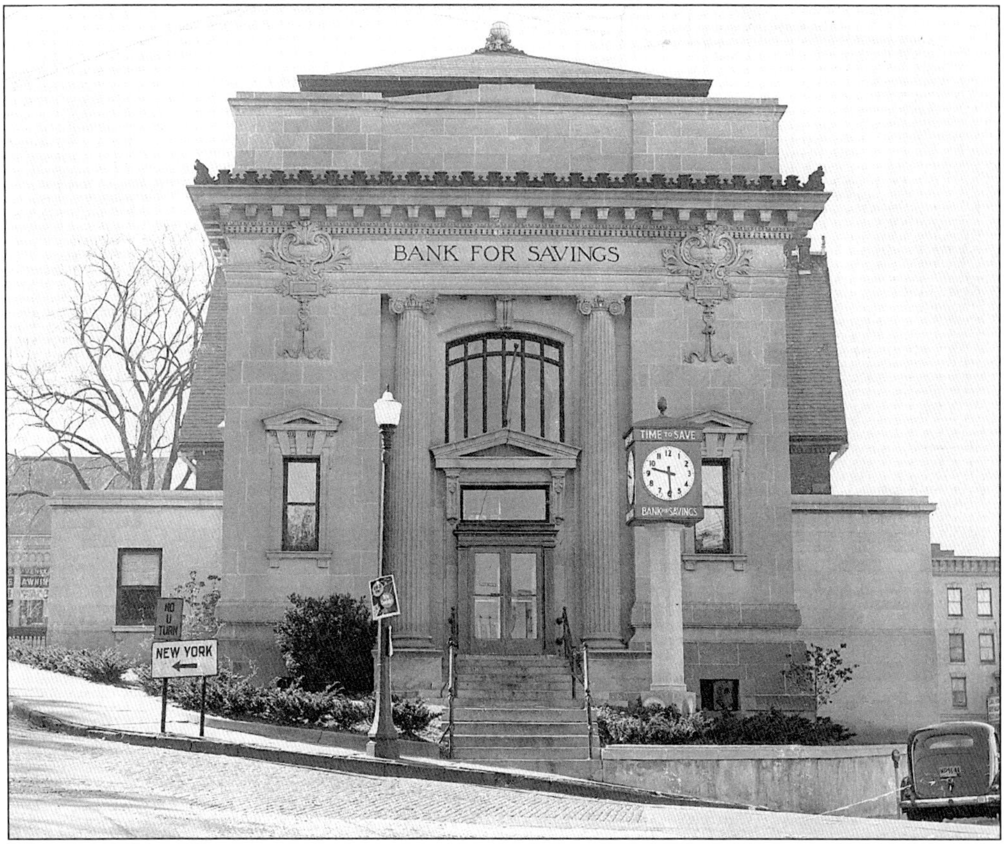

The exterior of the Bank for Savings remains essentially as it was built, except for window frames, glass, and the 1949 addition of two small wings at the rear of each side.

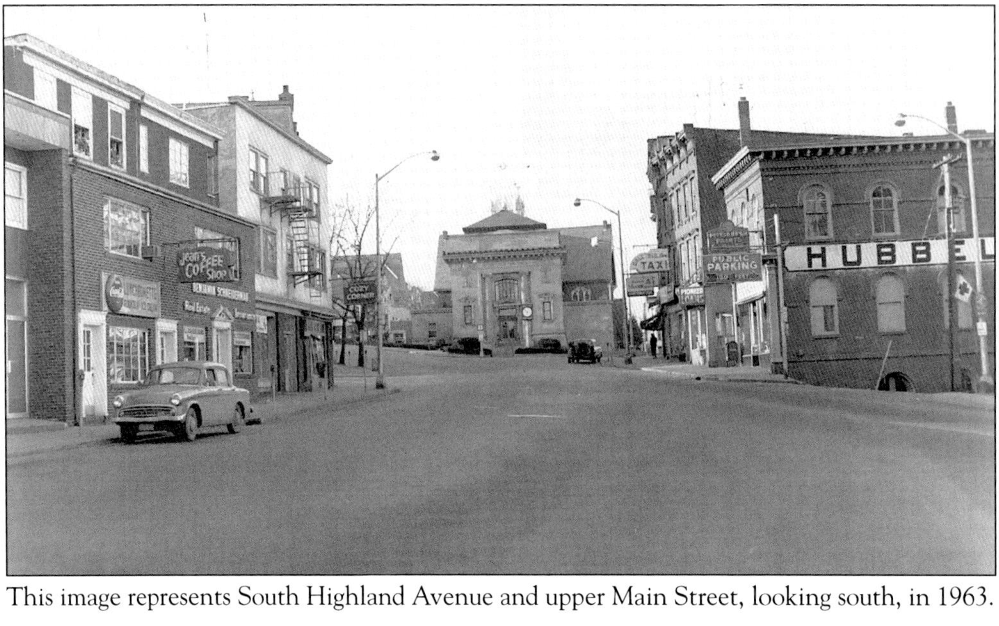

This image represents South Highland Avenue and upper Main Street, looking south, in 1963.

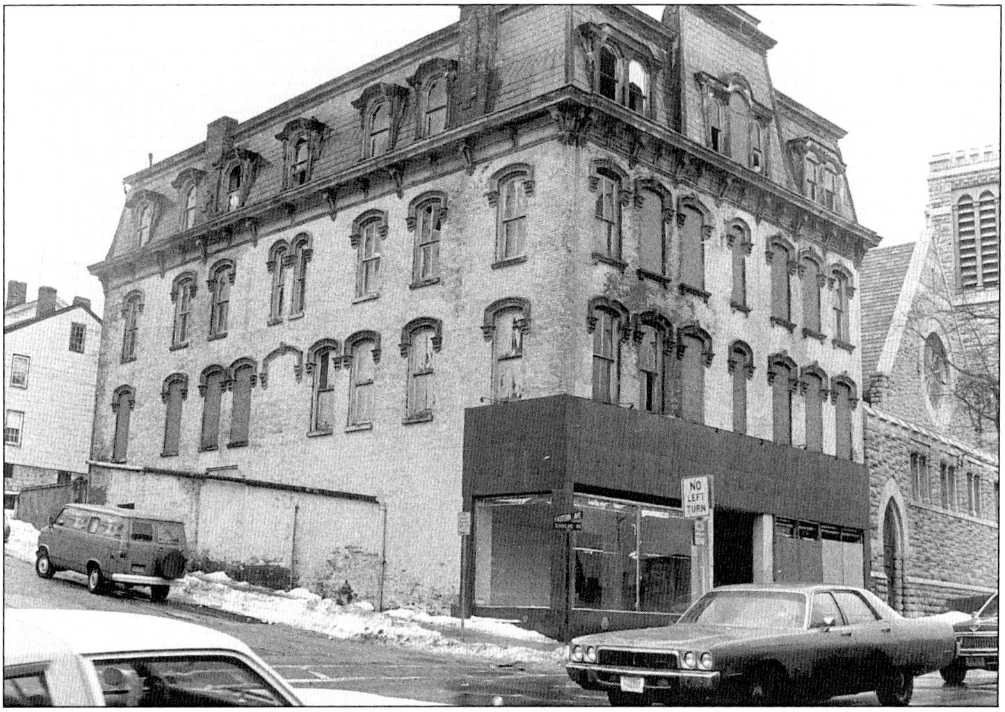

A superb example of the High Victorian Italianate style with a Mansard roof, this building stood on the corner of South Highland and Eastern Avenues, next to the Trinity Episcopal Church. It was erected around 1862 in a style not usually designed for commercial structures, which made it unique. During its long history, the building served as the village's first free dispensary, starting in 1886; a "Dramatic Hall" for lectures, dances, and concerts; a post office; and Arthur Curry's Auto Restaurant, which not only served chops and oysters, but it sold gasoline for the first motorcars in the community. Later, the building housed a furniture store and was eventually demolished in 1979.

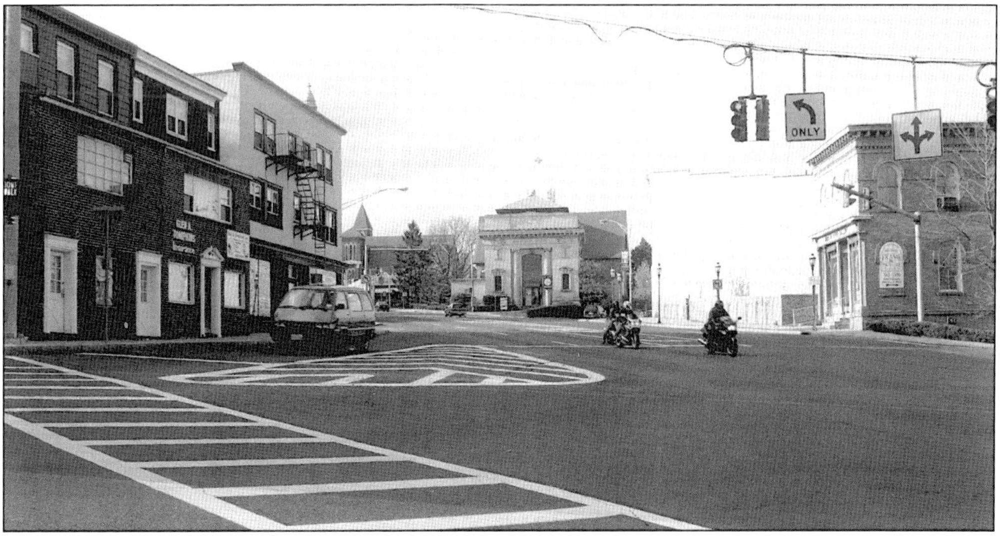

This photograph, taken in 1999, shows Pleasant Square in the foreground and the former "Bank with the Clock" in the background.

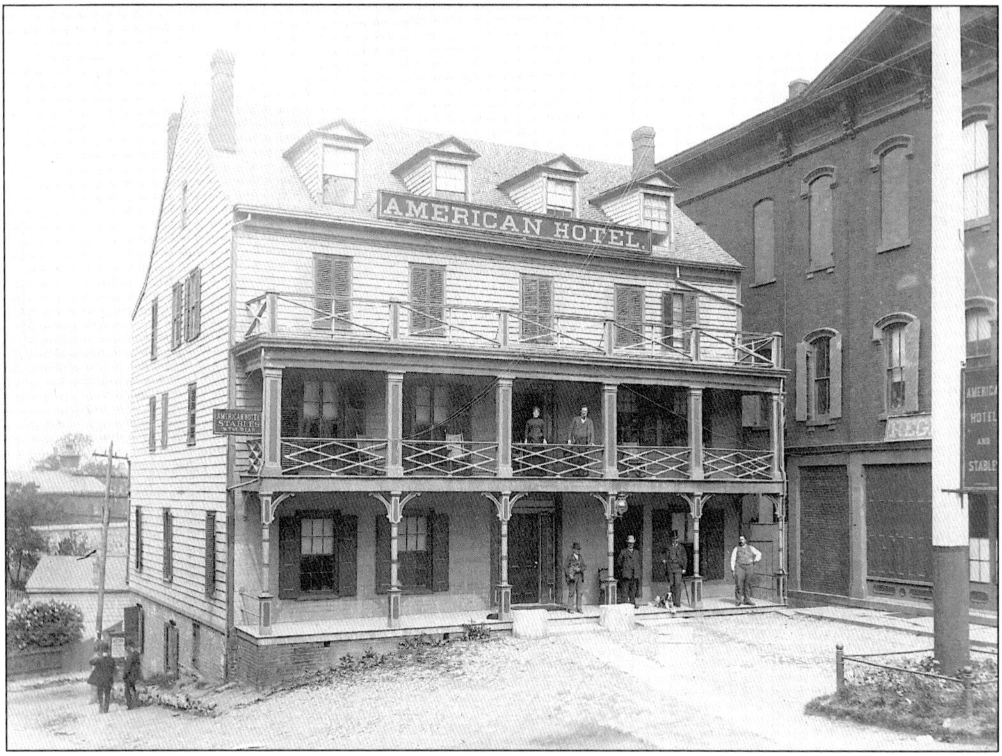

The American Hotel, on the northwest corner of North Highland Avenue and Broadway, is shown here in 1860. Built around 1800, the hotel was a "hotel in every best sense of the word" and featured a "large sample room for the accommodation of traveling men, a first-class cafe and billiard room." The hotel was also a stage house used by passengers traveling to Albany and New York City.

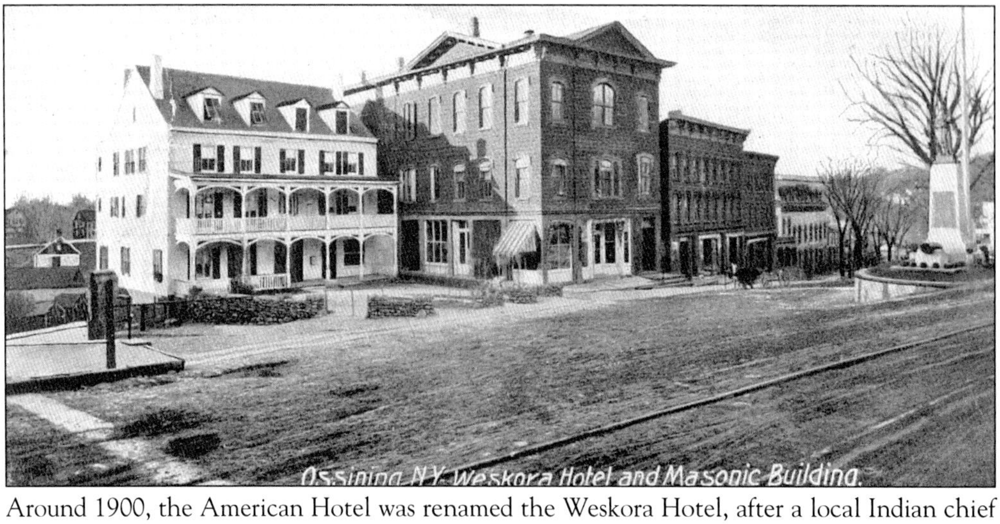

Around 1900, the American Hotel was renamed the Weskora Hotel, after a local Indian chief who sold the Ossining area to Lord of the Manor Frederick Philipse in 1685. The Weskora was destroyed by fire in 1928. The Masonic Hall Building was located next to the hotel. In the right corner of the photograph, the Soldier's Monument can be seen as well as trolley tracks heading up Croton Avenue (in the foreground).

Talcott Hall, on the northwest corner of North Highland Avenue, was built in 1861 and was the home of Sing Sing's local newspaper, the *Democratic Register*. In 1873, Talcott Hall became the home of Westchester Lodge of Free and Accepted Masons and was thereafter called Masonic Hall. The hall was the site of numerous businesses including a harness and saddle maker as well as many public, social, and political events, which were held in the upper floors. The building was demolished around 1973.

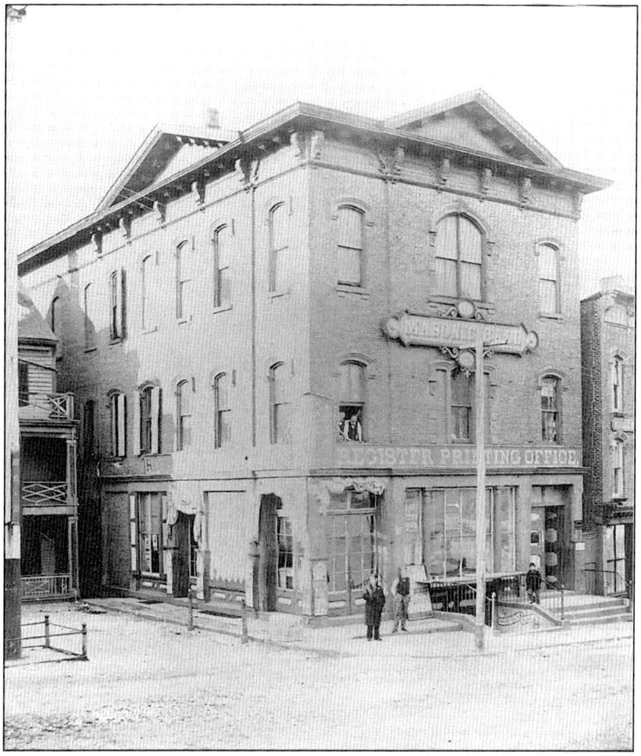

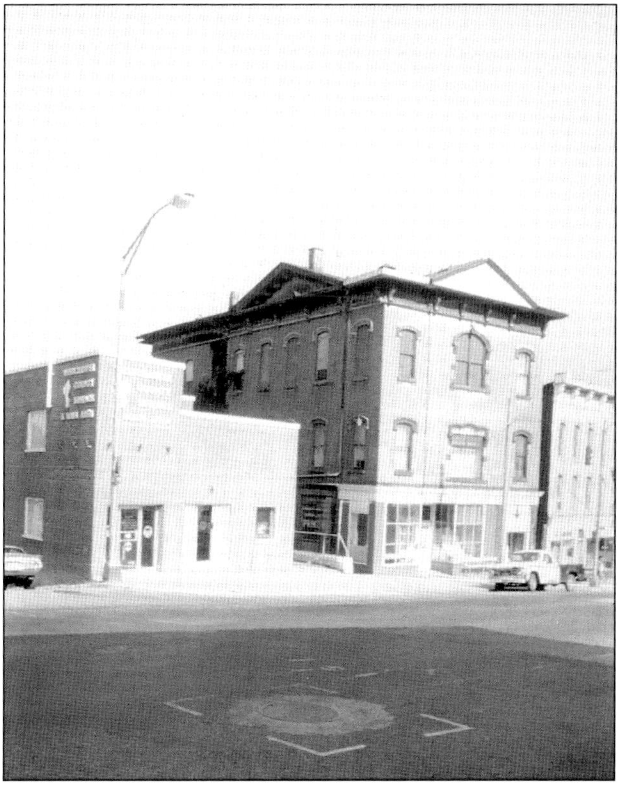

A new bank, the Westchester County Savings & Loan Association, was built on the site of the Weskora Hotel in the 1950s. The Masonic Hall stood to the right of the new bank, at the top of North Highland Avenue.

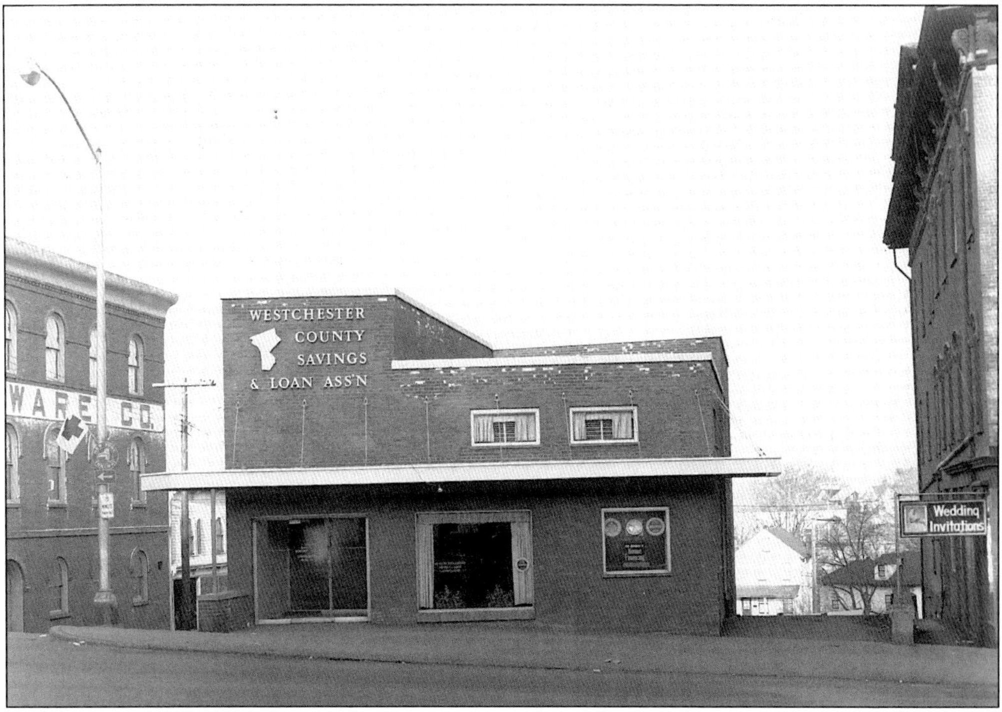

The Westchester County Savings & Loan Association, on the corner of Broadway and North Highland Avenue, is shown here in 1963. Hubbell's Hardware Store was to the left of the bank, and the Masonic Hall was to the right.

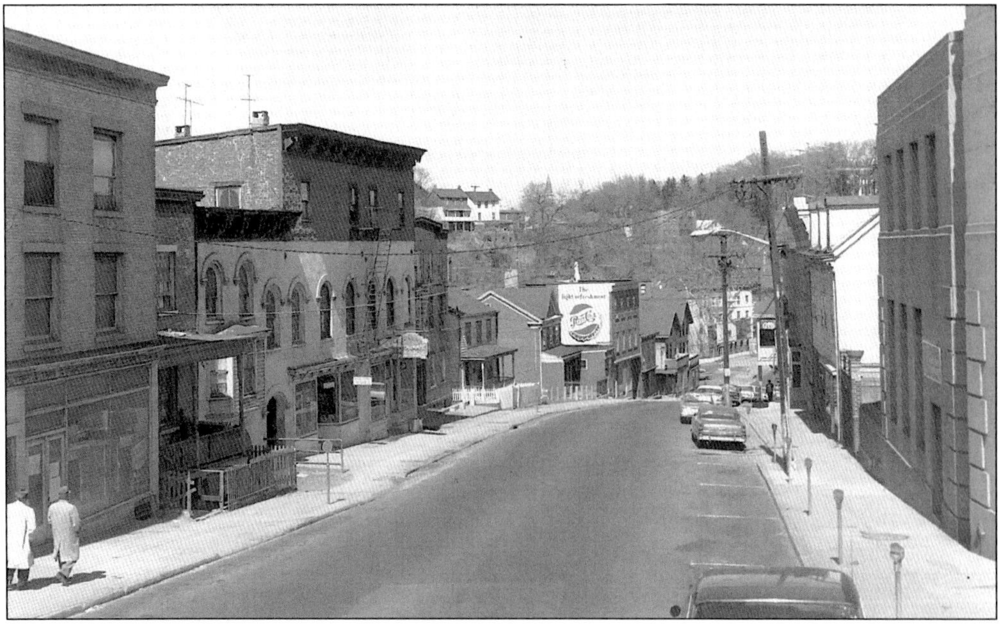

This is a view looking northwest down North Highland Avenue in 1963. In this view, the First National Bank is seen to the right, multi-use buildings are located to the left, and the spire of St. Augustine's Roman Catholic Church stands in the distance. All of the structures on the left side of this photograph have been torn down.

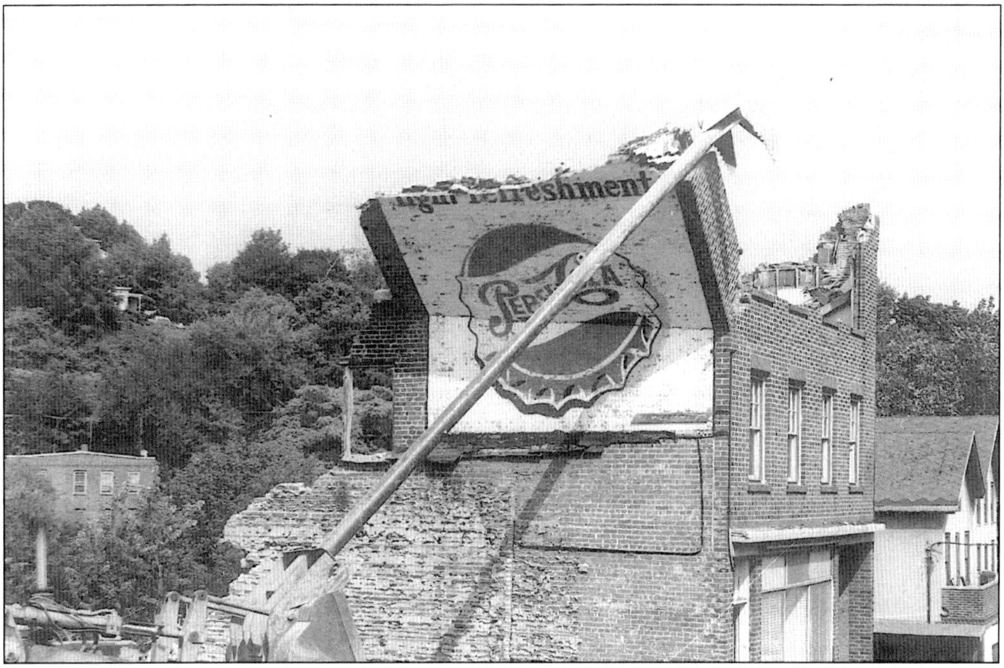

The razing of North Highland Avenue structures was part of the local urban renewal program in the 1970s.

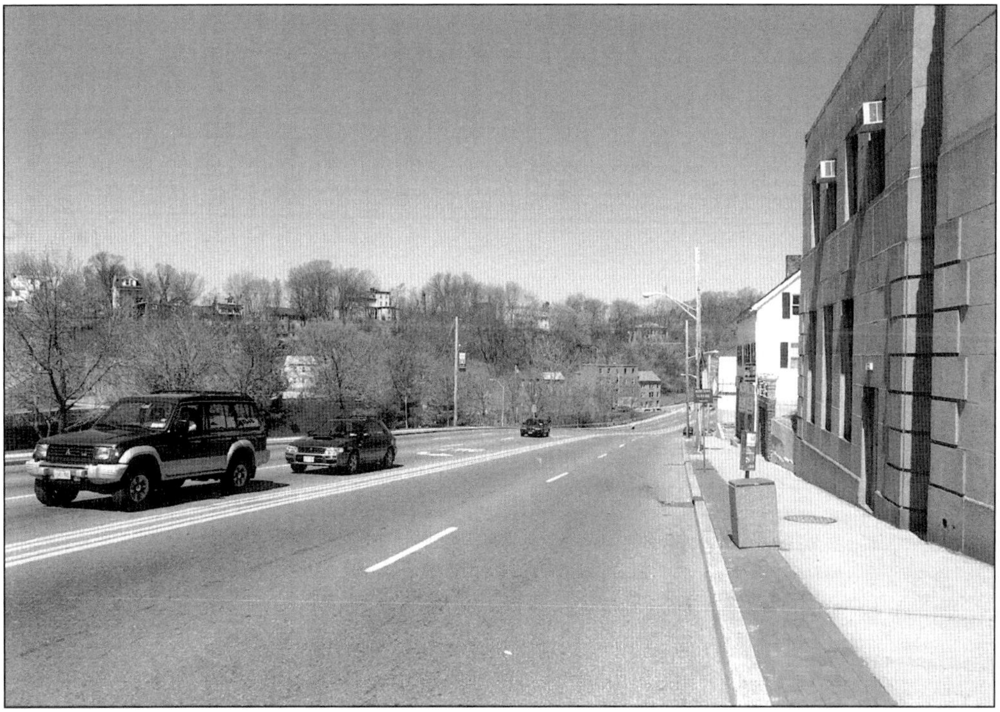

Shown here is a view looking down North Highland Avenue in 1999. The facade of the former First National Bank and Trust Company is to the right of the image.

I remember—

The Victoria Theater. There were steps in front of the Victoria Theater, as can be seen with ancient Roman buildings, and with brass handrails. The ticket window was inside the theater, on the right side of the sloped lobby. You knew just where to look for your friends, and sooner or later you met everyone you knew. Everyone went to the "Vic," and they had their favorite seats. The theater had a center aisle, and my favorite seat was the first one on the right of the aisle, row 12. At each side of the theater, the balcony reached forward toward the stage (like two thin arms) with just two seats in each row to create an extended loge. The phone number was 626. The show changed three times a week but always had a double feature—one bill from Sunday through Tuesday and another from Thursday through Saturday. Wednesday was a C-rated pair with limited appeal. Once in a while, a smash hit would lengthen a three-day bill to four days. The images were always projected while the curtain was closed. Then it dramatically opened to reveal its clear image. Uniformed ushers patrolled the theater in their brass buttons. No one went out of town for a movie. Although you had to wait until a movie left the first-run Times Square houses, eventually they all came to the Victoria. Unless you chose to go to Times Square to see the movie with its accompanying stage show, everyone seemed to go to the Victoria, at the intersection of Church and Main Streets, to see the show with its co-feature. The theater also featured Pathe and Movietone News—"The Eyes and Ears of the World." At Saturday matinees, you saved your ticket stub in the hopes of winning one of the prizes given each week by Ben's Stationary Store. I never won. The matinees were popular because of the serials shown each week such as Flash Gordon, Dick Tracy, and The Lone Ranger. Those cliffhangers brought you back every Saturday.

Woolworth's. Gold-colored Roman letters were set against a bright red background making up the Woolworth's emblem. So many things came from Woolworth's (at the top of Main Street), located two doors away from J.J. Newberry's, which was the other "Five-an-Ten." Merchandise in Woolworth's was displayed along the periphery, and the body of the store was divided into eighths, with a salesgirl in the center of each area. You knew exactly where items were located. Ten-cent goldfish were in a tank (in the front, left corner); school supplies were farther down the building on the left; 3-inch lead soldiers (among many other things) were found in the next-to-last section and cost a nickel apiece; balsa wood airplane models that you cut with a razor blade and put together with "airplane glue" were stacked on the rear shelf. There was a luncheonette counter that had an ever-present aroma of hot dogs and coffee. There was a "wave" in the center of the wooden floor that creaked. Christmastime at Woolworth's was irresistible. Lead tinsel on red-and-green ropes criss-crossing the store made the desirable toys all the more desirable. Snow-spray on the windows, candles and fake fireplaces, sparkles and glitter, red and green packages, images of reindeer and Santa on the walls, and trains and dolls and sleds were all on display. A kid naturally wanted everything there.

Hilliker's. Hilliker's was the town's classic department store. A big display window was situated on each side of the impressive entrance. It was a stately building that contained everything on one level, plus "the basement" stairs on the left. The salesladies wore black dresses with white collars and cuffs. Fine leather gloves were found in the case just inside the entrance. Mahogany and glass counters were all around. When you paid for your merchandise, your money and bill were placed inside a small cartridge at the counter that was sent upwards on tracks and then across the ceiling to the cashier in the far corner. There, the proper change was placed into the cartridge, which then journeyed back along the tracks like an electric train and stopped at its point of departure. There was an air of elegance about Hilliker's.

Kipp's. Working our way down Main Street, Kipp's was where everyone went for a Cherry Coke. It was one of several pharmacies in town, but it was the one with the most recognized name. Kipp's was housed in the most classical looking of all the buildings, with white, Greek Ionic columns that rose from the second story, unlike any other building on the street.

Ankerson's. Ankerson's, located on the corner of Spring and Main Streets, was the runner-up for popularity among the drug stores. There were two entrances to the small place, and the main entrance was located on the corner on the most famous of all intersections, Ossining's Broadway and 42nd Street. The soda fountain seemed to run the length of the store, and a hot chocolate with a dab of real whipped cream cost ten ¢.

Moses Myers. Moses Myers was located across the street from Ankerson's in its later years, but it originated a block lower on Main Street. The store was packed to the ceiling with toys and games of every size and description. Everything a child ever wanted could be found there. Bikes, electric trains, doll furniture, and Monopoly were all jammed in cases and on shelves as far as the eye could see. Seven daily newspapers were also on display.

The New York Store. Across the street from "Mo Myers" was an individually owned five-and-ten store unlike any other. The New York Store sold odd lots of chinaware and glassware, chipped "chemistry sets," and one-of-a-kind household items. The owner, Charlie Becker, was especially kind and patient with kids.

Ascherman's Bakery. Located on Spring Street, Ascherman's Bakery displayed endless goodies (with their tantalizing smells) in the window. Charlotte Russes created sponge cakes topped with whipped cream and a strawberry, which were contained in a cardboard cylinder. Decorated birthday cakes and apple turnovers were crafted by Karl the baker. There are fond memories of leaving Ossining High School (OHS) for lunch in the village. There was often a contest to see who could get to the downtown bakery the fastest to order the most fantastic sandwich. Some took Church Street, and others went via Maple Place. The sandwich was known as the Railroad. Half a loaf of fresh Italian bread was cut in half, laced with delicacies like ham, roast beef, salami, cheeses, lathered with thick layers of mayonnaise and mustard, and finally finished off with a cold Hires Root Beer. Lastly, there was a race back to sit on the school wall, luxuriating in every last bite.

Abelon. Abelon was every teenager's favorite, and only, record shop. All records, which were 78s back then, were sold individually in tan, paper sleeves with a die-cut circle in the center, showing the label. Columbia, Decca, Capitol, Bluebird, and Victor were some of the many labels featured at Abelon during the Big Band era. You waited for your favorite record to come in, and when it did, you played it over and over again until the sound became scratchy. Back then, there was no automatic placing of another record, and when a song finished, you picked up the record and placed another on the turntable, handling the "pickup" each time. Touch only the edges please. Abelon also had a three-day lending library for hardcover books or you could purchase them at ten ¢ per book.

Anna Bentz's Knit Shop. Located farther down Spring Street was Anna Bentz's Knit Shop. It seemed that at one time or another, every woman in town was in the narrow store knitting, buying yarn, or getting instructions. Chairs lined one wall of the store, where the women all sat. During WW II, knitting for the servicemen was a popular homespun activity, and wives and mothers spent hours knitting scarves, sweaters, and socks for the war effort.

One-O-Five and the Half Moon. Wintery Friday nights included attending the exciting Hudson River League basketball games in the old OHS gym. There were many hard fought battles with fierce rivals such as North Tarrytown, Washington Irving, Hastings, Croton, and Peekskill. Screaming after every point, among fellow spectators jammed into the balcony of a packed house, was a common activity. Spilling out into the cold night, there was total exhaustion after each game. Marching en masse down Church Street to Main and Spring Streets, you were drawn towards the strong odors of tomatoes, cheese, and garlic floating up the street. The two most popular pizza parlors (after we stopped calling it "LaBeetz" or "hot pie" and began calling it pizza) were One-O-Five and the Half Moon. There was a special identifying smell of "hot pie" like no other. After the games, piling through the front door to booths lining each side of the restaurants, or tables in the center, was the common trend. Six friends per booth made it a memorable evening. Walking home and saying goodnight to everyone as his or her street was reached often finished off the evening. Each person was sure to sleep soundly on those nights.

Two

ARCHITECTURAL TREASURES

Throughout the 1800s and the early 1900s, gracious homes and large estates were prevalent in communities along the Hudson River. In Ossining, mansions sat above the river with commanding views of the Hudson and surrounding countryside. The village streets, like Highland Avenue and State Street, were lined with homes of the wealthy and prosperous middle class that represented a variety of architectural styles of the time.

The exciting aspect of Ossining's architecture was that, like Westchester County, it contained a wide diversity of domestic structures of unusual breadth, style, and quality. Some of the oldest houses in the entire nation are located in our countryside, and the tradition of setting the theme for new shapes and fashions was born in our area. Also unique is the fact that one could venture down any number of Ossining streets and view a multitude of different forms standing in a line, from Greek Revival to Gothic to Victorian.

Those structures that remain today are a living connection to the incredible development of our village, first as Sing Sing and later Ossining. Some are still with us and offer a special look into what used to be. A distinct feeling can be captured by simply taking the time to walk by, look up, and imagine how exclusive they were at another time in history. They clearly show what a special suburban community we grew into and still are. In this chapter, we are able to tell about a few of these great houses.

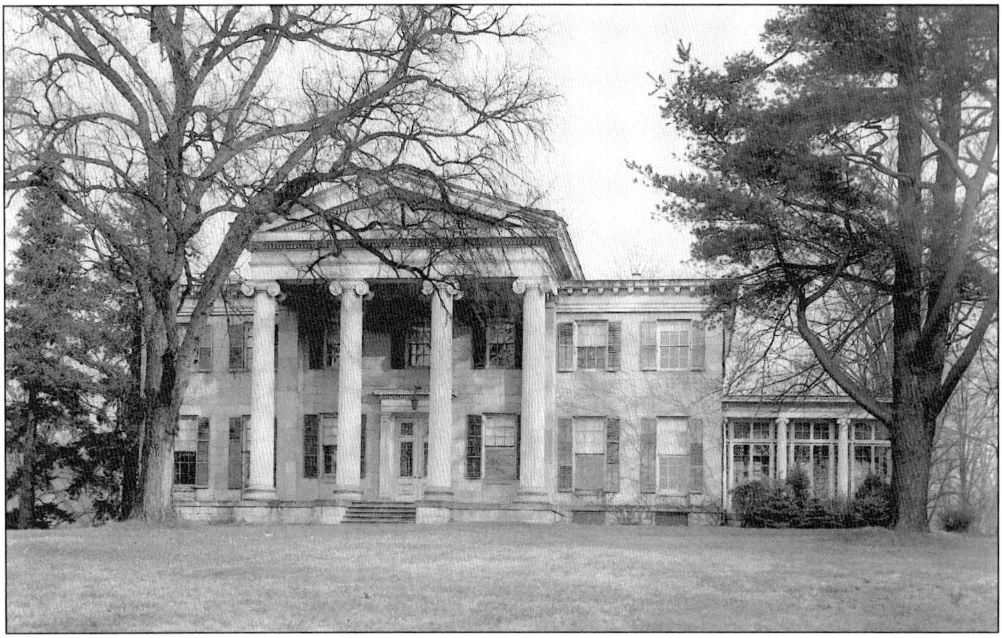

Careswell was the impressive Greek Revival mansion of General Aaron Ward. Ward, born in Sing Sing in 1790, served in the War of 1812. He was also a Westchester County district attorney and five-term congressman. Built in 1835 of Sing Sing marble, the structure was razed to make room for the expansion of the high school on South Highland Avenue.

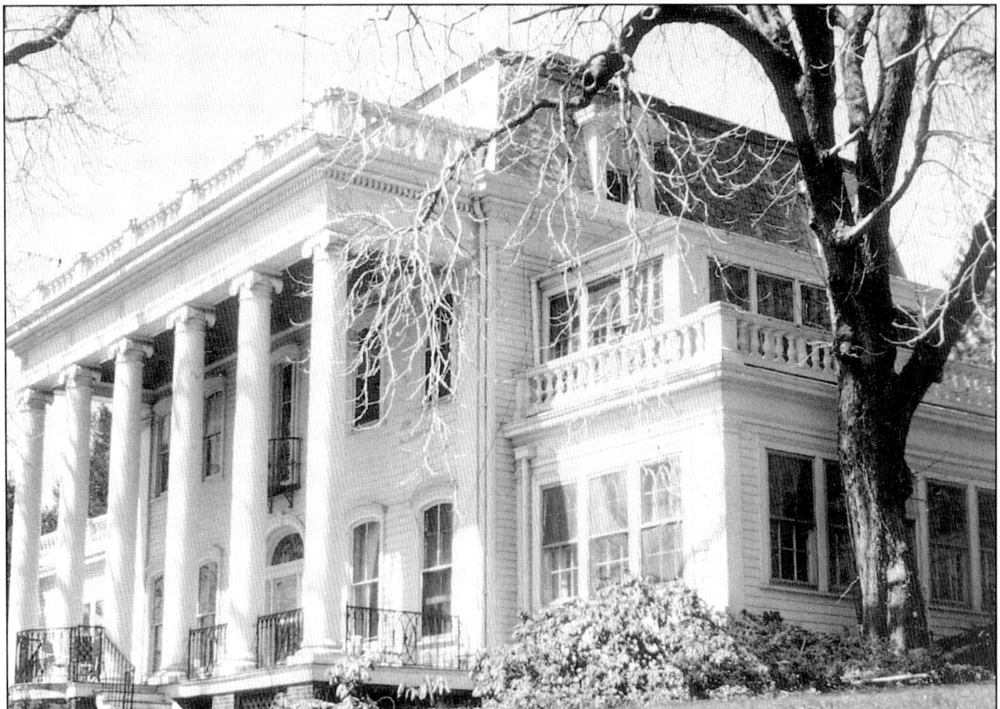

George D. Arthur built his impressive new home on the site of the Kemey house in 1870. The structure was razed to construct Kemey's Cove Condominiums.

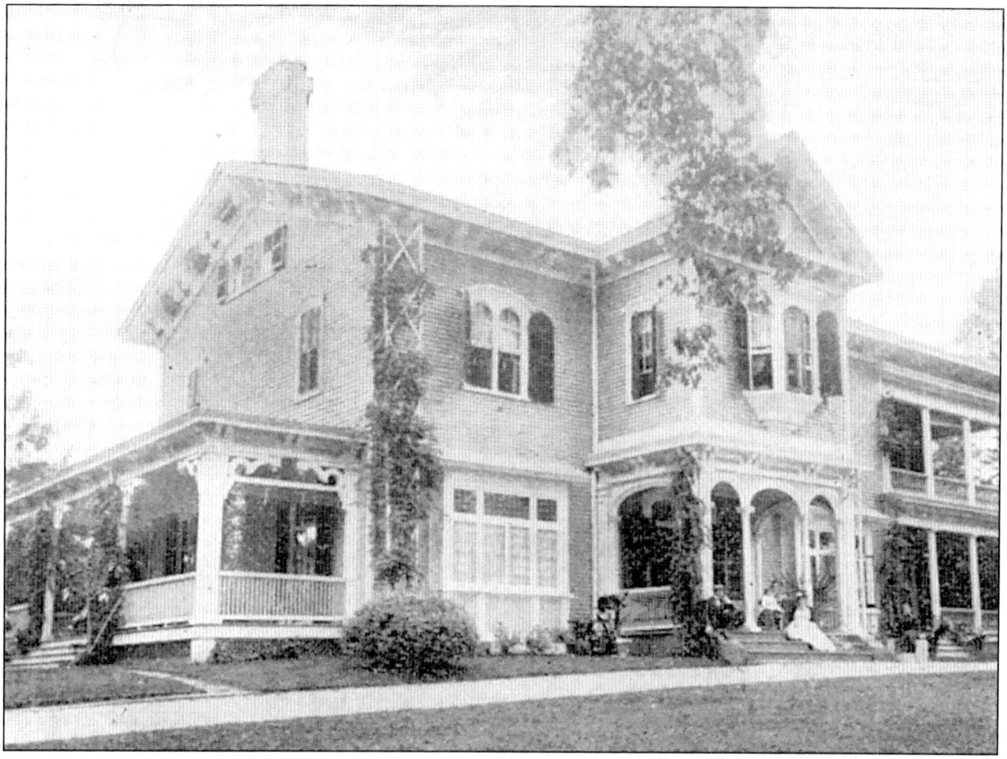

On the property next to Careswell was Lindwalden, the home of George F. Secor, one of many fine homes lining South Highland Avenue. The house was demolished to build Ossining High School in 1929.

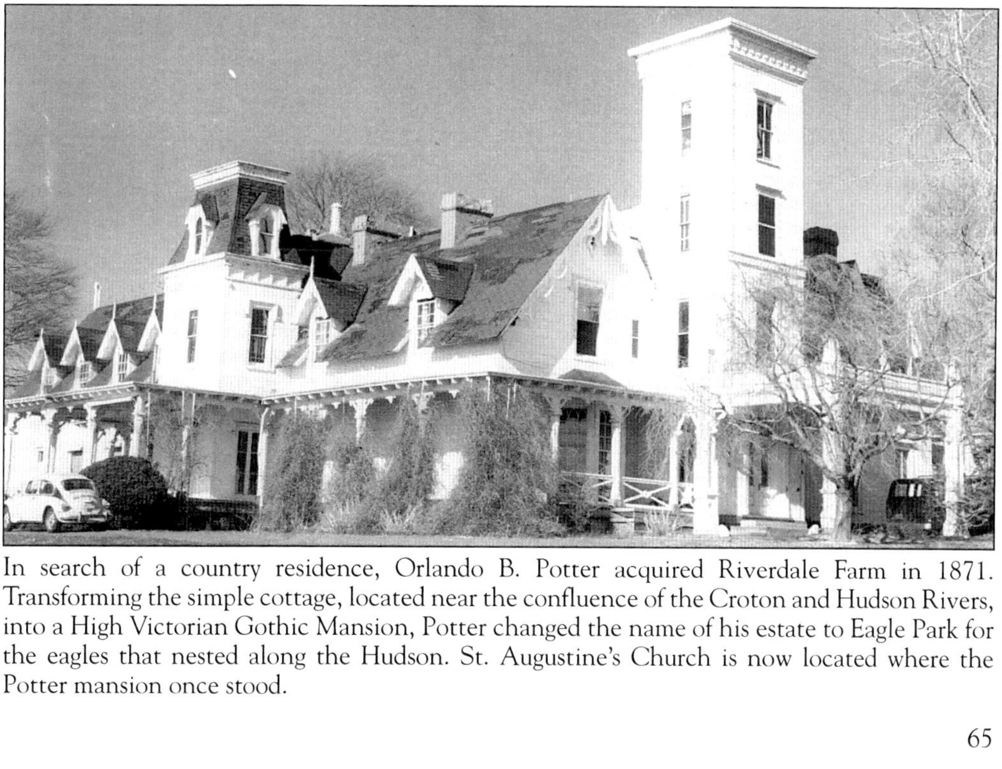

In search of a country residence, Orlando B. Potter acquired Riverdale Farm in 1871. Transforming the simple cottage, located near the confluence of the Croton and Hudson Rivers, into a High Victorian Gothic Mansion, Potter changed the name of his estate to Eagle Park for the eagles that nested along the Hudson. St. Augustine's Church is now located where the Potter mansion once stood.

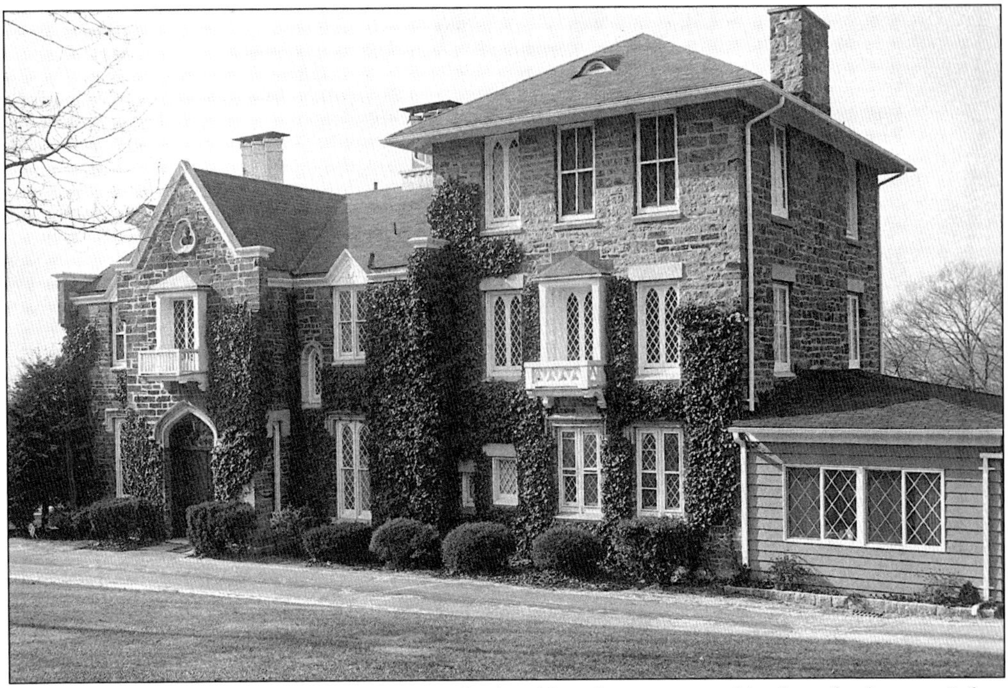

This c. 1845 Gothic Revival mansion was built of hand cut granite blocks, which were 2 feet thick, by John Innis Kane. Named Woodlawn, the country villa was situated on 46 acres stretching from Highland Avenue to the Hudson River. The estate stayed in the Kane family for nearly 100 years. The building is now owned by the Engelhard Corporation.

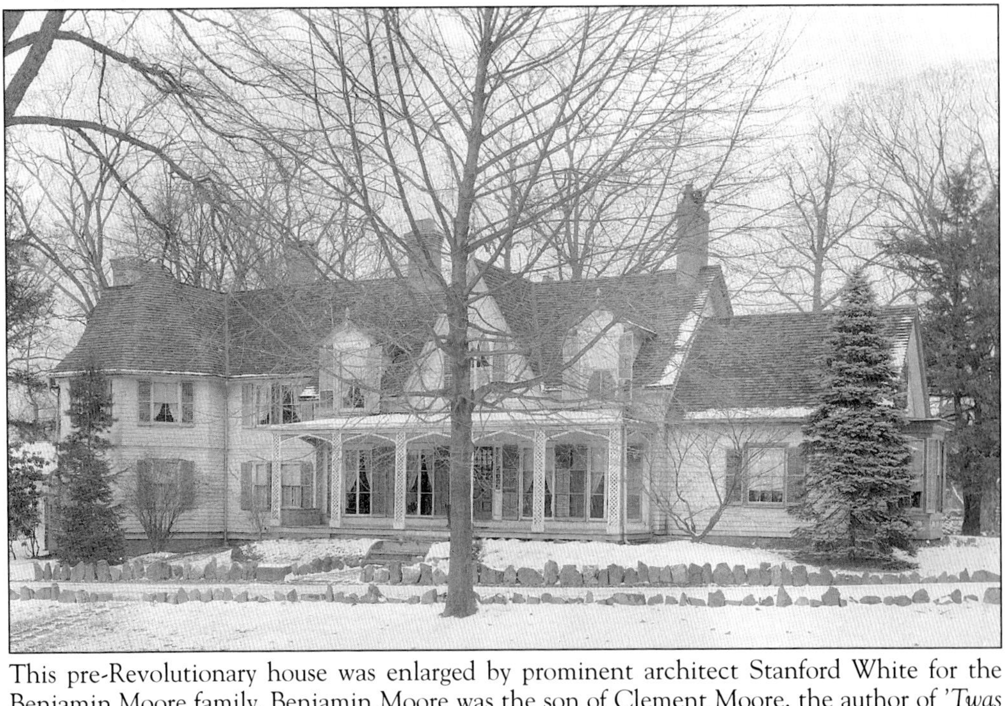

This pre-Revolutionary house was enlarged by prominent architect Stanford White for the Benjamin Moore family. Benjamin Moore was the son of Clement Moore, the author of *'Twas the Night Before Christmas*. Known as Moorehaven, this house is located on Beach Road.

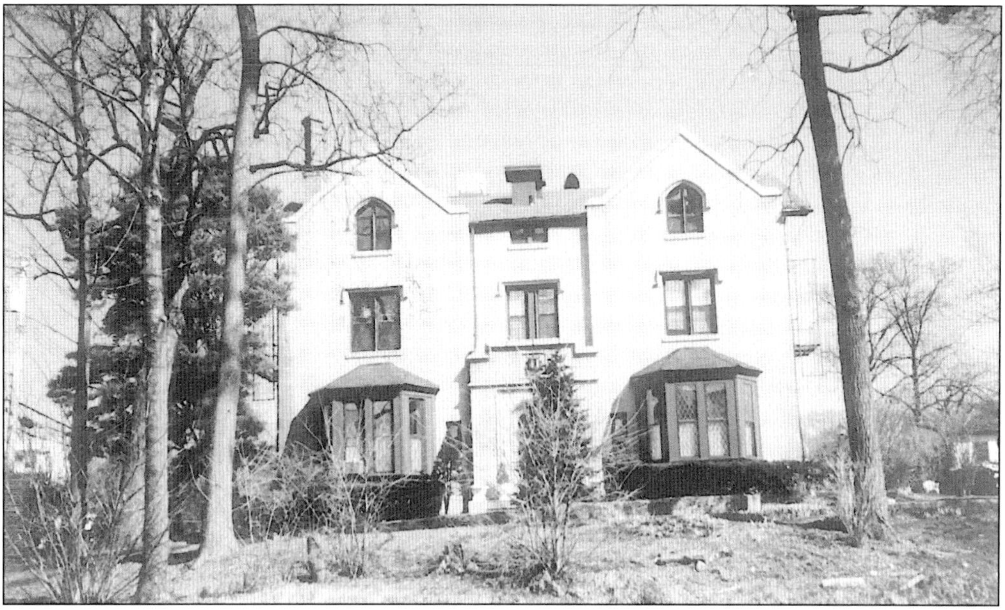

This Gothic Revival mansion is built of Sing Sing marble. The Thedford or Larkin house is on Emwilton Place on property that originally extended to South Highland Avenue.

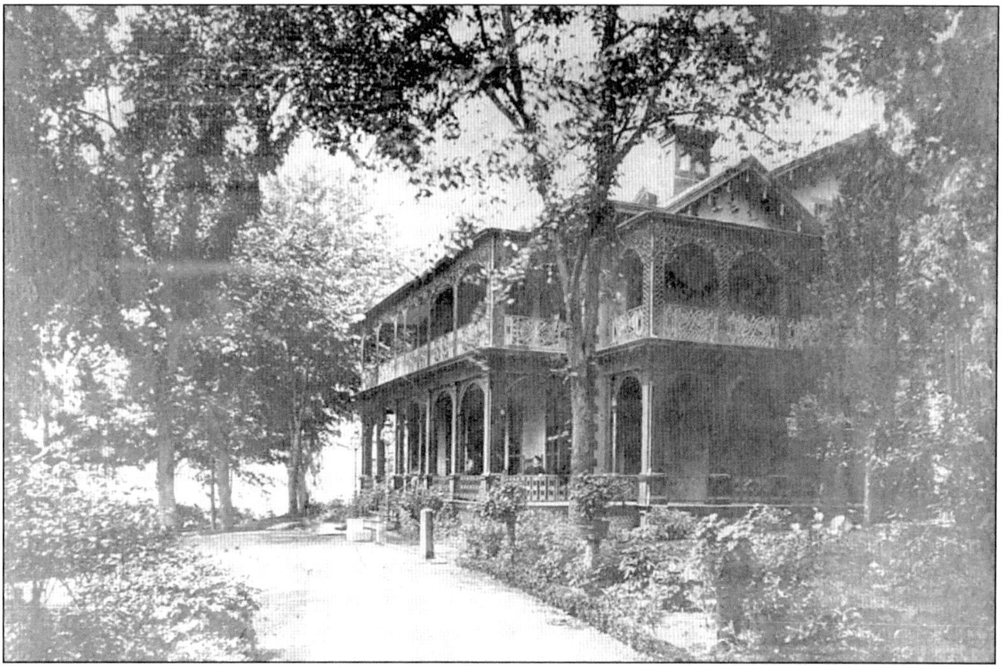

Influenced by the decorative ironwork of homes in New Orleans, Benjamin Brandreth incorporated large verandas with fanciful gingerbread trim into the design of Glyndon. Situated close to the railroad tracks, the mansion contained 35 rooms and 18 baths, unheard of in a house built in 1850. The mansion was later demolished.

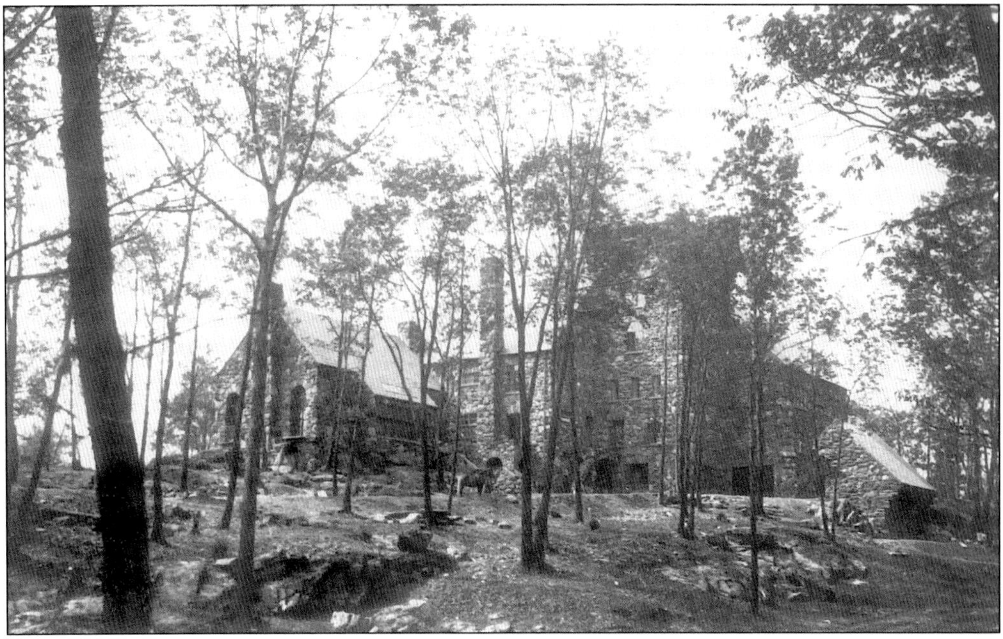

David T. Abercrombie of Abercrombie and Fitch built this retirement home on Croton Dam Road in 1925. The estate derives its name, Elda, from the initials of the names of the four Abercrombie children. The 25-room castle was built, surrounded by woods, at the end of a half-mile-long drive with ponds, reflecting pool, and spring-fed swimming pool.

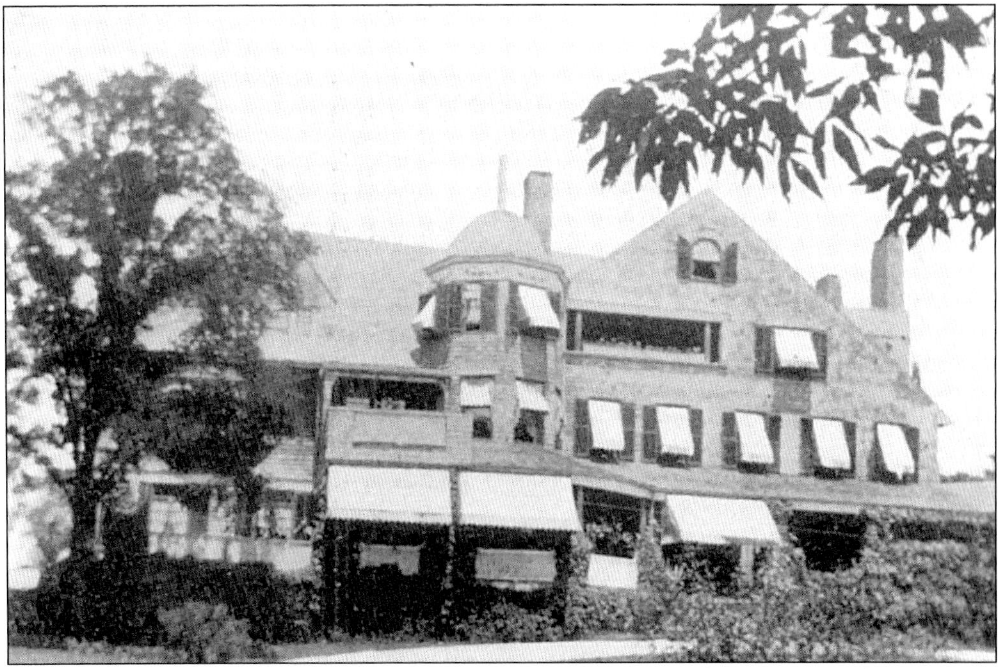

Colonel E.A. McAlpin built Hillside in 1889, on 15 acres adjoining Snowden Avenue, Broadway, North Malcolm, and Matilda Streets. Located on the site of an existing estate, Rock Spur, the front of the house extended 100 feet across. Hillside continues to serve as a residence as the Victoria Home for Retired Men and Women.

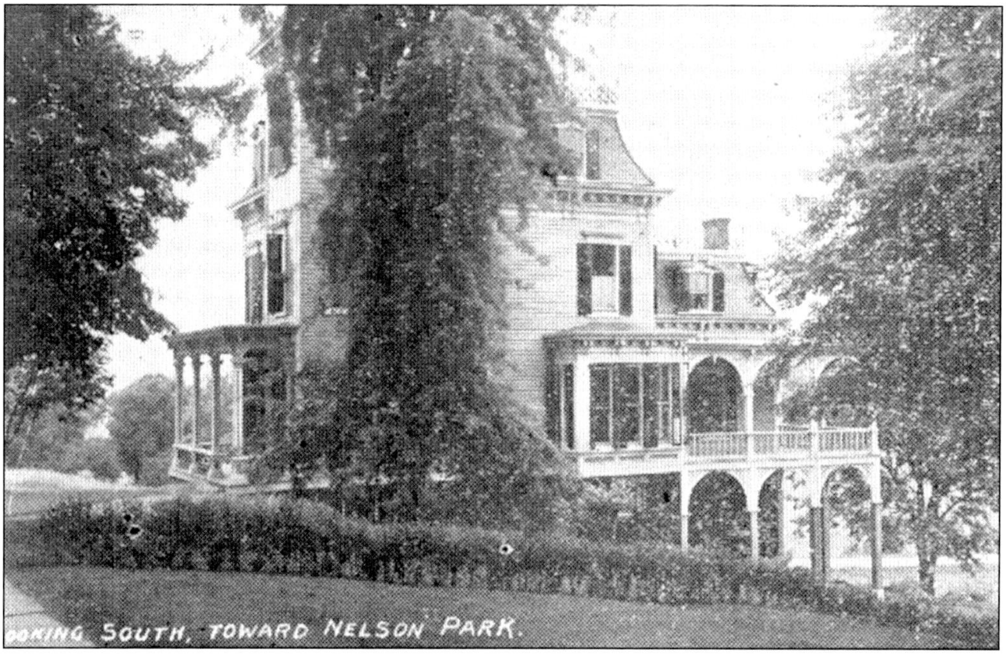

Village architect S. Marvin McCord, whose career spanned more than 45 years, built his home on South Highland Avenue, at the corner of Washington Avenue, overlooking Nelson Park. The house was built in the Second Empire style in 1891. McCord's most noteworthy work is the design of Highland Cottage.

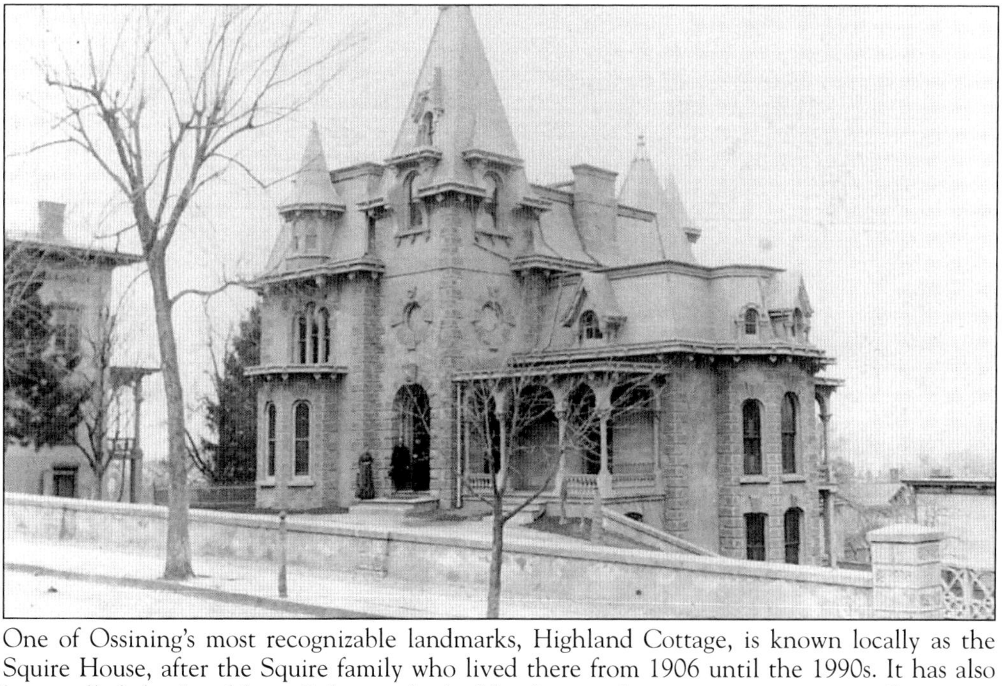

One of Ossining's most recognizable landmarks, Highland Cottage, is known locally as the Squire House, after the Squire family who lived there from 1906 until the 1990s. It has also been called the "mud house" due to the building's poured concrete construction. Consisting of an elaborate blend of turrets, towers, bay windows, and gables, this home, built in the early 1870s, portrays the romantic style once popular in the Hudson Valley.

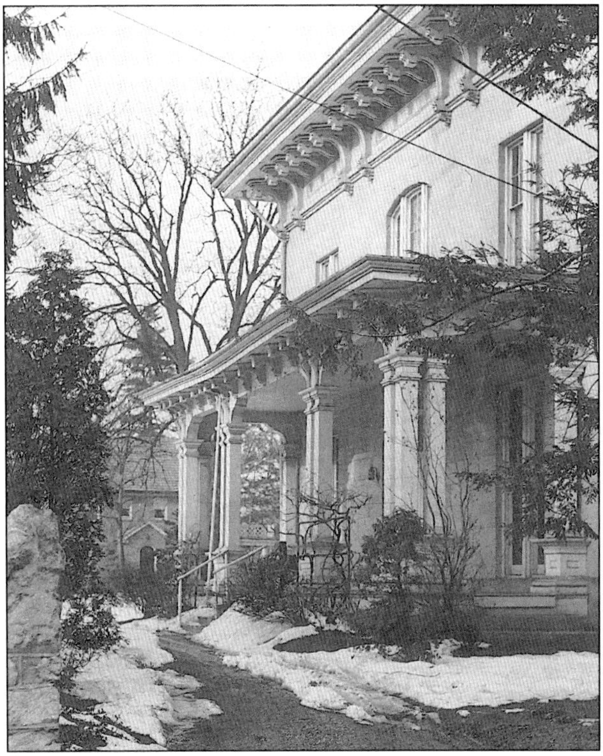

The Marcius Cobb, or Madden house, is located on Lincoln Place. It was built in 1850, of locally quarried Sing Sing marble.

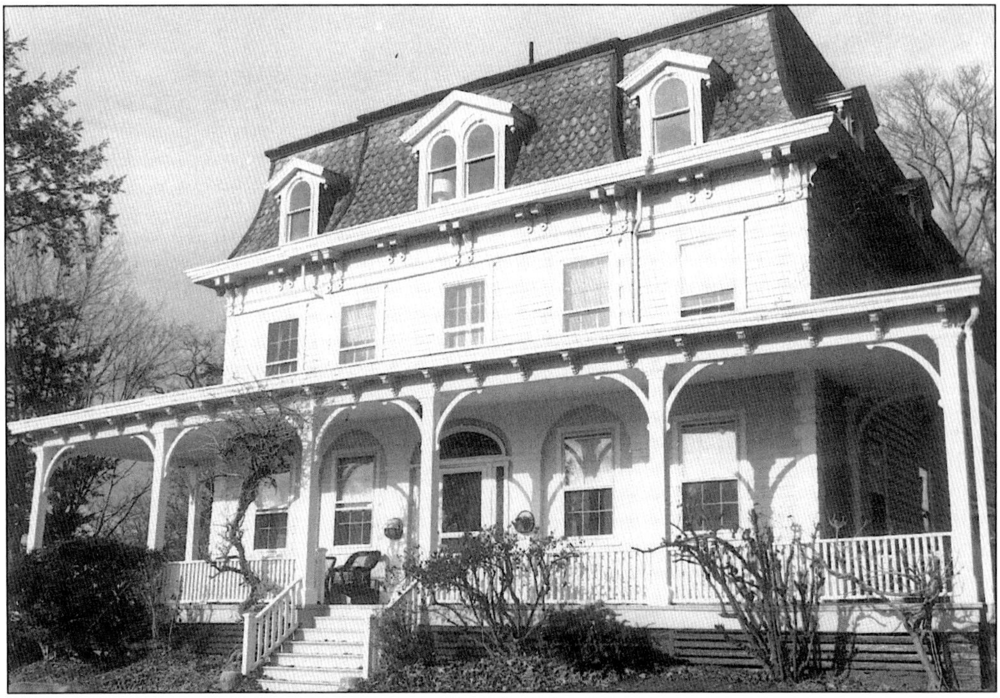

Built in 1812, Grove Hill, as it was originally called, has had a number of renovations including the addition of a mansard roof and a third floor (probably in the 1870s). The house has been in the Brandreth family since the early 1900s and was renamed Boxwood.

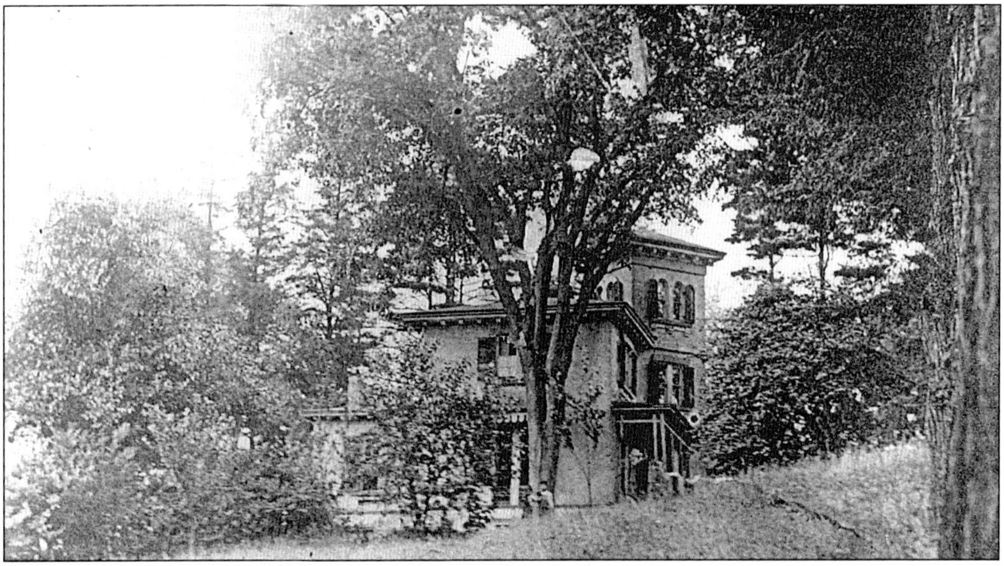

This modest mid-19th-century estate was the summer home of our 21st president, Chester Arthur. The house was built in the Italianate style at the end of Havell Street. The tower was set at an angle to the body of the house and had a staircase that wound to the top. The house was demolished in 1999, to make way for a subdivision of new homes.

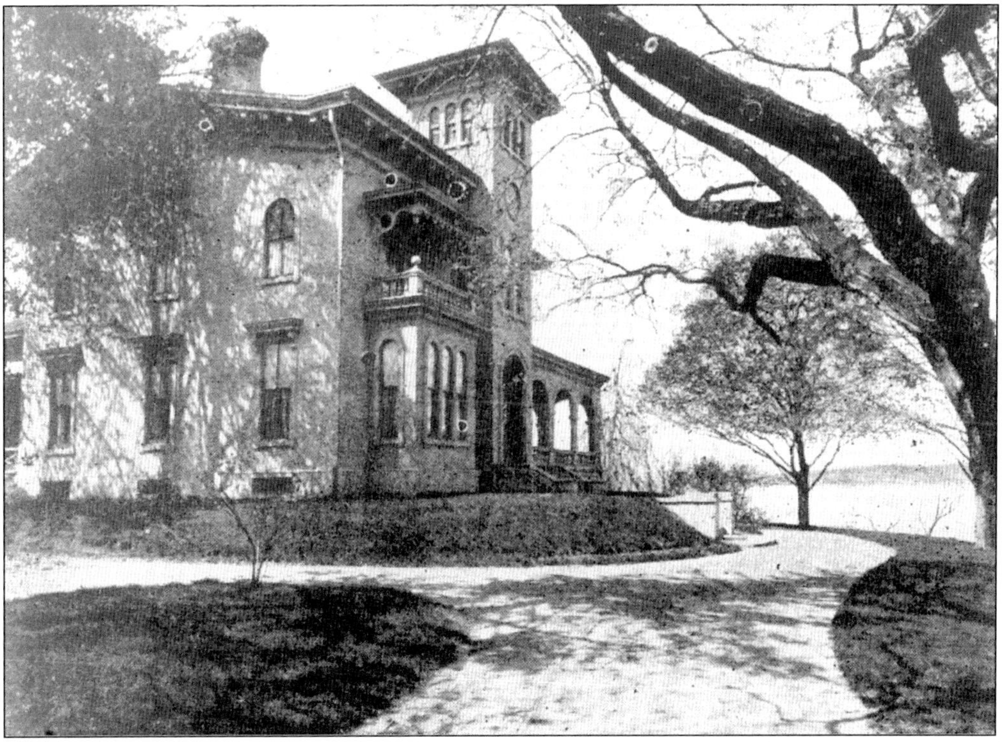

The Carpenter residence, built by 1867 on a promontory above Main Street in the center of the village, was situated on several acres. High above the Hudson, this residence incorporated many balconies and verandas to take advantage of the scenic views. It was formerly the Elks lodge B.P.O.E. 1496.

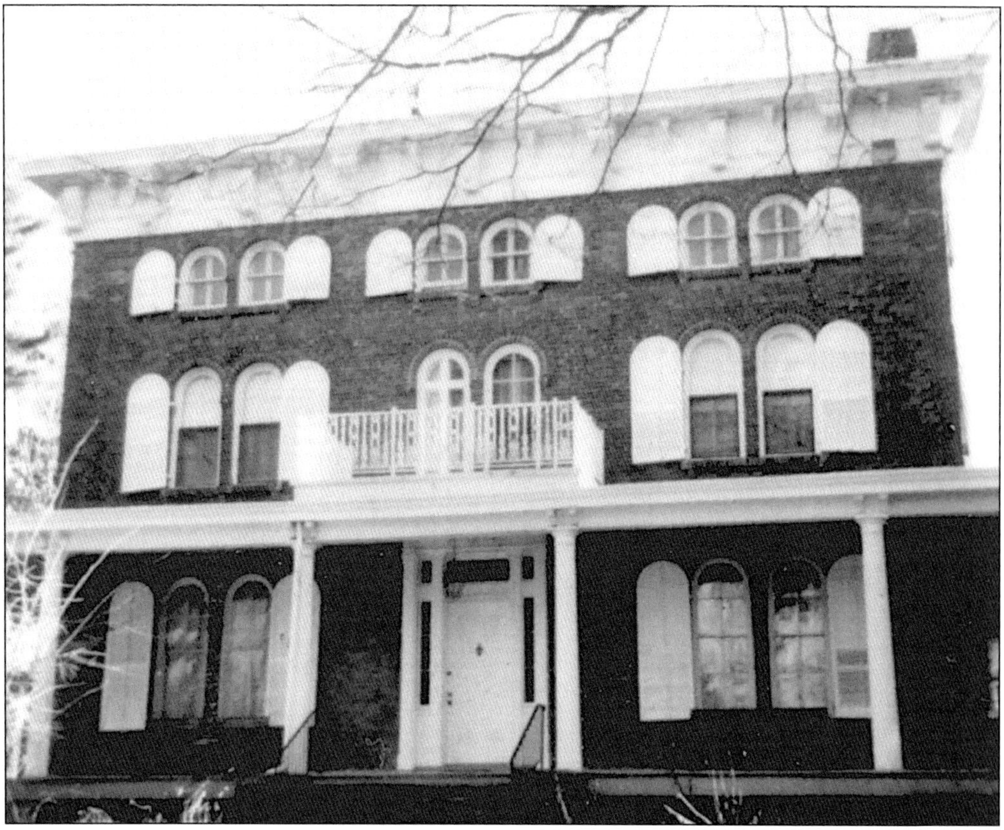

Torbank was the gracious brick home of Peter Donald, which was built on property extending from St. Paul's on the Hill Church to Route 9A. Scottish born Donald was a successful importer of linens. The mid-19th-century house was built with a large holding tank in the attic story to collect rainwater. The water was then supplied throughout the house by gravity.

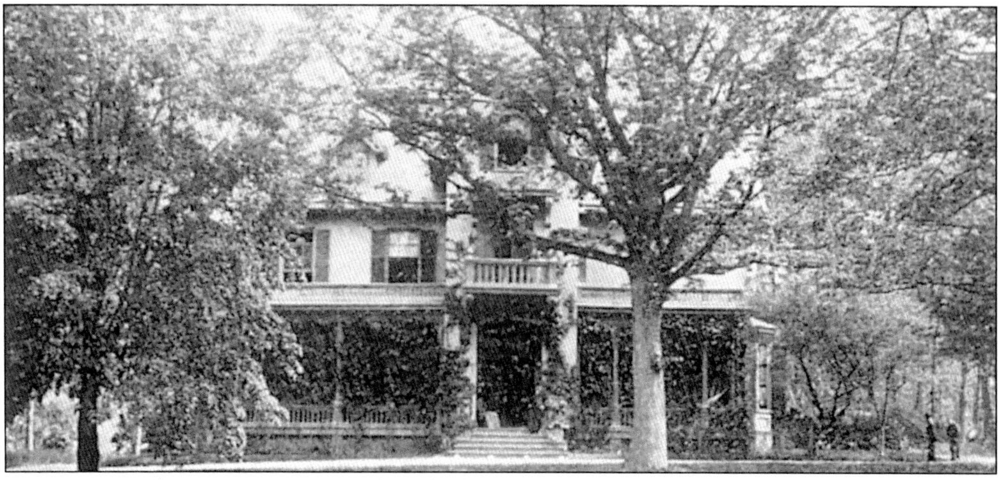

In a 1901 article, Greenmount was described as "one of the most beautiful smaller places on the Hudson." Dr. Horace Green built Greenmount in 1863 to accommodate his large family. The residence was situated on a rise above North Highland Avenue in the middle of 20 landscaped acres. It was demolished in the 1970s to build Claremont Gardens.

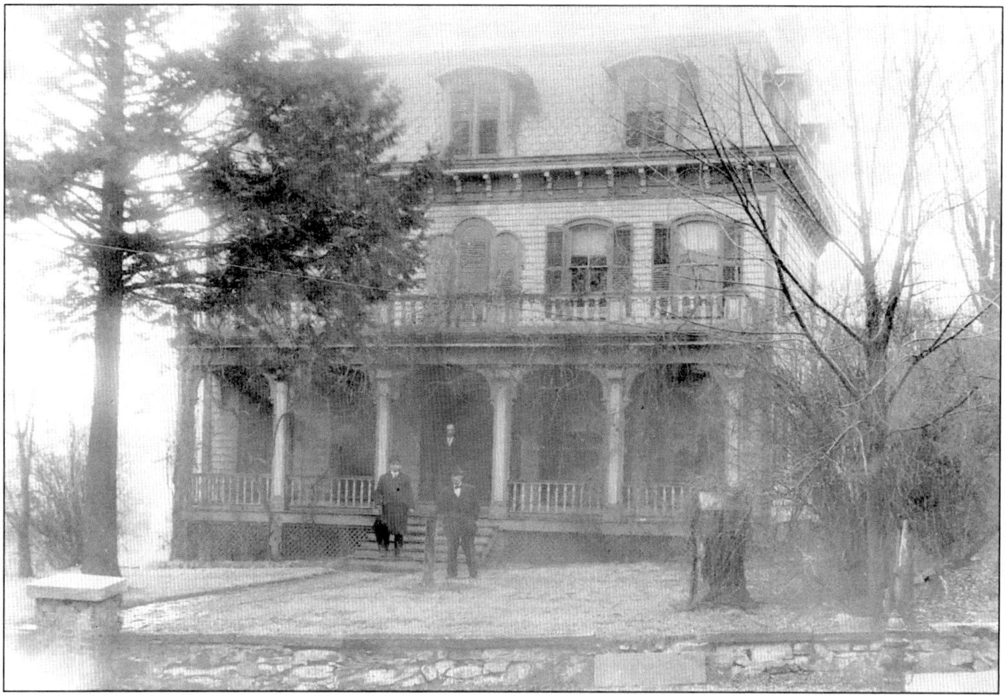

The Stephen Auser house, which dates from the 1860s, is located at 175 Croton Avenue.

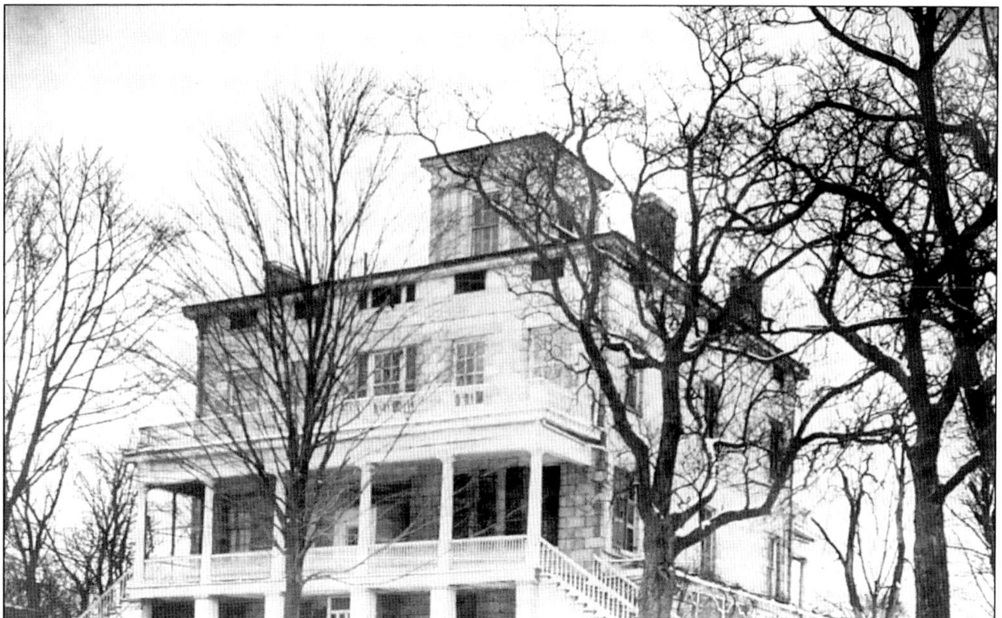

This early-19th-century mansion stands at the end of Broad Avenue on State Street. Built by James Smith of Sing Sing marble and later owned by James Robinson, the grounds once extended to Highland Avenue and included acres of orchards.

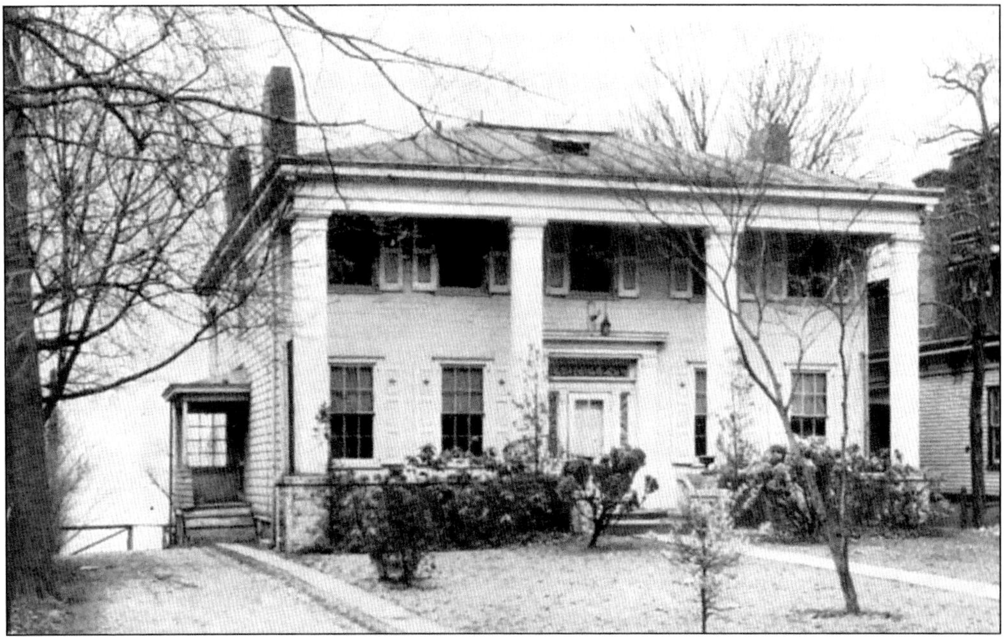

Located at 30 State Street, this colonial residence is best known as the home of Dr. George W. Hill, an outstanding Black physician and community leader in Ossining for over 30 years.

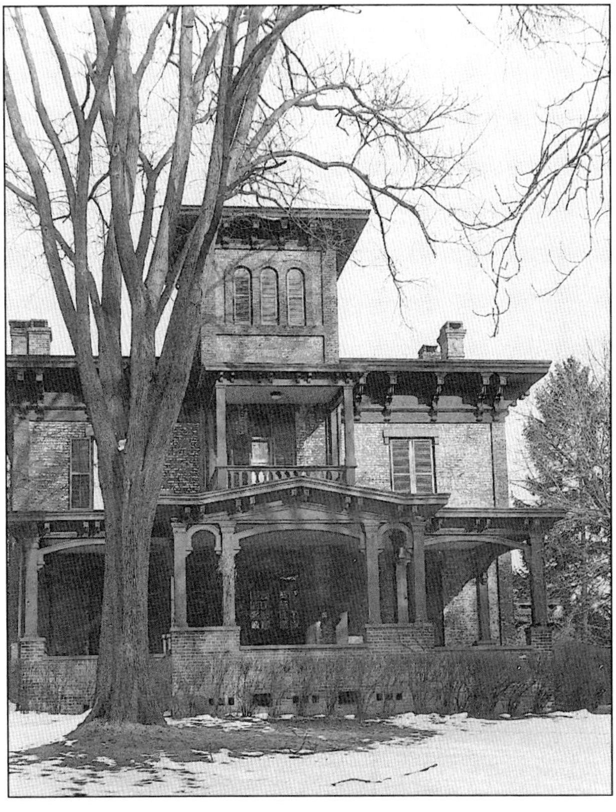

The Sir Tabot Ewart house, formerly known as the Henop house, was located on South Highland Avenue opposite Everett Avenue. The mid-19th-century brick and fieldstone Italian villa passed into the hands of a developer upon Ewart's death around 1960. The building was razed to build the Surray Oaks development.

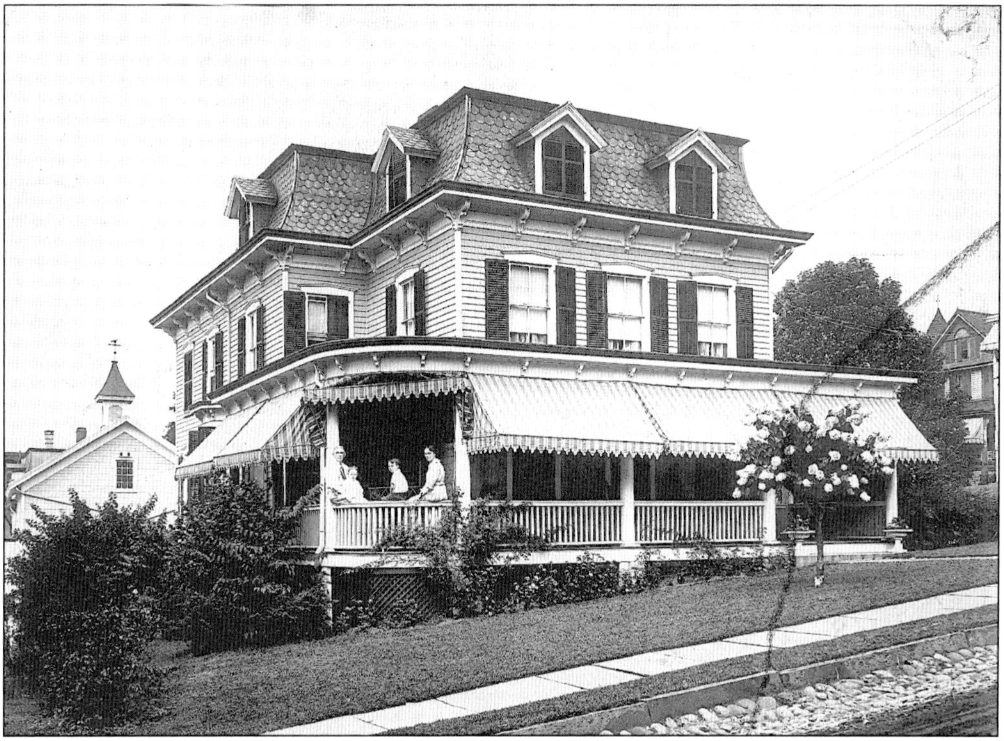

An excellent example of Victorian village architecture, this house is located at 27 Clinton Avenue on the corner of Linden Avenue, shown here the way it looked in the late 1800s.

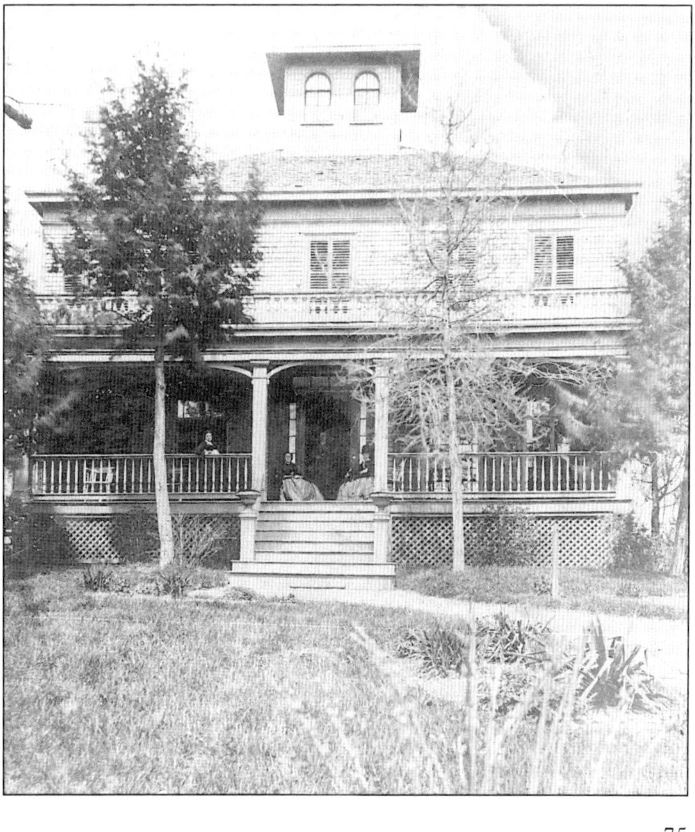

The home of Robert Havell, known as Rocky Mount, is an early example of cube-form architecture. The house was built in 1841 and occupied until 1857 by this world-famous John James Audubon engraver and noted local artist. The home was demolished in 1998.

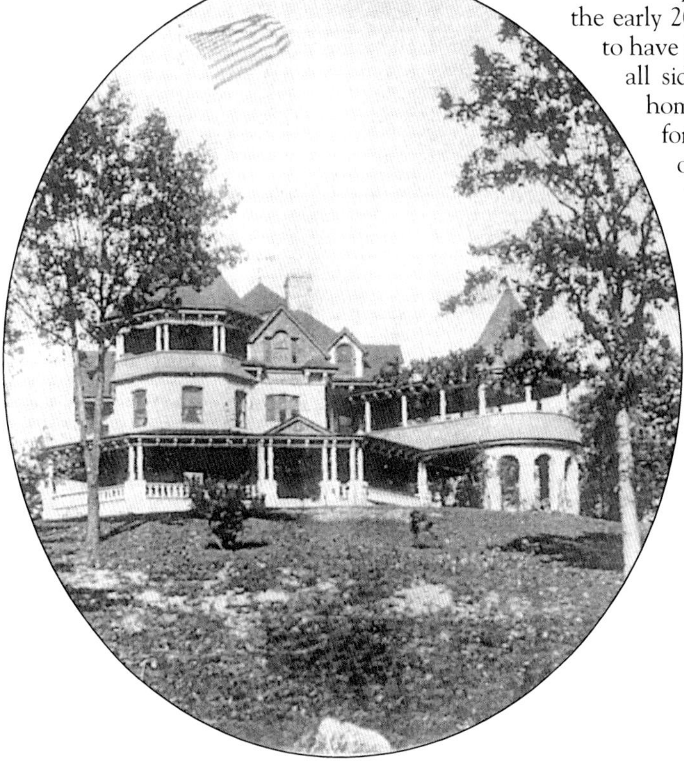

Situated on top of Mt. Murray on 12 acres in the early 20th century, Rockladge is said to have had views of the Hudson from all sides. Clinton Arnold built his home of rose granite, a rare stone for this area that was quarried on the property. Rockledge featured large verandas, up to 100 feet in length and 20 feet wide, and a semi-circular porte-cochere. The house was demolished to build Scarborough Manor.

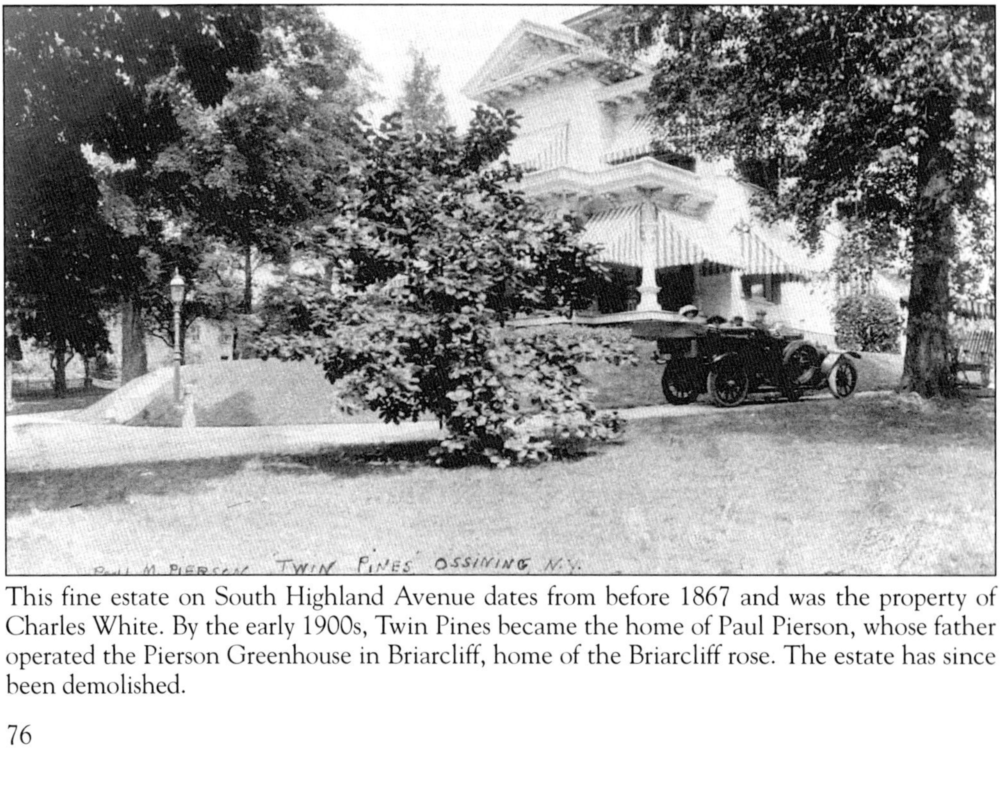

This fine estate on South Highland Avenue dates from before 1867 and was the property of Charles White. By the early 1900s, Twin Pines became the home of Paul Pierson, whose father operated the Pierson Greenhouse in Briarcliff, home of the Briarcliff rose. The estate has since been demolished.

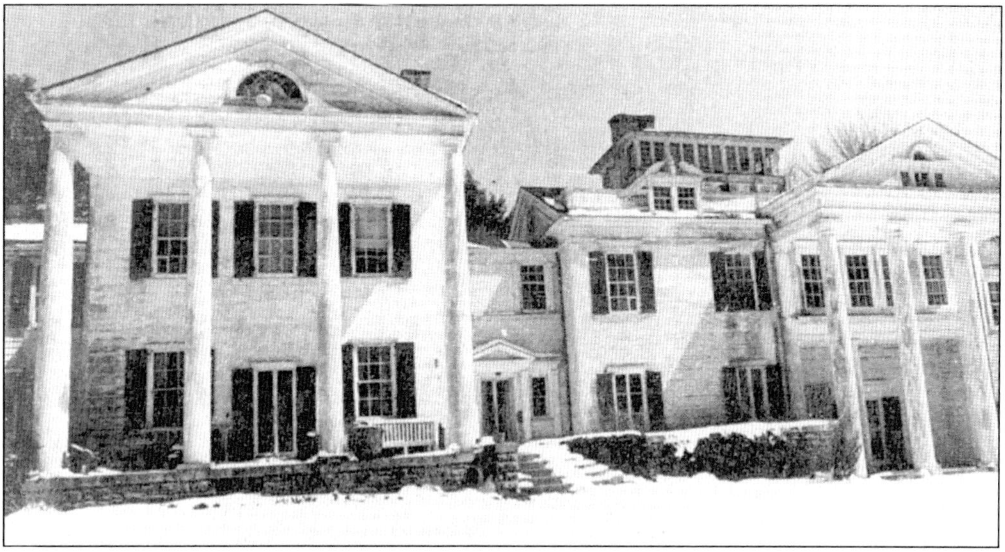

The Beechwood estate, located in Scarborough, was the home of Frank A. Vanderlip during the early 20th century. Vanderlip, who worked his way up to president of the National Bank of New York, is responsible for the restoration and rehabilitation of many of the homes that make up the Sparta Historic District.

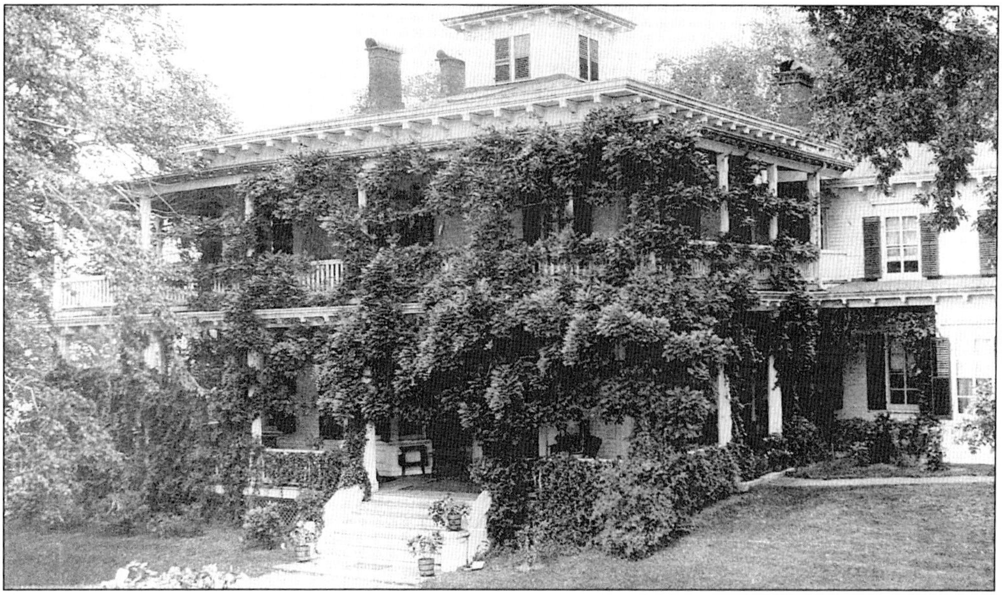

Called Sunnyside by John Aaron Browning and Sharborn by Noel Macy, this mansion has been home to a number of Ossining's prominent families. Built about 1850 and later improved, the mansion grew to contain some 50 rooms. The Briar Crest Nursing Home has occupied the property since 1951.

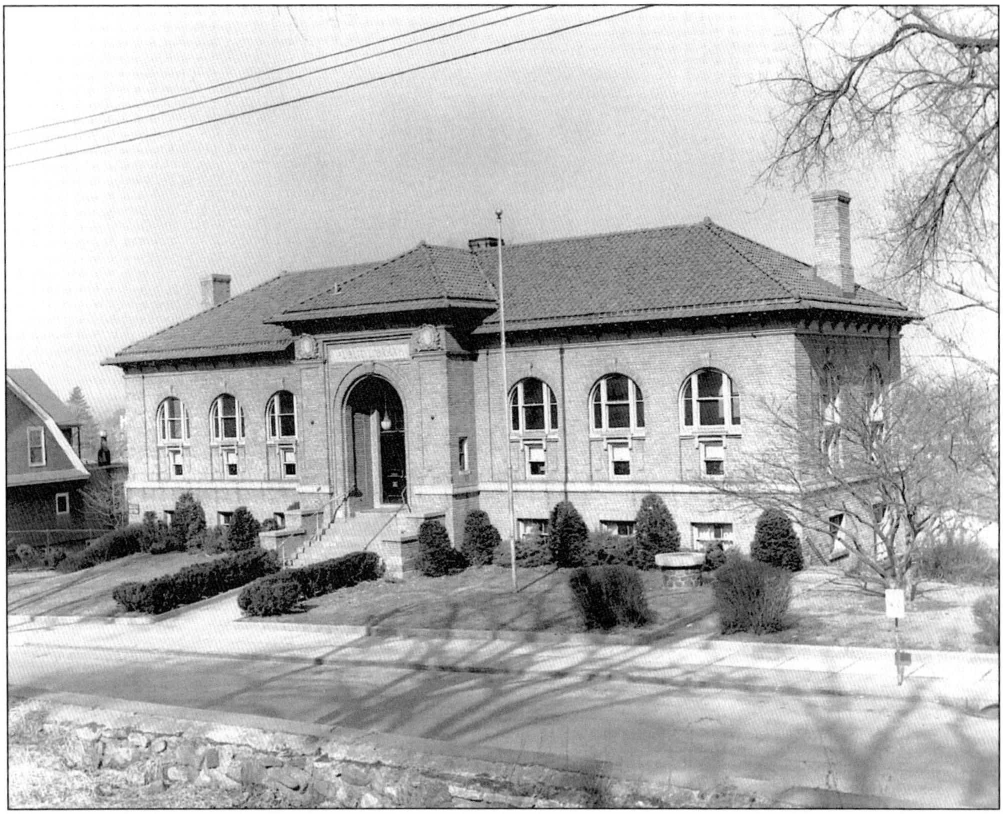

The Ossining Public Library was chartered in 1893 with a book collection of 2,000 volumes, which were kept in the superintendent's office in the Broadway School. The library was later moved to Park School and as the need expanded, the library moved to the Twiggar Building and YMCA, both on Church Street. In 1912, Dr. Albert W. Twiggar wrote to industrialist Andrew Carnegie, who had given money to other communities for new public library buildings. Carnegie's reply was: "If Ossining agrees to maintain a free public library and provide a suitable site for a building, I will be glad to give $26,000 to the community." This structure was opened on Croton Avenue in 1914 and demolished after many years of service, in 1968, to make way for the present institution.

I remember—

THE PUBLIC LIBRARY. A long flight of wide stone steps lead to the entrance door. Windsor chairs were situated at each table and oak window seats made reading special, on rainy days. Fiction was arranged alphabetically (by author) around the room, beginning in the near corner on the left side of the library. The library editions featured embossed lettering on the covers. Sabatini was found toward the back of the room, to the right. Theater materials were located straight ahead from the entrance, beyond and a little to the right of the librarian's desk (who allowed no talking). Newspapers were hung horizontally, at the folds, with long wooden spears on racks. The children's room was located downstairs and contained books of many different sizes and colors, more appealing to the eye than in the adult section. Five books were allowed out at a time. The strict librarian marked a small piece of paper that was glued on the first page with a stamp, which was connected to the end of a pencil. When the paper was filled with dated stamps, it was replaced with a fresh sheet, and the stamping process began anew.

Three

Service for the Public Good

As the small village of Sing Sing grew in the late 1800s, there was a predictable rhythm to the pattern of daily life that bred confidence in the natural order of things. This rhythm was upset by village's changes and weakened by its losses. Local pride and boosterism were solid as things were always being improved upon and spruced up. As the community grew so did property values and the necessity for an operating government, police force, fire department, and medical dispensary. By the early 1900s, Ossining was well on its way to economic interdependency. Public services, however, retained their individualistic touch. The lawyer in his office across from the Municipal Building, the real estate agent above the bank, and the doctor who routinely made house calls, all remained part of the daily scene. Local citizens exhibited a deep and proud attachment to the community and to family ties. Once settled in, most families tended to remain that way, entirely willing to invest a lot of time and energy into making Ossining a better place to live and grow.

With the coming of the two World Wars, Ossining readily supported the common cause for freedom. Because the fighting was far away and there were only so many production jobs for the war effort to go around, many people felt frustrated. Trying to be part of the action, citizens bought War Bonds, grew their own food in Victory Gardens, and formed a Civilian Defense corps. Air raid wardens enforced unnecessary blackouts while spotters scanned the skies for hostile craft and volunteered with the American Red Cross. Children saved their empty toothpaste tubes and adults went on scavenger hunts, ransacking their attics for discarded overshoes, rusty baby carriages, aluminum pots, tin cans, and anything else that could be turned into armaments. Citizens dealt with rationing (a mess of little books and stamps that limited the food or gas they could buy). Through all of this turmoil, the survival of the nation was paramount. Ossining remained strong and united, and to this day, service for the public good is a strong value shared by all.

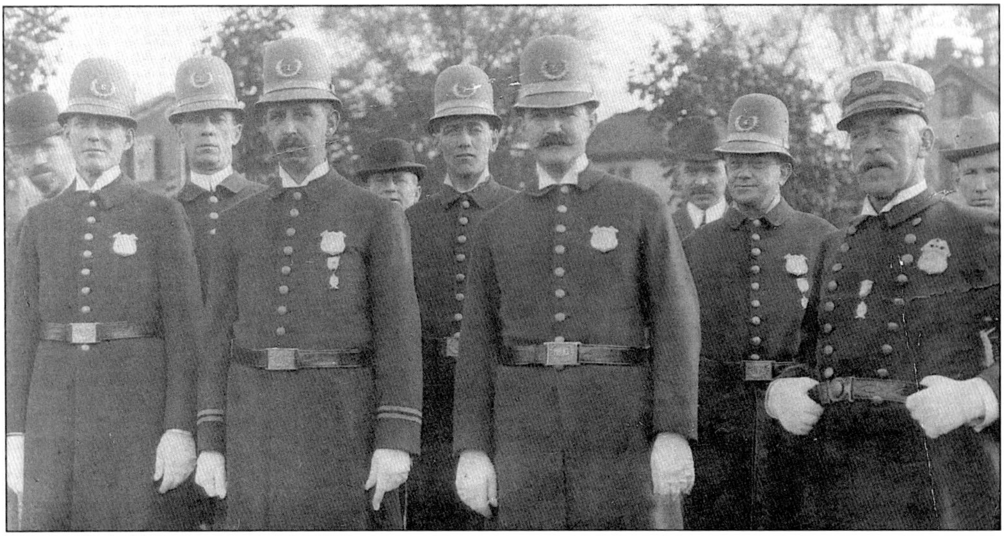

The Ossining police wore long coats, helmets, and handlebar mustaches in 1910, by which time the department had been in existence only 16 years. Between 1910 and 1920, the police were starting to encounter a new problem that required different tactics—the coming of the automobile. The force included, from left to right, Nicholas Murphy, James Irving, Frank Minnerly, Harry Keenan, John Wescott, Lorenzo Sniffen, and Chief James W. Tompkins.

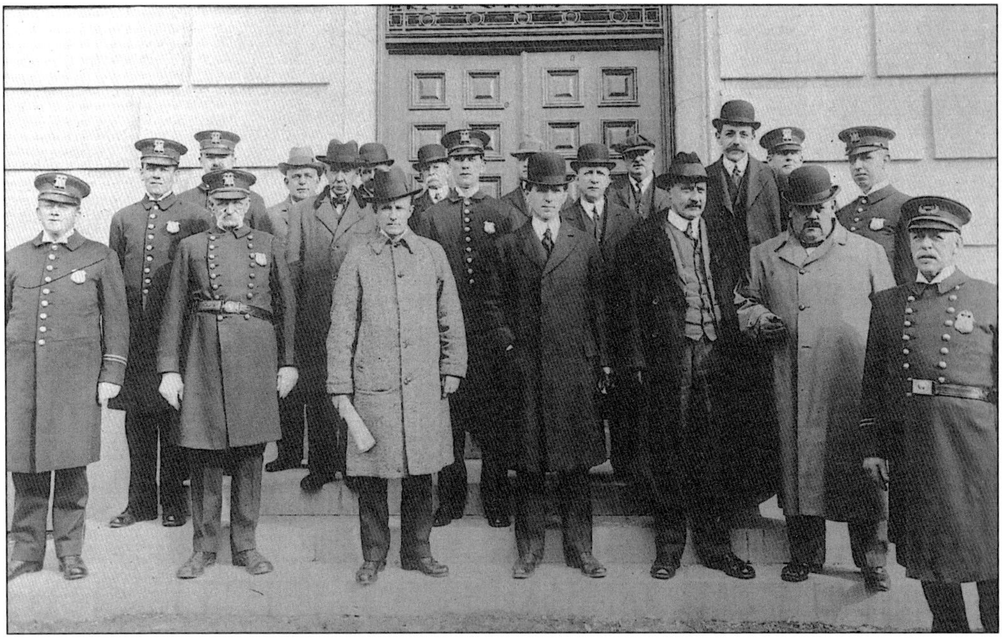

Elected village officials pose in front of the newly constructed Municipal Building on Croton Avenue during the 1915 dedication ceremony. The new structure was needed after the community population passed 13,000. By 1900, there were major discussions centering on changing the name of the village from Sing Sing to Ossining. The name Sing Sing was being confused with the state prison, which upset many citizens and business people. After repeated meetings and petitions, a law was passed in 1901 changing the town's name from Sing Sing to Ossining.

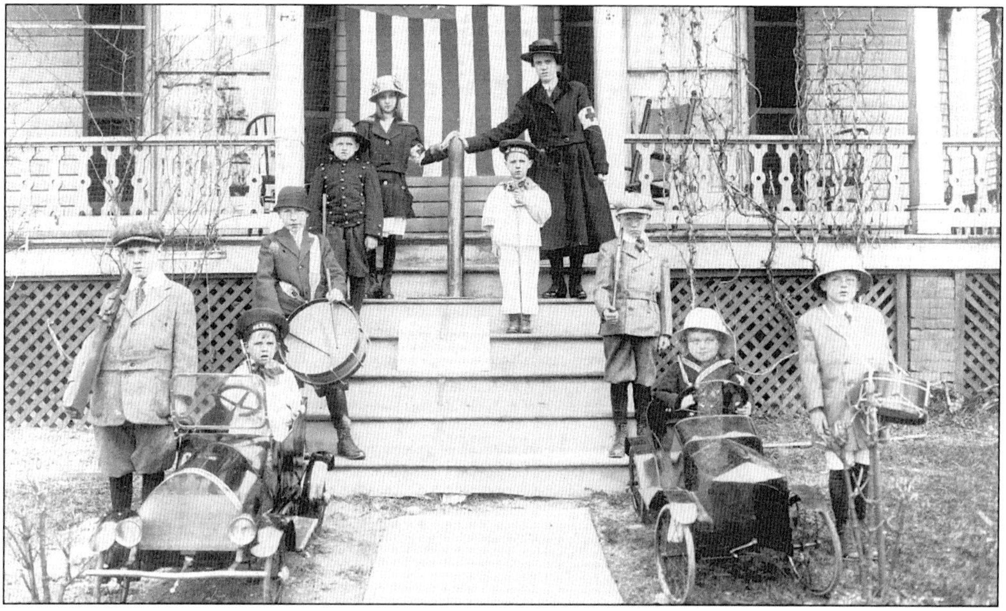

In 1916, America was preparing for the coming of WW I, which came the following year. Patriotic fervor on the home front is illustrated in this photograph as these "little soldiers" pose on the lawn of the Valentine house on Spring Street. The sign on the step reads: "We are ready to enlist—are you? We are Americans." Many local citizens owning large plots of land loaned them for community gardens in which high school students signed up to work. During the war years, hundreds of barrels of potatoes and other vegetables were grown. A common slogan was: "Raise all you can, can all you raise."

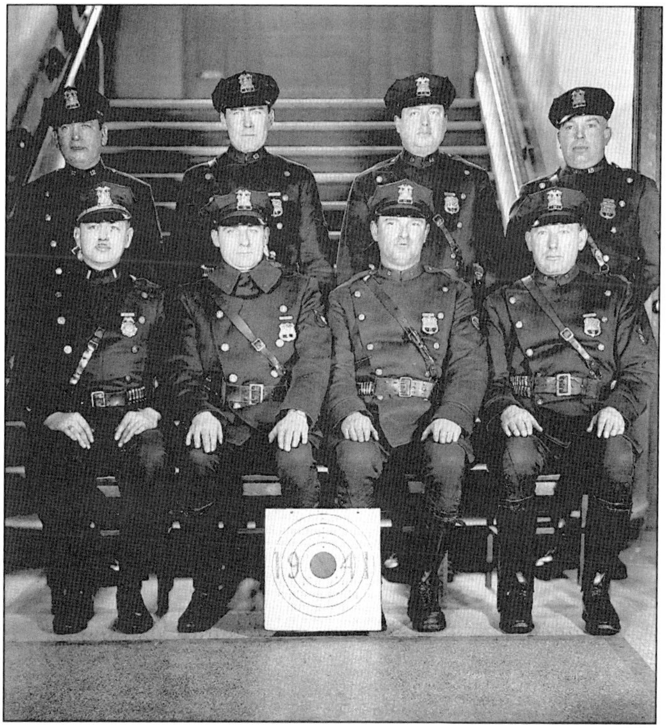

Members of the Ossining Police Department inside the front entrance of the Municipal Building at 26 Croton Avenue in 1941 are shown here, from left to right, as follows: (first row) Arthur Meade, Henry Bell, Norman Cypher, and William Nelson; (second row) Ralph Knapp, James Fagan, Samuel Rubin, and Peter Florian. Officer Fagan and Prison Guard John Hartye gave their lives in the line of duty during a Sing Sing Prison escape attempt in the same year this photograph was taken.

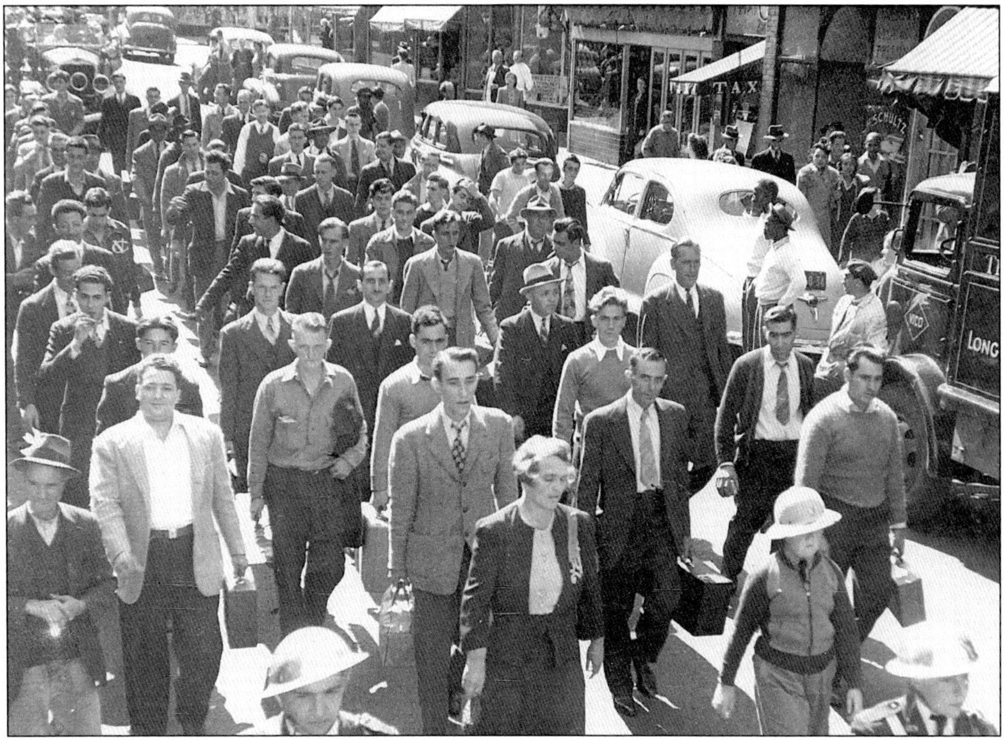

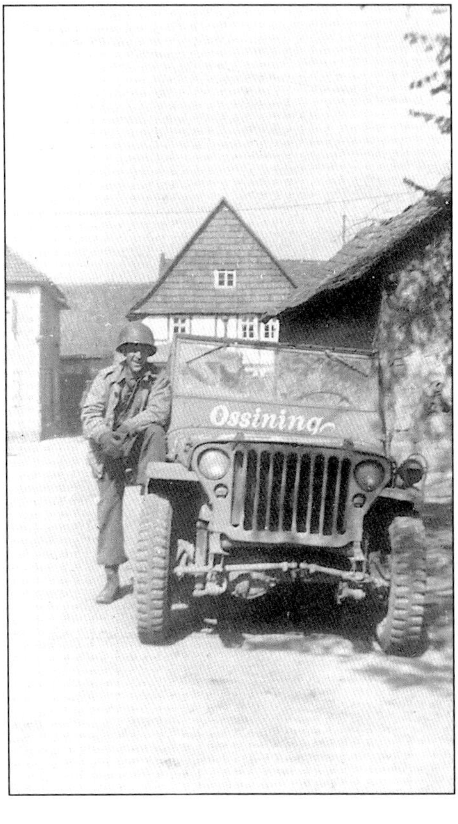

New recruits march in their civilian clothes with overnight bags down Spring Street at the start of WW II. Most Ossining males were part of the War Department's manpower drive, which was launched immediately after Pearl Harbor in 1940. Men between the ages of 18 and 36 discovered a fateful notice in their morning mail that began with the words, "Greetings, you are hereby notified that you have now been selected for training and service in the land or naval forces of the United States."

Corporal Aldo DiNolfo is shown here standing next to his jeep *Ossining* outside Trier, Germany, in 1944. DiNolfo was a member of the 1271st Combat Engineers attached to General George Patton's 3rd Army, and one of his unofficial assignments was that of lettering the names of wives, girlfriends, and hometowns on jeeps and trucks in his unit. A few weeks after this photograph was taken, the jeep was destroyed in a German ambush while driving along the Autobahn. DiNolfo was injured but returned to duty and came home after the war was over. One reason DiNolfo painted his jeep was to use it as a sort of advertisement in finding other GIs from Westchester County.

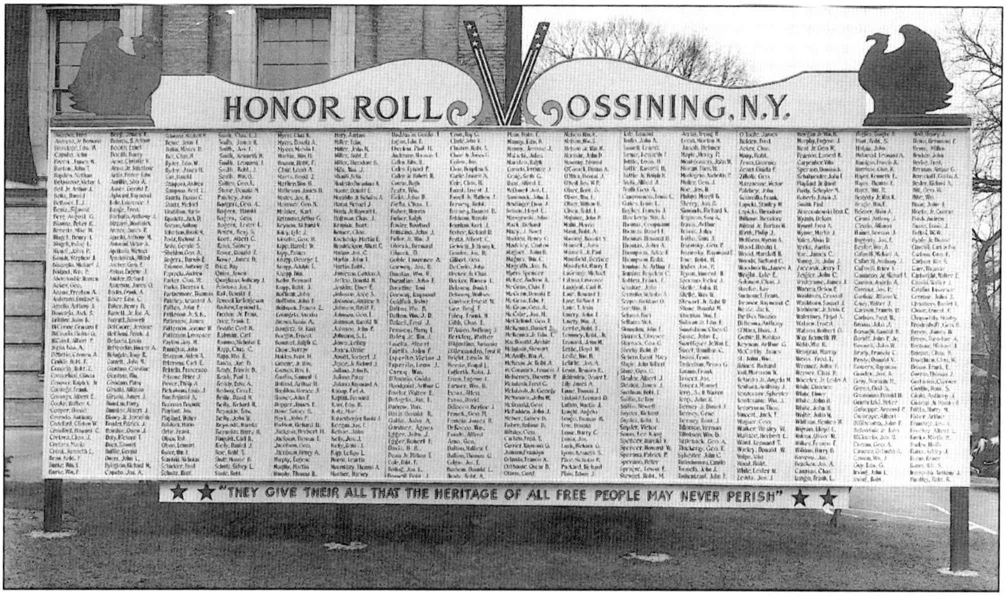

During WW II, the community proudly erected honor roll displays on the front lawn of the Municipal Building. There were two displays of equal size built by Sing Sing Prison inmates, and each included 800 names of men and women serving from the local area. The inscription at the bottom read: "They give their all that the heritage of all free people may never perish."

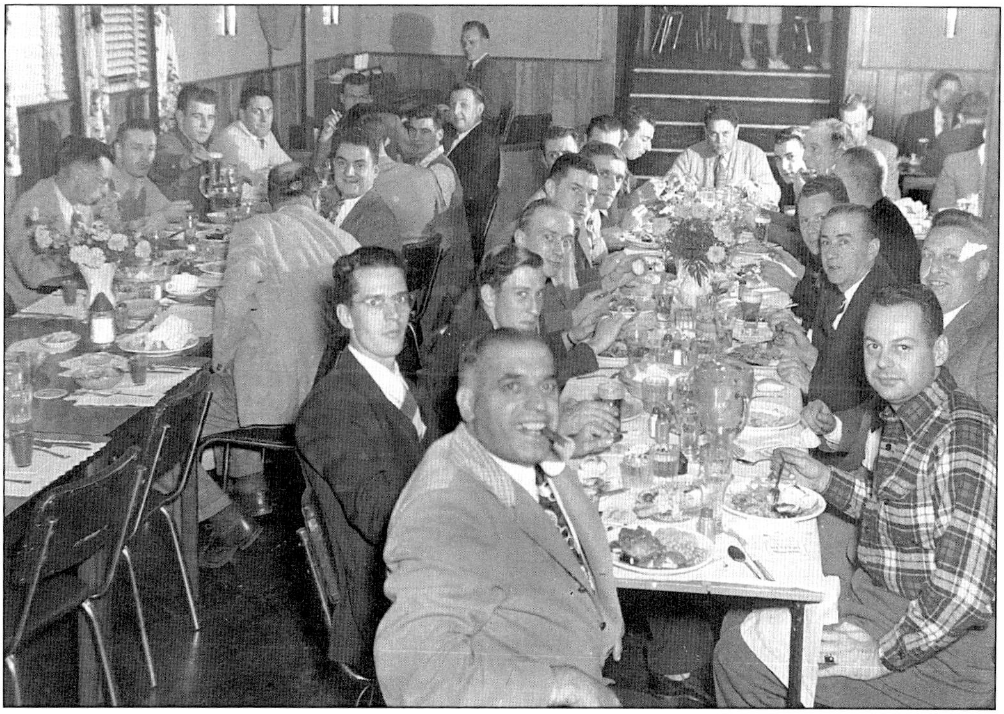

In 1946, WW II ended and the soldiers returned home. Shown here enjoying the festivities, at Pete LaLuna's Pine Tree Restaurant on Rockledge Avenue, are veterans of the conflict, all of whom were members of the Holla Hose fire department on State Street. Pete was known for his Italian menu, and his restaurant was a local mainstay.

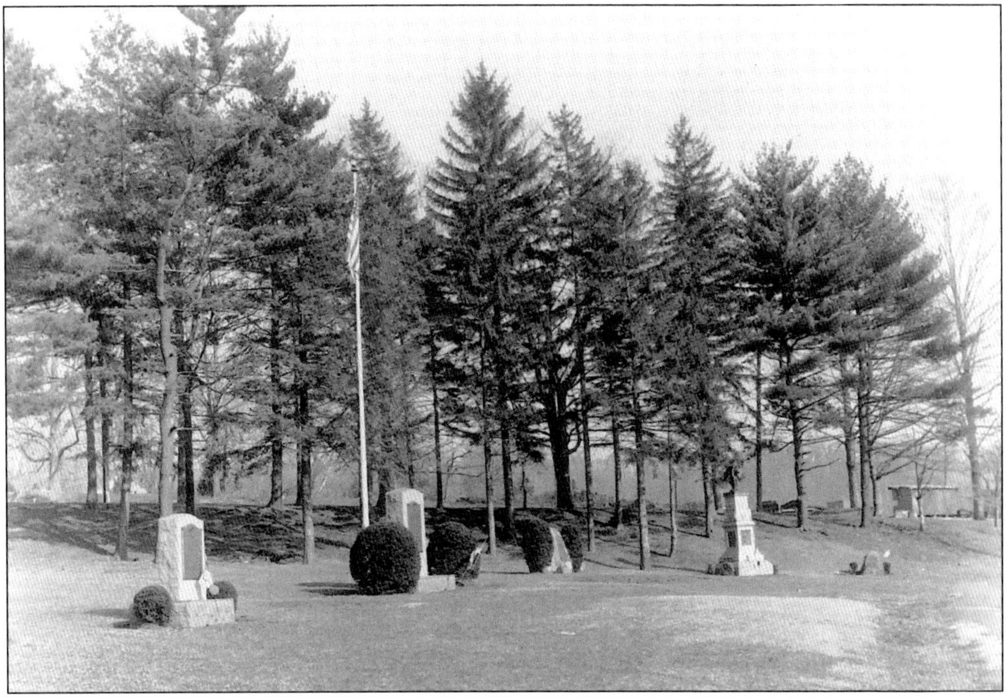

The Nelson Memorial Park on South Highland Avenue was named after State Senator Henry Clay Nelson, who succeeded in having this property deeded to the village in 1882. The park is Ossining's salute to fallen heroes. Thirty-eight evergreen trees were planted by the Daughters of the American Revolution representing the soldiers of WW I who sacrificed their lives. The multiple stone monuments honor the 193 men and women from the town of Ossining and the villages of Ossining and Briarcliff Manor who were casualties of the Revolutionary War, Civil War, WW I, WW II, Korean War, Vietnam War, as well as the Beirut, Lebanon conflict.

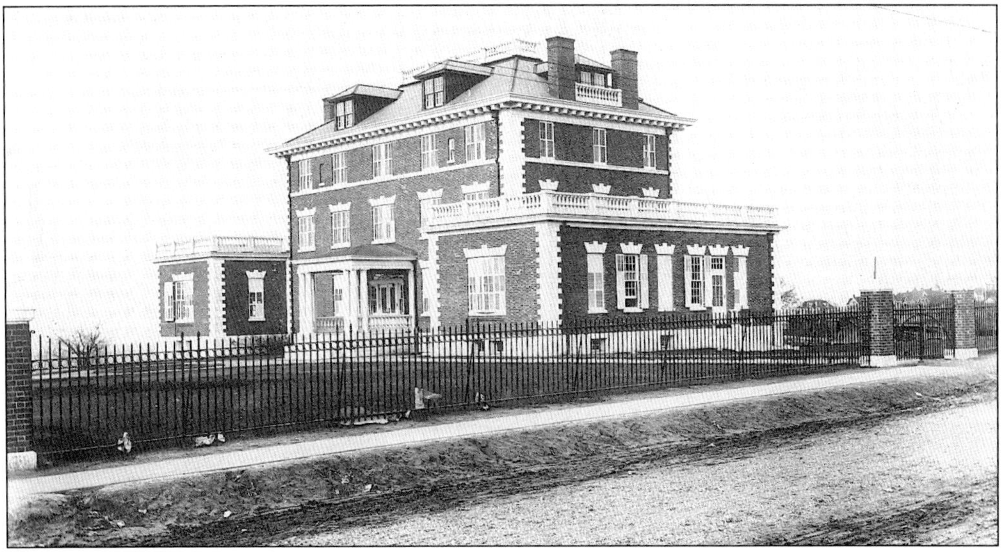

Shown here is the Ossining Hospital on Spring Street. Built in 1906, on land donated by the Potter family, the hospital served the community until 1956 when the new Phelps Memorial Hospital was built in Sleepy Hollow.

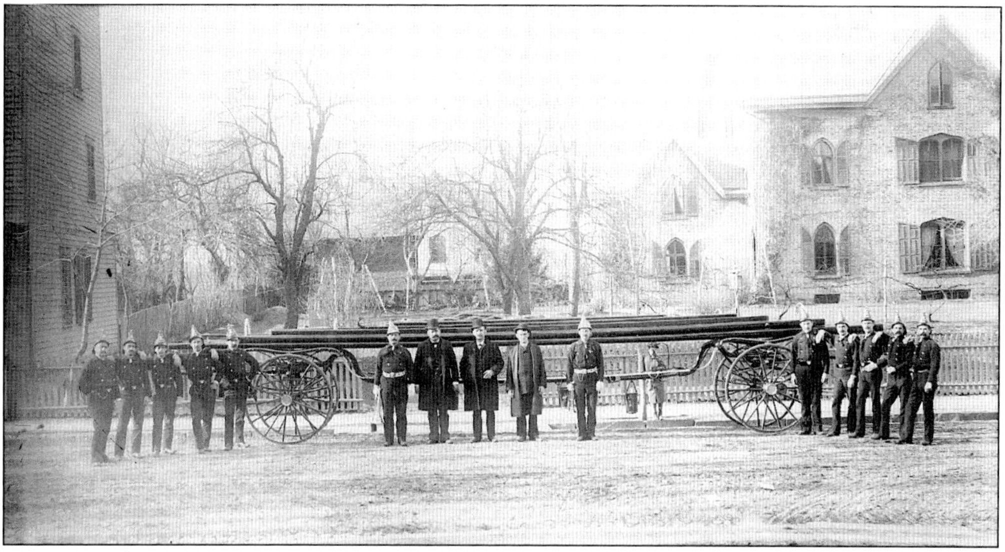

In 1812, a fire company was organized in the village of Sing Sing. The company purchased a hand engine in New York City ornamented with a drawing of George Washington, thus the name Washington Engine Company Number 1. In 1812, a fire company was organized in the village of Sing Sing. The company purchased a hand engine in New York City ornamented with a drawing of George Washington, thus the name Washington Engine Company No. 1. The hand-drawn apparatus pictured was later elongated and converted to horse-drawn and the name changed to Washington Hook and Ladder Company No. 2.

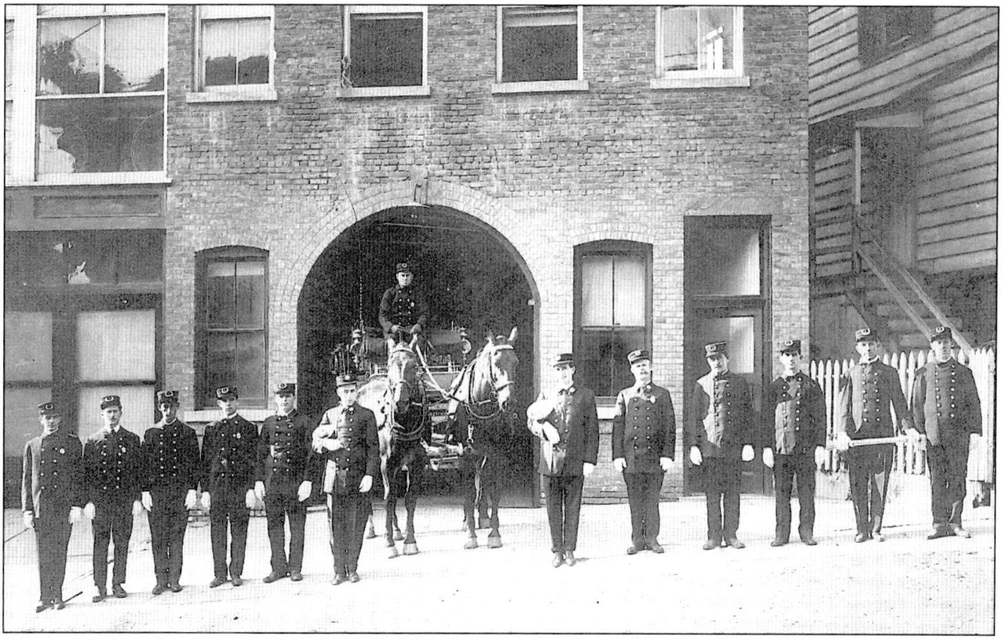

In 1856, a hand engine and hose carriage were purchased. The hand engine went to Washington Engine Company Number 1 and the Ossining Hose Company Number 1 was formed to operate the hose carriage. From about 1873, both of these companies were housed on the north side of the village. In 1893, Ossining Hose Company was given quarters on North Highland Avenue. A horse-drawn apparatus was acquired in 1905.

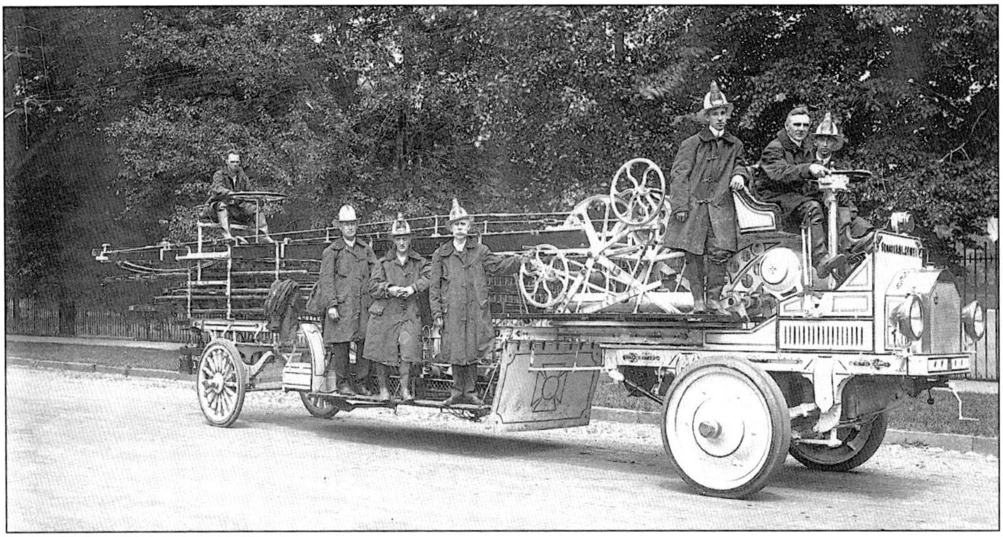

In 1857, a petition was sent to Albany stating that much state property had been saved by the many responses of the local fire department at the prison. The village requested a fire engine and other equipment to be used at the prison and in the community. The legislature passed the request, and the new equipment became Senate Hook and Ladder Company Number 1. This 75 horsepower, 4-cylinder motor tractor with 55-foot aerial ladder was bought in 1922, motorized in 1936, and remained with the Senate Hook and Ladder Company until 1940.

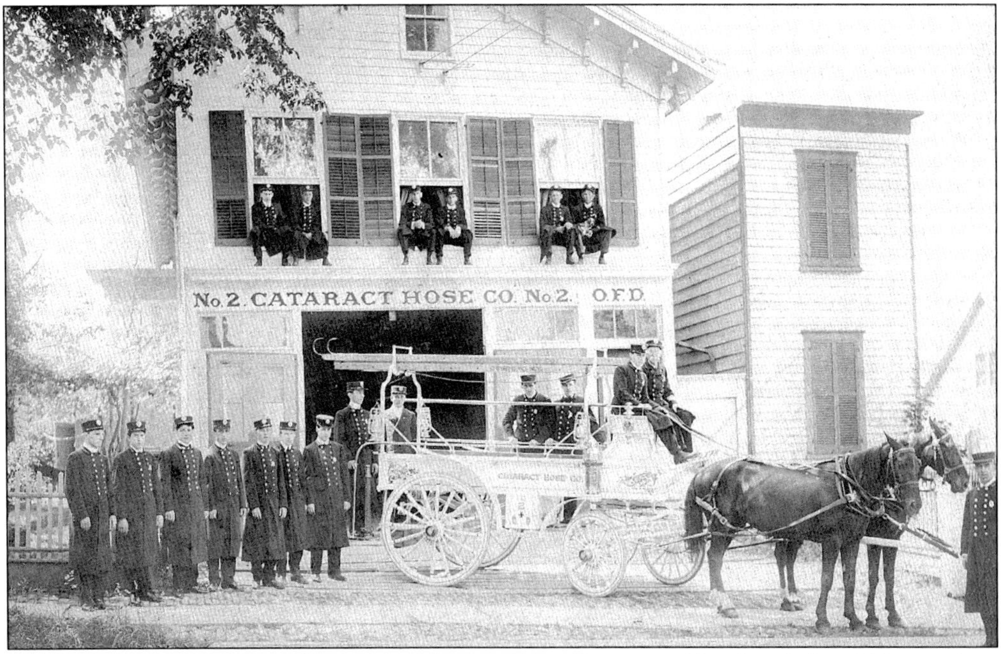

The hand engine was turned over to Protection Hose Company Number 3. In 1890, members decided to change their name to Cataract Hose Company Number 2. In 1909, Cataract's hose wagon was equipped with two copper fire extinguishers, a 12-foot ladder, a 20-foot extension ladder, ax, crowbar, four lanterns, and 800 feet of hose. The horses in the photograph were known as "Barney" and "Jack." In 1922, the first automotive pumper was put in service by the Cataract Hose Company.

In 1876, a steam fire engine was exhibited in the village, a fire broke out on Main Street, and the engine was put to use. Soon after, a steam fire engine was bought and Sing Sing Steamer Company Number 1 was organized. In 1901, the name was changed to Ossining Steamer Company Number 1. Numerous fires struck the village downtown and along the waterfront in the late 1800s. In 1891, Monitor Hose Company Number 4, whose name was taken from the Monitor Iron Foundry on Water Street (as many of the volunteers worked at the factory), was founded. The two-wheel apparatus shown here was the first equipment used by the Monitor Hose Company.

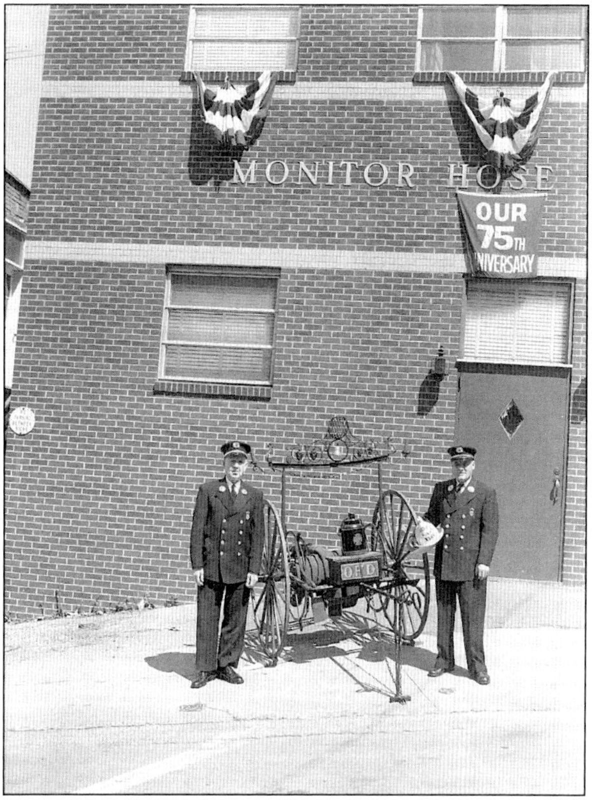

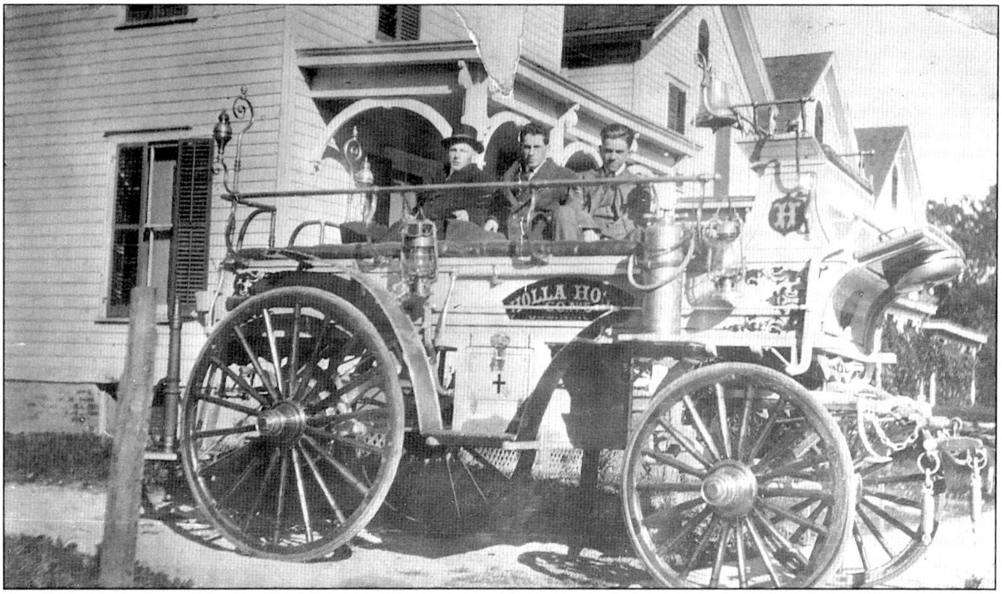

In 1900, Holla Hose Company Number 5 was started and named for J. Edward Holla, then village president. Holla had pressed for fire protection for citizens living in the south end of the community. This horse-drawn wagon was purchased from Phoenix Hose Company of Tarrytown in 1914.

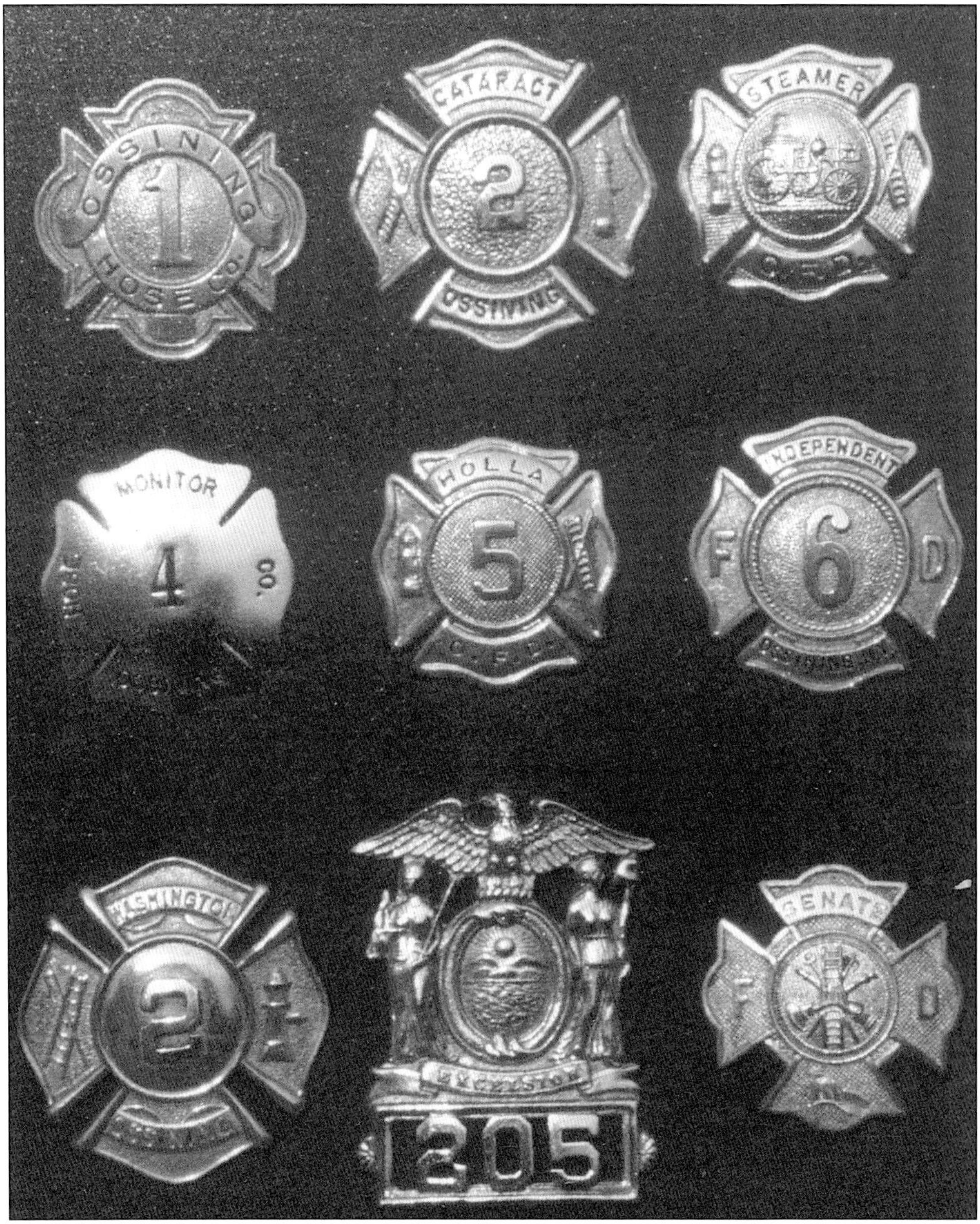

Ossining Volunteer Fire Department Hat Badges are shown here, from left to right, as follows: (first row) Ossining Hose Company Number 1, 23 Snowden Avenue, organized September 8, 1856; Cataract Hose Company Number 2, 6 Waller Avenue, organized May 25, 1857; and Ossining Steamer Company Number 1, 115 Main Street, organized June 3, 1876; (second row) Monitor Hose Company Number 4, 57 Central Avenue, organized July 7, 1891; Holla Hose Company Number 5, State Street, organized April 24, 1900, and Independent Hose Company Number 6, Campwoods Road, organized March 11, 1911; (third row) Washington Hook and Ladder Company Number 2, 23 Snowden Avenue, organized May 12, 1812; Fire Police and Emergency, 21 State Street, organized December 15, 1922; and Senate Hook and Ladder Company Number 1, 115 Main Street, organized May 12, 1857.

Four

Young Ladies, Cadets, and Indians

The history of education in Ossining was a mirror of what took place throughout New York State in the 19th and 20th centuries. The earliest institutions were not public but private academies that were supported by wealthy individuals within the community. Free public schools maintained by citizen taxes started in the county around 1815. In 1825, a compulsory education law for early grades was passed in the state. Ossining, like neighboring villages, was divided into a district, and small one-room schoolhouses were built. These early structures contained one large open space that allowed for a multitude of uses, including social and governmental gatherings.

One of those early schools was the Camp Meeting Ground facility, located near the Methodist property on Campwoods Road. When small neighborhood schools were first formed, they were considered private institutions until taken in by the local public school administration. Exactly where the first schools started in Sing Sing is not known, but it is thought there was a one-room building in the village as early as 1800. The Trustees of the Common School did lease rooms at the Mount Pleasant Military Academy on State Street in the 1820s. The Sparta schoolhouse on lower Spring Street, at the corner of Fairview Place, opened about 1847. This was the same year that school trustees decided to set aside a classroom to be devoted exclusively to girls and hire a female teacher.

Ossining has been home to an impressive number of preparatory schools for girls and military academies for boys. All of these institutions featured students who boarded, which was a major difference from the public schools. Clearly, Ossining has throughout the years supported education in varied forms—private, parochial, and public. Ossining has been a major force in establishing and maintaining our nation's constitutional and cultural heritage.

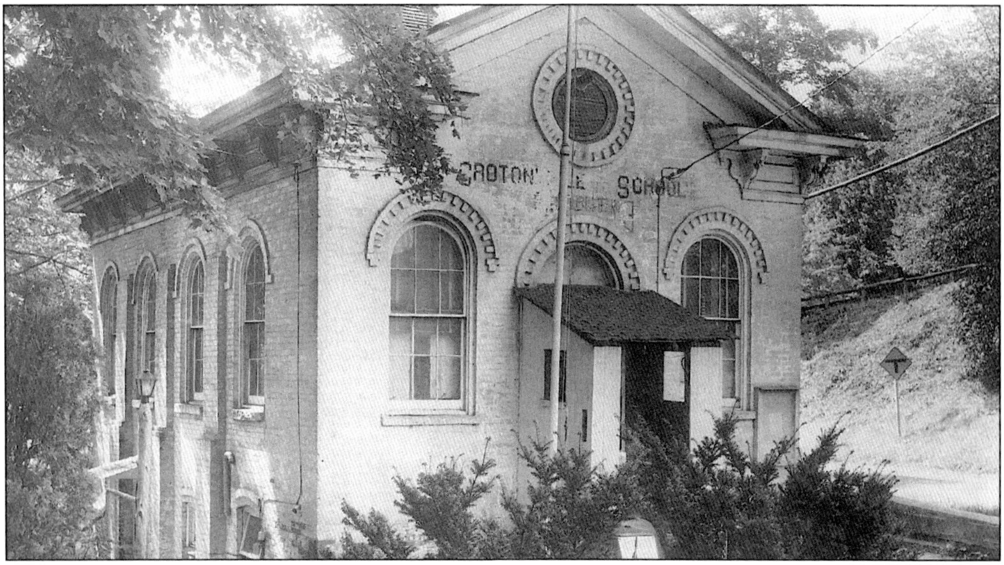

The Crotonville school was opened about 1860, and it was known as School Number 5. The school was part of the local district, known as a "branch" school for students living nearby. It was located 2 miles from downtown. The architecture is notable, as it is more stylistic than most schoolhouses. The architecture features brackets, fancy brickwork, rounded arches over wall openings, Italianate Revival cornices, and a round bull's eye in the front gable. It is located on Albany Post Road and today is an American Legion hall.

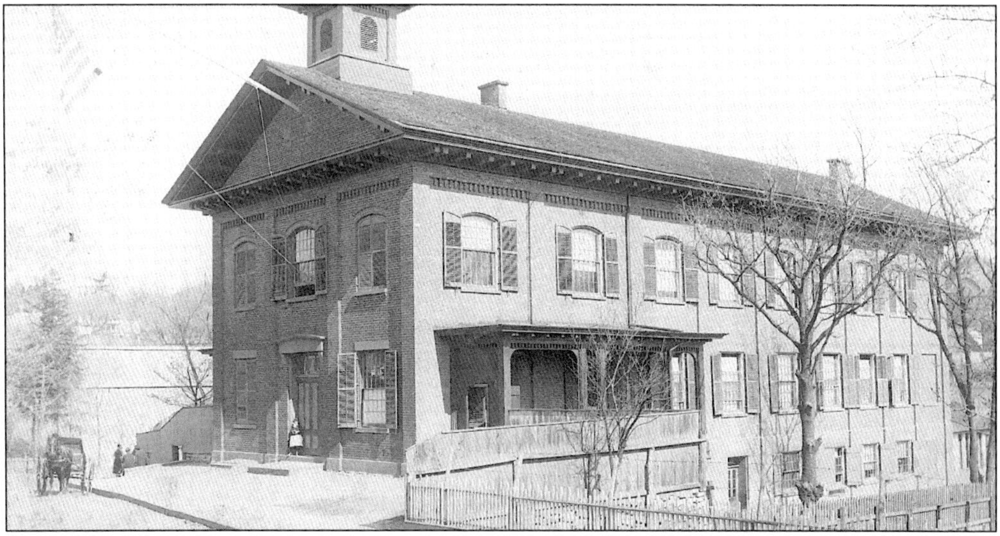

Completed in 1858, this building was the first central schoolhouse in Union Free School District Number 1. Originally known as the Broadway School, in 1909, it underwent a face lifting and was renamed Lincoln School. This was the result of a nationwide effort on the part of Civil War veterans to have each municipality name a school in honor of Abraham Lincoln. For many years, the bell that hung in the belfry summoned students to study. The bell had done service on the steam engine *Constitution*, which pulled Lincoln's train down the Hudson on his way to Washington, D.C., to assume duties as president in 1860. In 1921, an Americanization School started here to care for foreign-born students. It is located on the corner of Broadway and Brandreth Street.

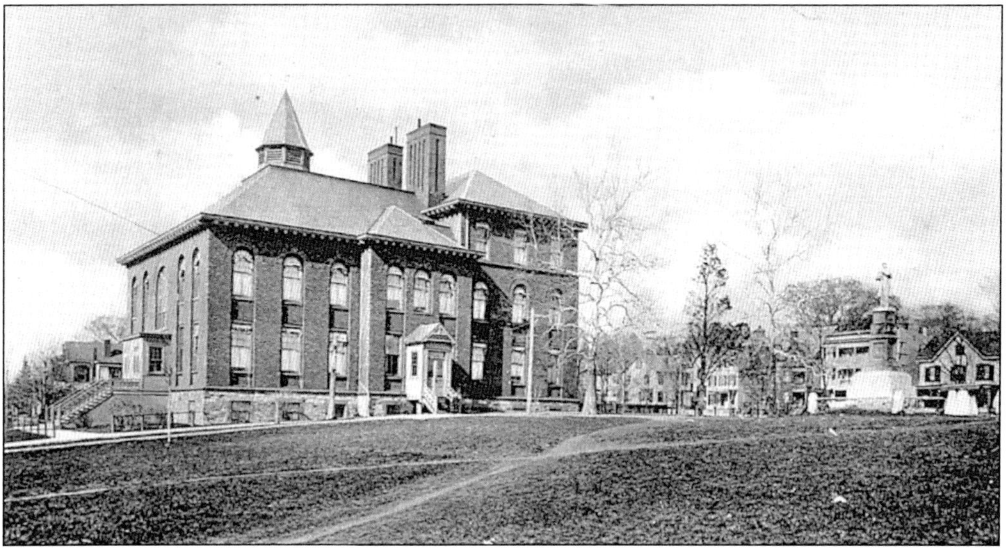

This is the first Park School on Edward Street. In 1885, the district purchased a part of the Robinson family property adjacent to Nelson Park for $4,800. Just before it opened in 1889, as a primary school, it burned to the ground and was rebuilt. The building cost $25,000 to construct, and it housed the public library for many years. A local newspaper article pointed out: "Visitors to the school are always sure of a cordial welcome. The orderly dismissal forms a beautiful sight. Hundreds of pupils march out in step to a piano. The happy faces indicate the fact that 'Rule by Love' is the school's motto."

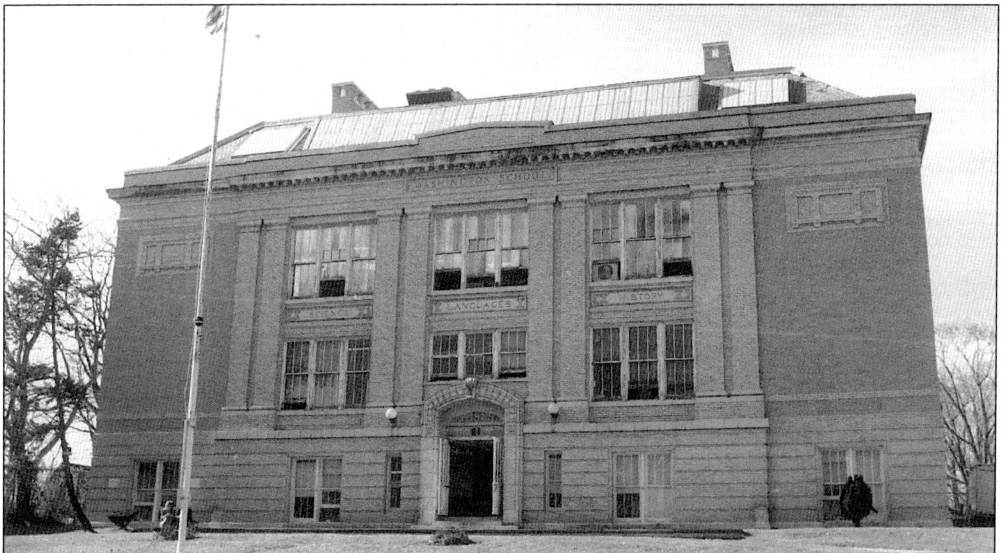

By 1910, the first high school, Broadway, was so crowded that temporary classroom space in the village was being rented. In 1907, local voters approved this new building on Croton Avenue, part of the Gilbert Todd farm and it was named Ossining High School. With the opening of the new high school edifice on South Highland Avenue in 1929, this building was renamed Washington School and turned into an elementary grade facility. It is an example of the Beaux-Arts style, which at this time was at its peak. Grand Central Station was under construction and another building, the New York Public Library, had just been completed.

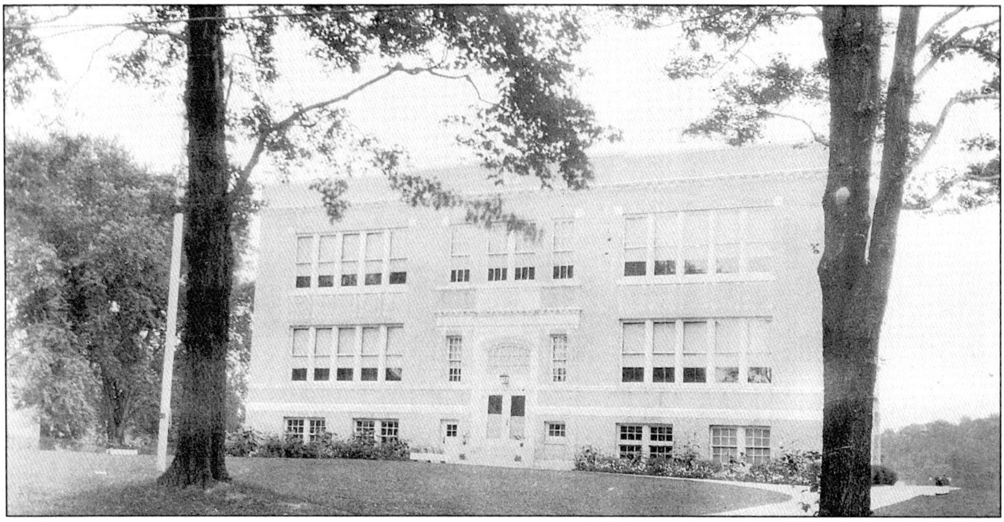

The school district continued to grow in population and geographic area that it served, so it became necessary to build Roosevelt School on Croton Avenue. The school opened in 1922, at a cost of $60,000 for grades one through eight. Milk was served daily to all children in the lower grades. The first full-time nurse was hired to visit each school, and, in 1927, an oral-hygienist was on staff also moving from school to school. A full-time doctor was on the job by 1929. An annex was completed in 1937. The two dates of construction can be seen at opposite ends of the front facade of the school.

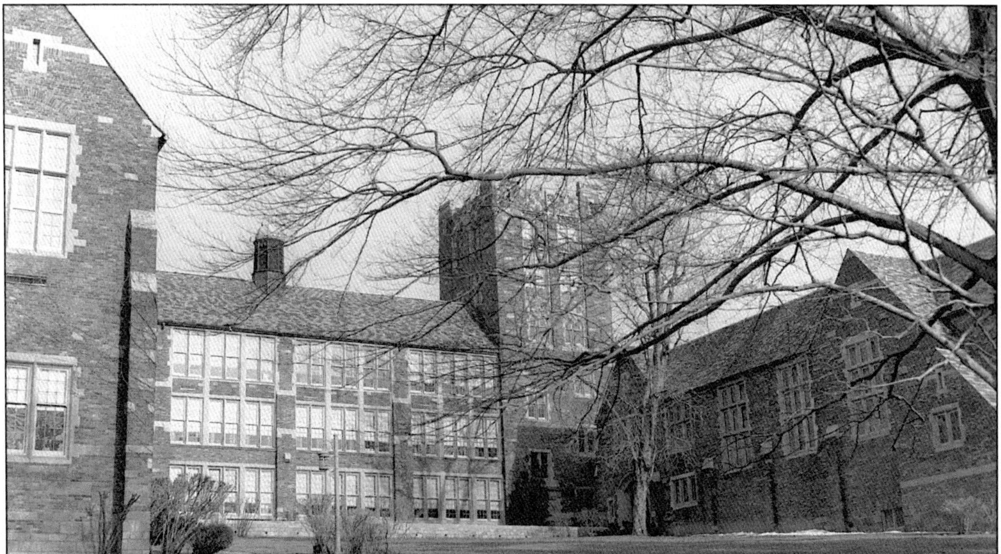

In 1927, two special meetings were held at which time propositions for a new high school were defeated. In 1928, the sum of $750,000 was put forth and passed, and the junior/senior high school opened in 1929. The new building accommodated 900 students, but by 1937, the enrollment was over 1,300. There was much discussion centering on the floor plan of the building, which is an excellent example of the Gothic Revival style. The tower with extra classroom space for later expansion was voted into the design over the objections of residents who favored an indoor swimming pool. A new wing for junior high school students was added in 1957.

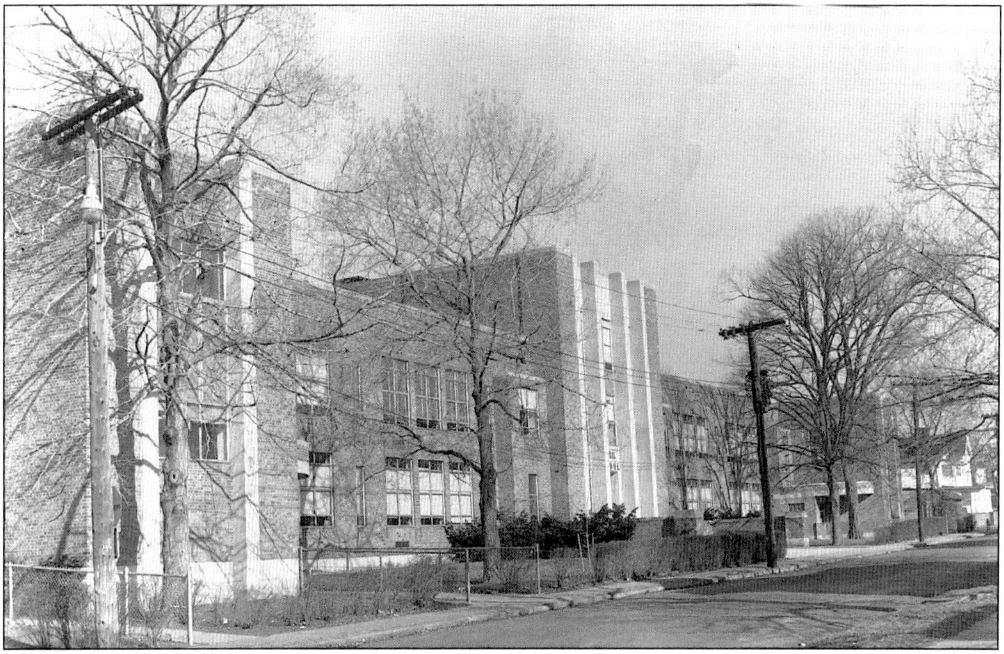

The new Park School, on the same site as the original, was built in 1939, to replace the old structure. It is a wonderful example of the commercially popular Art Deco style of the 1930s. The building entrance features Deco spirals and chevrons. The Park School clearly breaks out of the traditional mold of school design.

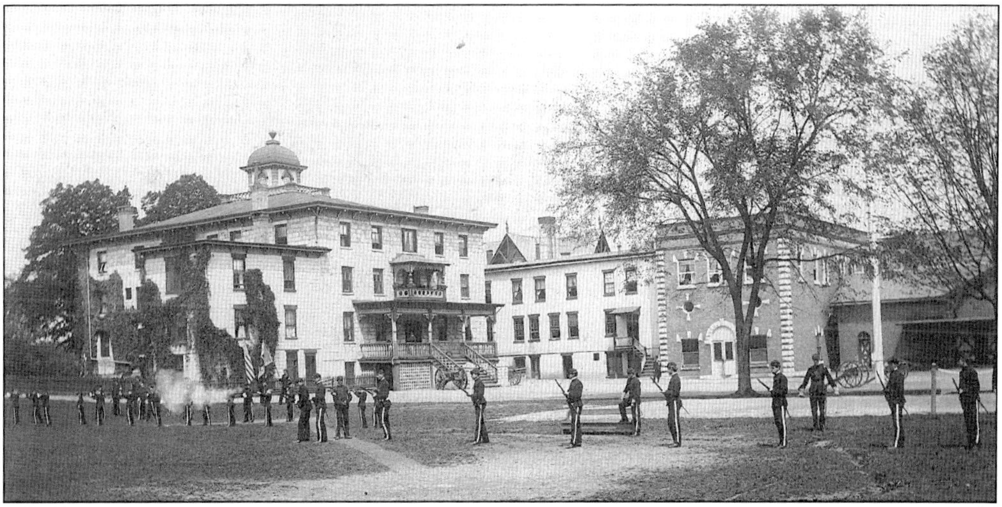

The Mount Pleasant Military Academy was established in 1814, through financial contributions from the community. It was located on State Street near Broad Avenue and was first operated as a day school. By 1848, military schools were very popular and so it was turned into an academy. A female department, started years earlier, was not successful and so was closed. The academy taught boys aged 6 through 17 and was "of the first order where young men might be prepared for college or university, or for active business life, and where the influences thrown around the students should be such as to inspire gentlemanly conduct." The school stayed in operation until 1925. The former library, at 23 State Street, is the only surviving building from the original campus. The nearby Academy Place is named after the school.

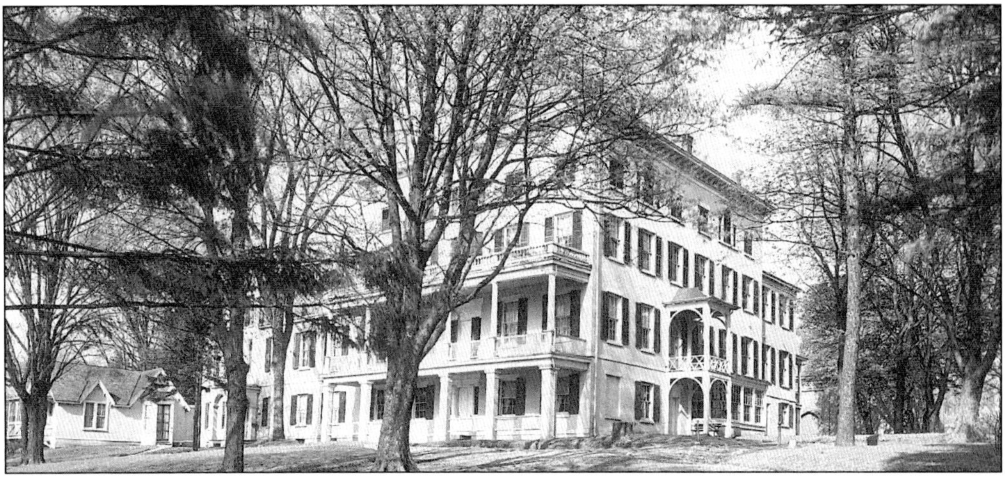

St. John's Military Academy School was founded in 1842, and it was known as the Mountain Institute. In the beginning, the school was for girls only and then a hotel, before Marlborough Churchill bought the land on Eastern Avenue and changed its name. St. John's included 6 acres of campus, an average of 90 students (most of whom boarded), and prided itself on furnishing officers for the Union cause during the Civil War. Its most notable student was President Theodore Roosevelt. The school closed in 1948, and the buildings were razed in 1958 to make way for St. Ann's Parochial School.

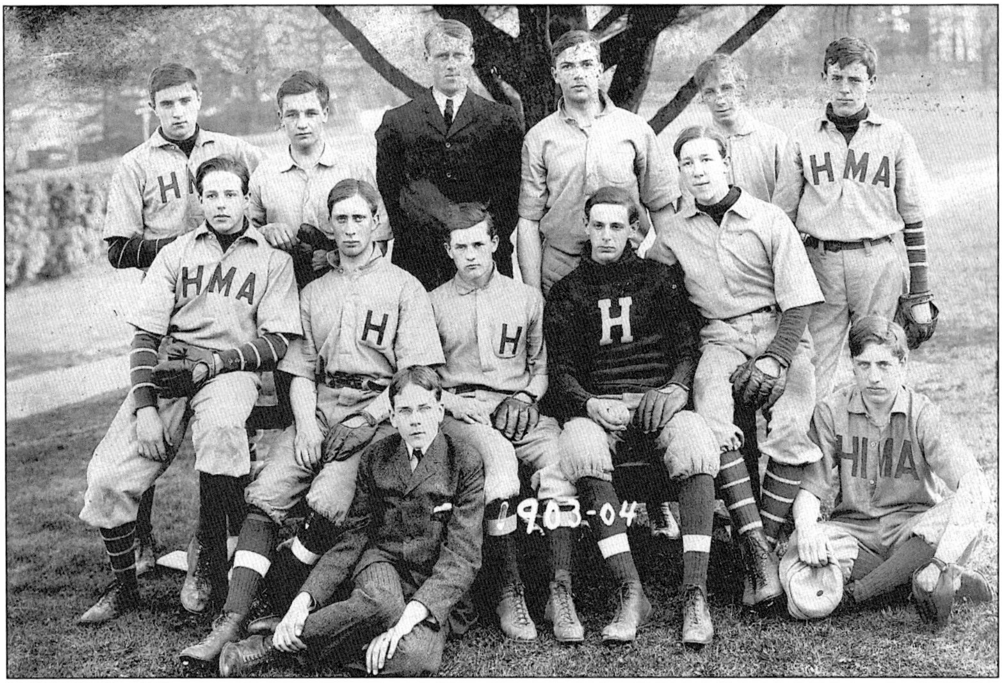

Dr. Holbrook's Military Academy and Classical School was founded around 1860, as a seminary for young women on 10 acres of land, where part of the Chilmark development stands today. The academy was turned into a boy's school and enlarged in 1866, by Reverend D.A. Holbrook, an educator from Brooklyn. It was strictly a boarding school with a population of 60 students. The curriculum included "all the English branches, Latin, Greek, French, German, chemistry, natural philosophy, music, and military tactics." The academy was closed in the 1920s.

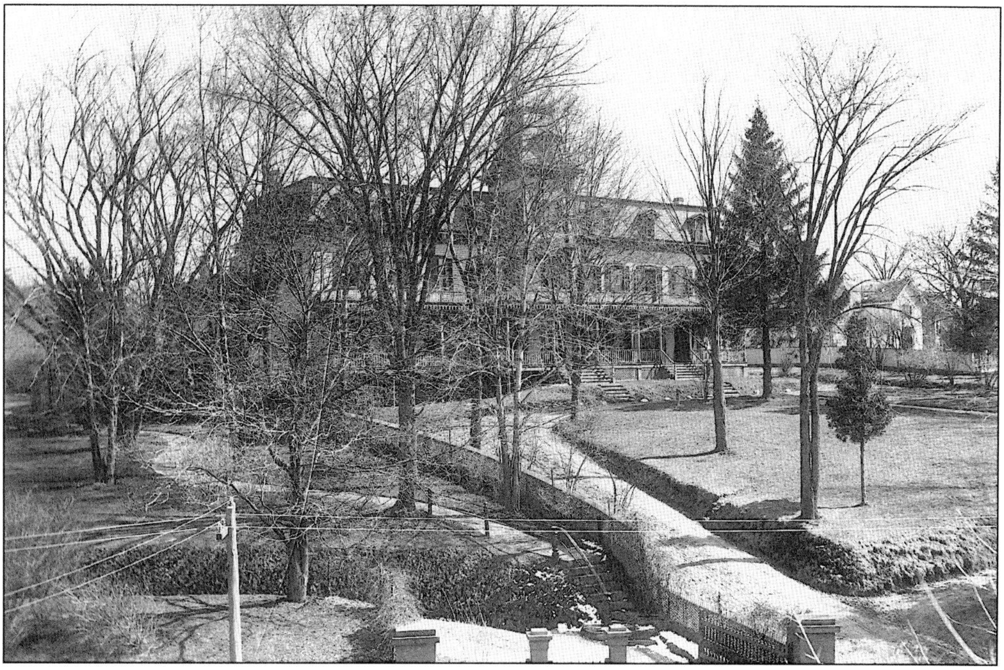

The Ossining School for Girls, which was in operation from 1869 until 1932, was located on Croton Avenue, opposite the public library, and maintained as a school for boarders and day pupils. Its purpose was "To surround its members with the influence of an attractive Christian home and so to make their association helpful, not only in elevating and strengthening their mind and character, but also in acquiring grace, dignity and refinement of bearing and manner." Today, it is an apartment complex that includes two buildings named after school officials—Clara Fuller and Mary Hampton.

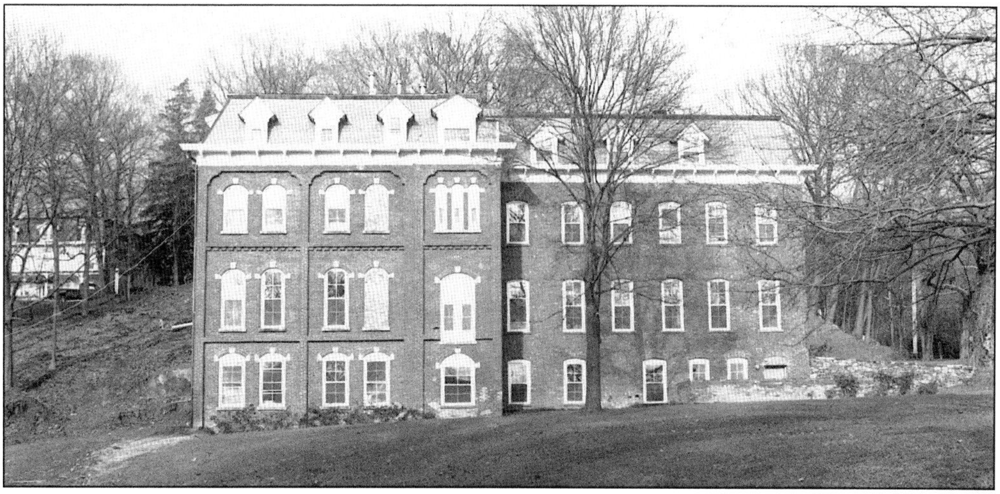

Vireun, a small military school for boys at the foot of Snowden Avenue, was founded by H.C. Symonds, a former West Point officer and English professor, in 1870. The higher standards for admission to West Point and Annapolis, which had been brought on by the Civil War, opened a field for the private school especially around the areas closest to the nation's academies. Vireun's major function was "To prepare the boys for the severe examinations of the military academies." Today, the building is a condominium.

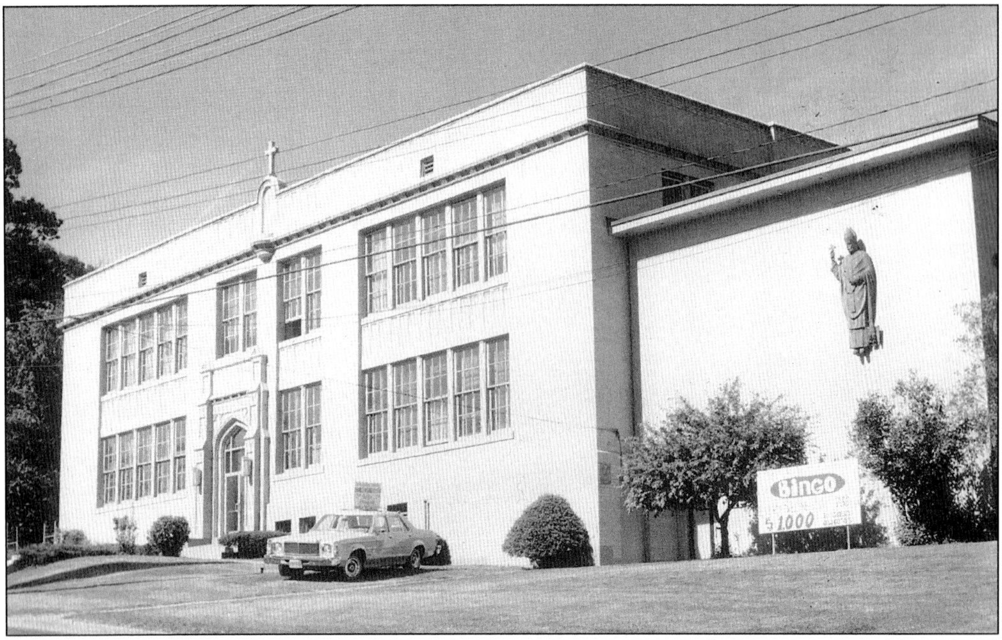

Saint Augustine's School, on North Highland Avenue, was started in 1878 as a public school (at the rear of the church across the street) with a population of 125 students. In 1892, it became the first parochial school in Sing Sing. There were 275 pupils and the Sisters of Charity were the teachers. This building was erected in 1925, and enrollment increased to the point that the annex to the right was constructed in 1960. The building included an auditorium and gymnasium and was partially demolished in 1980. Today, it is the home of Media One.

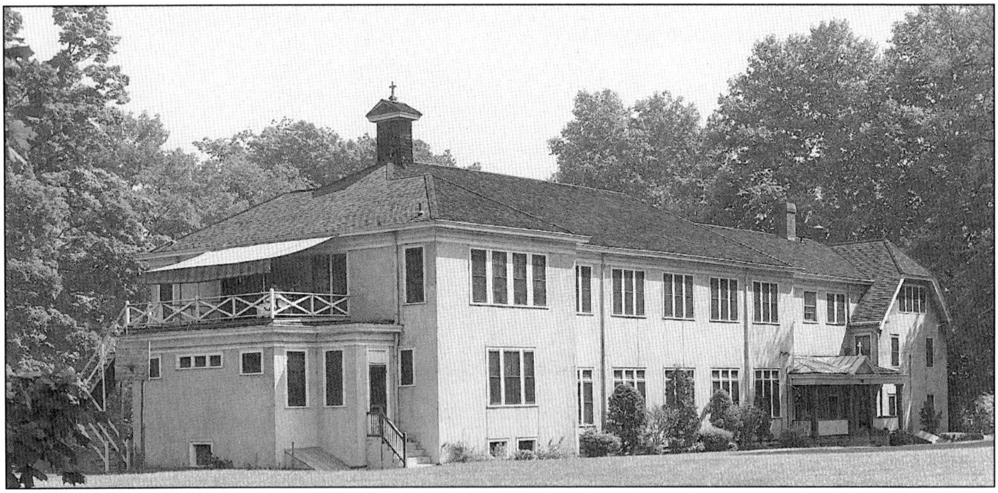

Mary Immaculate School at Eagle Park on Albany Post Road was started in 1915, when the Order of Dominican Sisters of Ohio bought the property from the estate of Orlando Potter (whose family owned the land since 1870). The enrollment at the Catholic school increased to a high of 327 in 1967, and new buildings were added to the campus. The girl's boarding school ranged from 1st through 12th grade. This photograph is of Aquinas Hall, where classes were first held. The hall also served as a dormitory and chapel. The property was purchased by St. Augustine's in 1978, after their church and school were torn down due to the widening of Route 9.

Five

VILLAGE OF CHURCHES

Our village is unique in the Hudson River Valley, as it is home to a truly impressive number of religious structures, all within easy walking distance of downtown. When the community was first settled and began to grow in the early 1800s, houses of worship were among the very first structures to be constructed. They were not only utilized for prayer but as gathering places for various social and governmental events. The earliest citizens to locate here placed a special emphasis upon making their ecclesiastical buildings the best that money could afford. Their design, materials, and interior decorations were a sight to behold. A great deal of love and care went into their upkeep from the very start.

Since religious and social freedom had always been a mainstay of Ossining's multicultural population, the growth of a wide variety of architectural styles in the area of religious edifices took place. Of particular pride is the fact that a number of local houses of worship have been designated as historic landmarks, more so than in other metropolitan communities of similar size.

One area that must be mentioned is the Sing Sing Camp Meeting Society, which was established in 1831 and held meetings in the locust grove (north of Croton Avenue on Campwoods Road). The uniquely American camp meeting started in Westchester in Carmel in 1804, Croton in 1805, and Haverstraw in 1825. Land was bought in 1834, and the formation of the Mount Pleasant Episcopal Church Meeting Society took place. During the Civil War period, yearly meetings were attended by as many as 15,000 followers. Many came by steamboat and stayed in cottages and tents on the grounds. The meetings lasted about ten days, the ministers preaching with "eloquence and power holding the great congregation to rapt attention."

Two other areas needing attention are the Dale Cemetery Association, founded in 1851, and Saint Augustine's Cemetery, started in 1847. The background and architectural history of Ossining's religious structures are well worth presenting.

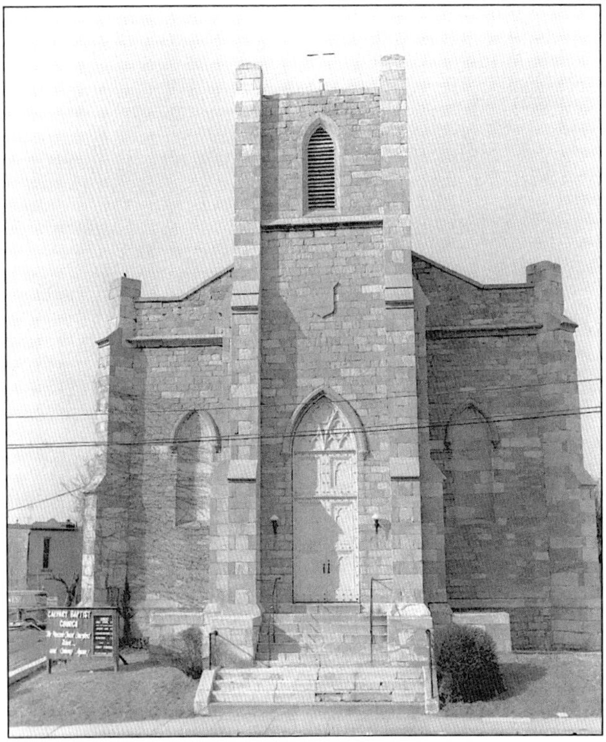

Originally named St. Paul's Episcopal Church, when it was completed in 1836, this building was designed by noted New York City architect Calvin Pollard, with walls and tower built of locally quarried Sing Sing marble. The spire was removed in the late 1930s. The church is an example of Gothic Revival architecture and is listed on the National Register of Historic Places. In 1956, St. Paul's on the Hill began worship in a former hay barn atop Ganung Drive, part of the former Torbank estate. Their new church was dedicated in 1961. Today, this building is Calvary Baptist Church on St. Paul's Place.

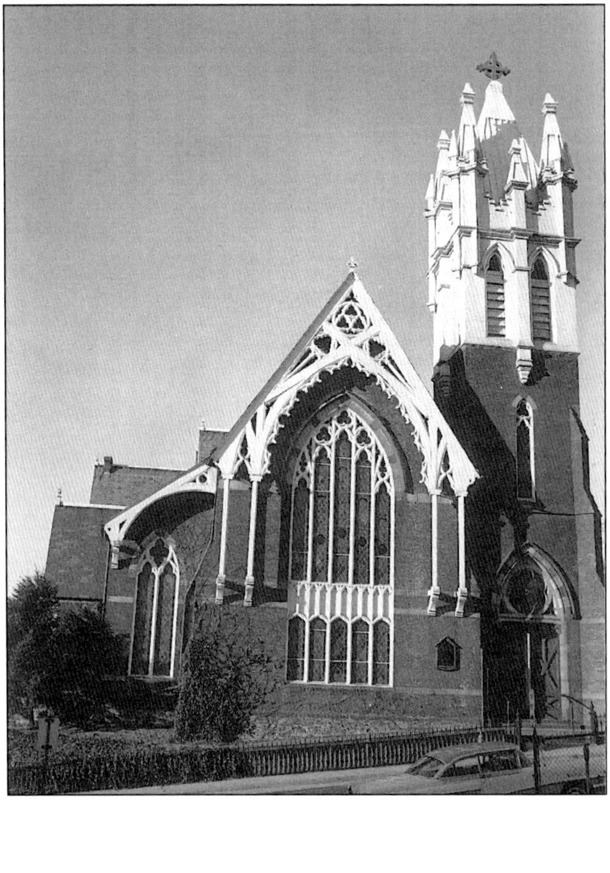

The First Baptist Church, on Church Street and Route 9, was the second edifice on this site. The first was Greek Revival in style and used from 1815 until 1871. The local Baptist congregation was formed in 1790. This structure was dedicated in 1874 and featured a 150-foot-high octagonal spire, which was blown down in 1884, and replaced by the present 100-foot massive tower. The church is an example of the High Victorian Gothic style with an outstanding sculptured interior. It is listed on the National Register of Historic Places.

Located on the corner of South Highland Avenue and Maple Place, the First Presbyterian Church is the oldest congregation in Ossining, formed in 1763. The first building was constructed in 1768, on the site of Sparta Cemetery, and was badly damaged during the Revolutionary War. The present edifice was consecrated in 1870 and features an octagonal spire, high mansard roof, iron cresting along the roof ridges, and elaborate stone work on the pointed entrance doors.

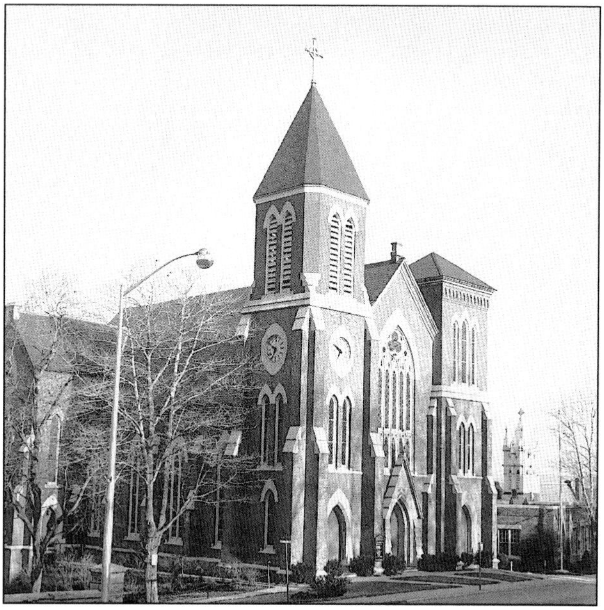

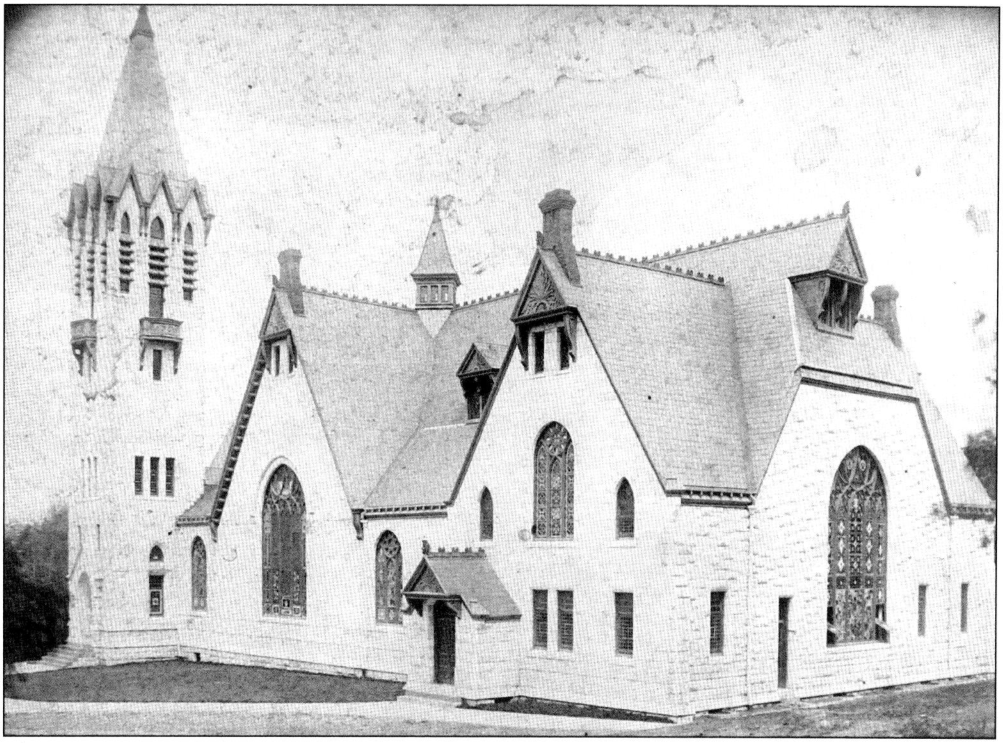

This High Victorian Gothic church was dedicated in 1889 and represents a congregation that dates to 1787, when itinerant Methodist ministers preached to a small society that met in a local cider mill. Today, the Ossining United Methodist Church includes 40 stained-glass memorial windows, featuring a large Tiffany Glass Company centerpiece, and a massive tower with unusual cross gables. The church is located on the corner of Emwilton Place and South Highland Avenue.

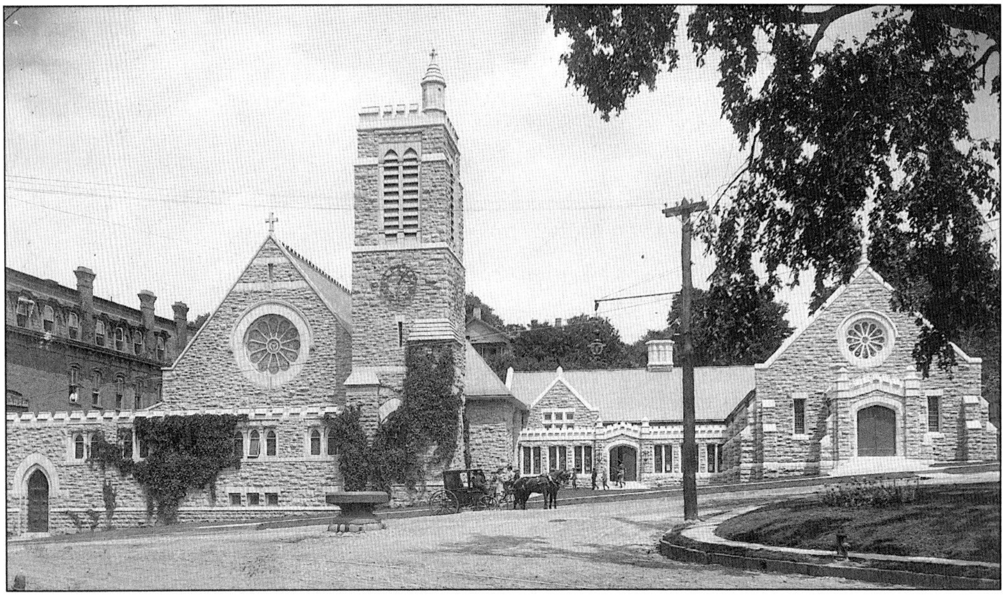

The Trinity Episcopal Church, on South Highland Avenue, was constructed, in 1892, of grey marble by New York City architect Robert W. Gibson. The church is a fine example of the Neo-Gothic Revival style, featuring careful reproduction of details and building methods of Old English prototypes. Most of the stained-glass windows are by Tiffany of New York City. Additions were constructed in 1907 to form a roughly shaped "U" plan around the courtyard.

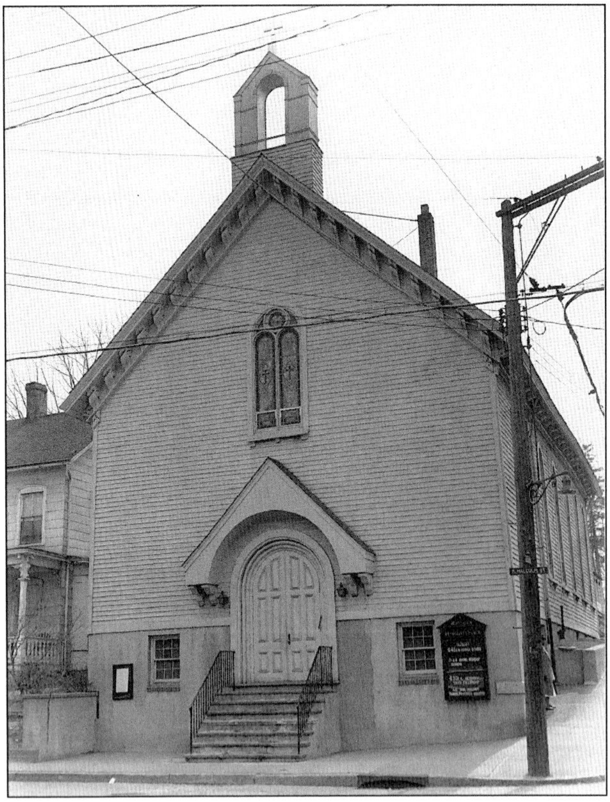

The North Sing Sing Methodist Church was erected in 1870. The church was first organized as the Sing Sing Mission with initial meetings held in a building on Broadway. Formal organization of St. Matthew's Methodist Church came in 1900, when the growing congregation moved to its present address, on the corner of Ann and North Malcolm Street. The first parsonage was located at 24 Sarah Street.

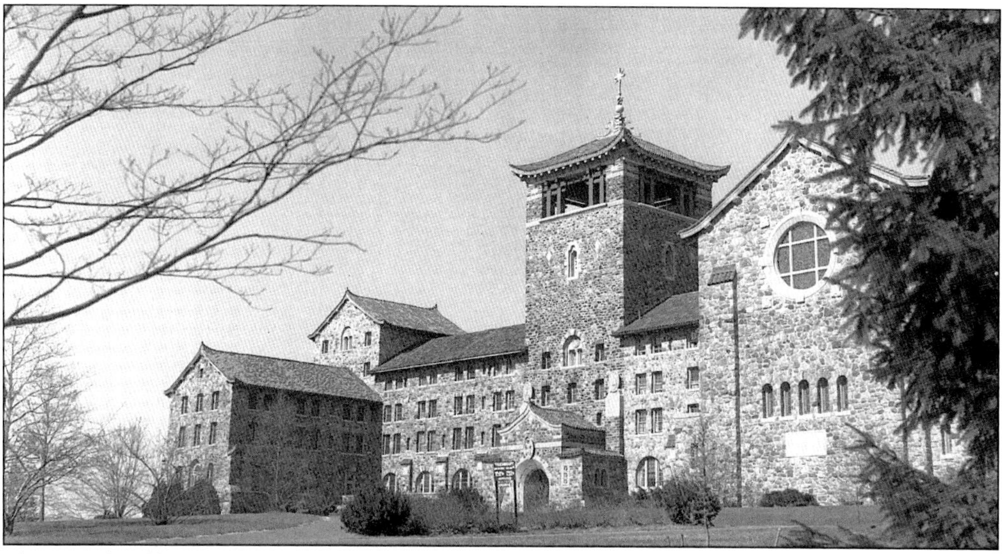

The Maryknoll Seminary, on Sunset Hill (off of Ryder Road), was built in 1920, with the wings and chapel added in 1956. The firm of Maginnis and Walsh designed the structure, along with 114 others in America. They believed that the Gothic style was purely Protestant and that Catholics needed a style they could identify with. They chose pre-Gothic Early Byzantine style, from northern Italy and Sicily, featuring rounded arches with mosaic decoration. Maryknoll goes beyond early Christian themes to include Oriental influences, especially roofs and the tower. This is a reflection of the seminary's purpose, which was the training of missionaries for foreign posts, including many in the Far East. The Catholic Foreign Mission Society of America was formed in 1911.

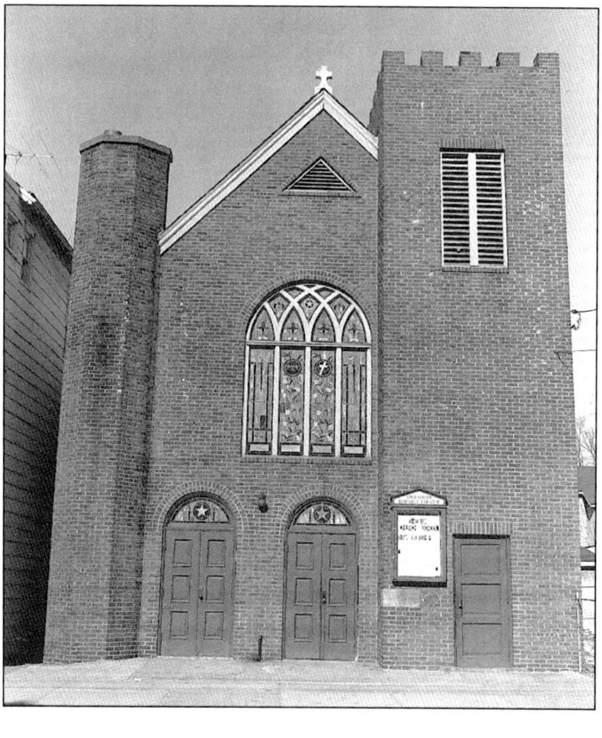

Spring Street was the site of the Star of Bethlehem Baptist Church, founded by Reverend Henry E. Duers, who was a former slave and fought with the Union Army in the Civil War. Brother Duers came to Ossining in 1889 to start a mission. Membership grew so much that in 1890 he organized the Centennial Star of Bethlehem Church and completed this building in 1892. Duers Circle, at the intersection of Ann and Brandreth Streets and Broadway, is named in his honor. In 1998, a majestic new church was erected on Spring Street, on the site of the former Ossining Hospital.

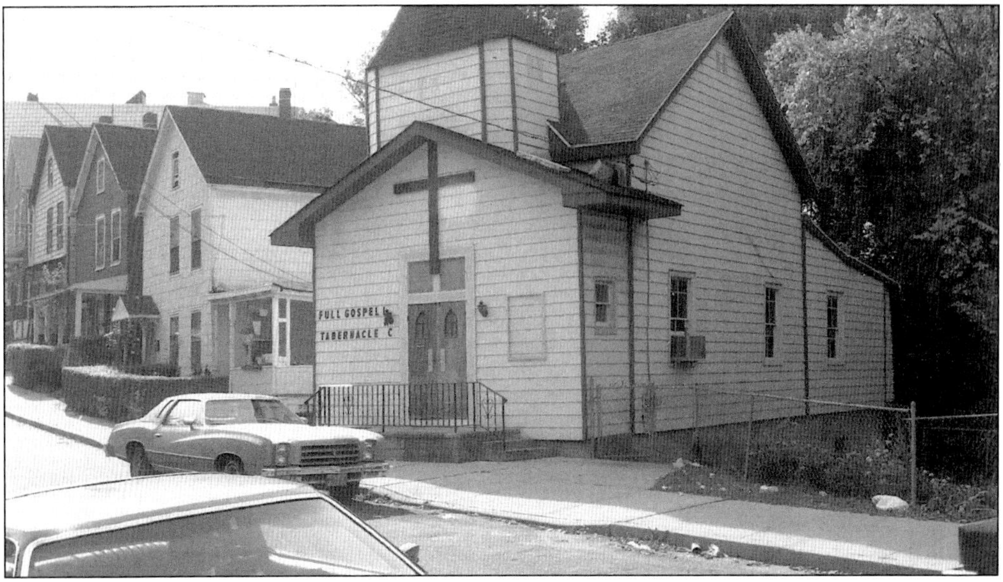

The Full Gospel Tabernacle Church was founded in 1931, by John and Nellie Sharrock, on Aqueduct Street. As the congregation prospered, the church moved to larger quarters on Leonard Street, followed by Central Avenue. This present edifice was purchased in 1941 and is located on Brandreth Street.

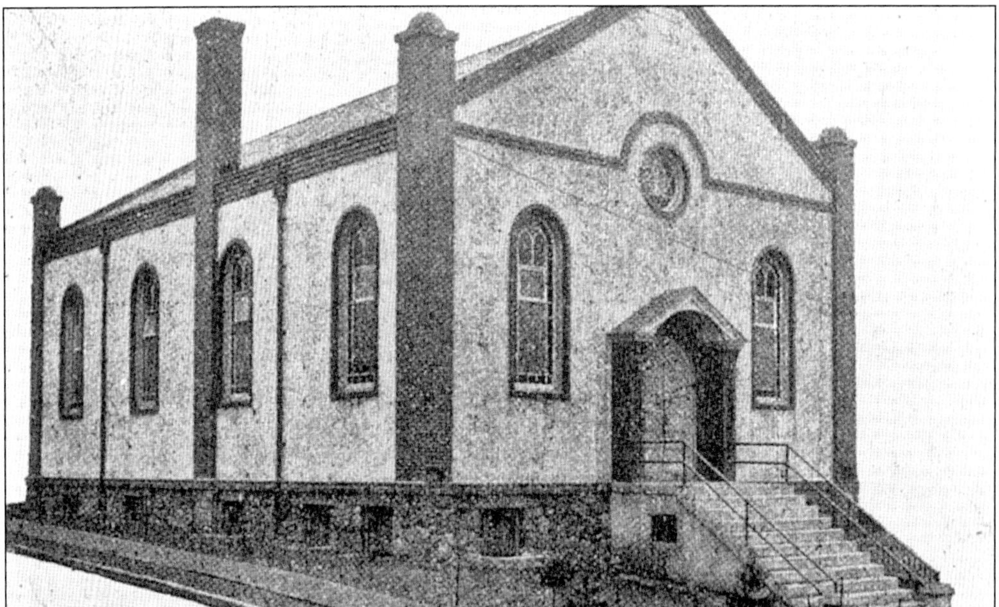

The first Jewish families arrived in Ossining in the 1890s, creating a religious entity known as the Sons of Israel in 1893 as well as a Mutual Aid Society called B'Nai B'Rith, or the Sons of the Covenant. Early services were held in a house on Hunter Street that was purchased by members. In 1921, the congregation had grown to 45 families and the need for expansion became clear. Congregation Sons of Israel constructed this new synagogue on Waller Avenue, holding their first services in 1924. In 1960, a modern synagogue was built on an 11-acre site, once the Meade family farm, on Pleasantville Road.

Prior to the establishment of St. Augustine's as a parish, Sing Sing village Catholics were part of a mission of St. Patrick's Church in Verplanck. Most worshippers were Irish-immigrant laborers constructing the first Croton Aqueduct and Hudson River Railroad between 1837 and 1855. Initial local masses were celebrated in 1845 in a house on Cedar Lane. Land on the Highland Turnpike was purchased in 1854, and this structure opened in 1857. It was demolished in 1980 with the congregation moving to Eagle Park. A new church was constructed on the property of the former Mary Immaculate School.

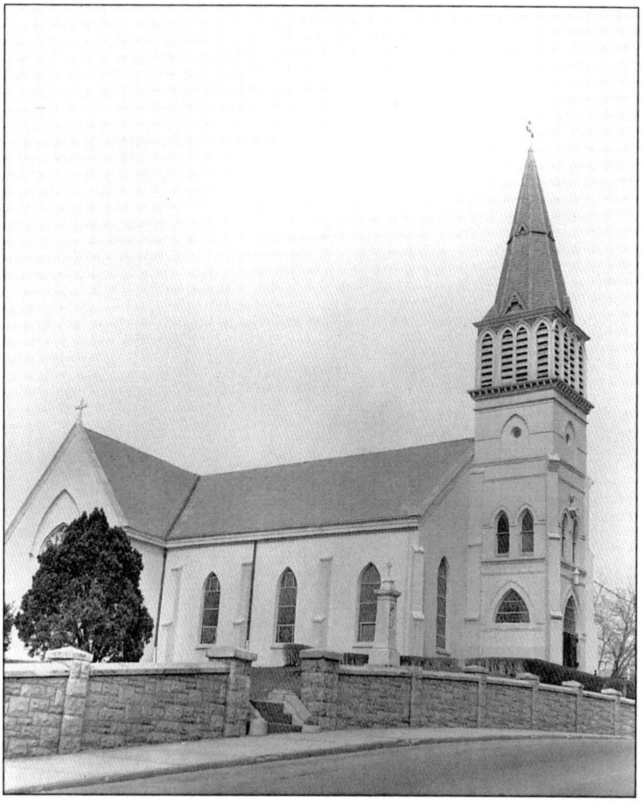

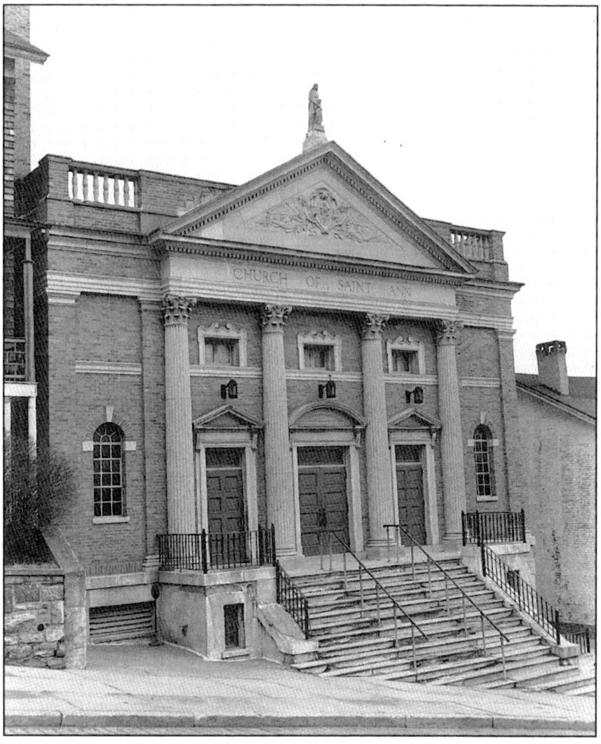

St. Ann's Roman Catholic Church on Eastern Avenue was founded to serve the needs of the large number of Italian immigrants who had settled in this area seeking work in the construction of the New Croton Aqueduct and Cornell Dam in the early 1900s. The first Mass was celebrated in 1927 in a store at the corner of Central Avenue and Brandreth Street. The congregation then moved to the vacant Parthenon Theatre on Main Street. This structure was opened in 1928. It is an interesting mixture of Greek Revival and Romanesque styles with unusual Corinthian pilasters and pediment on the front facade.

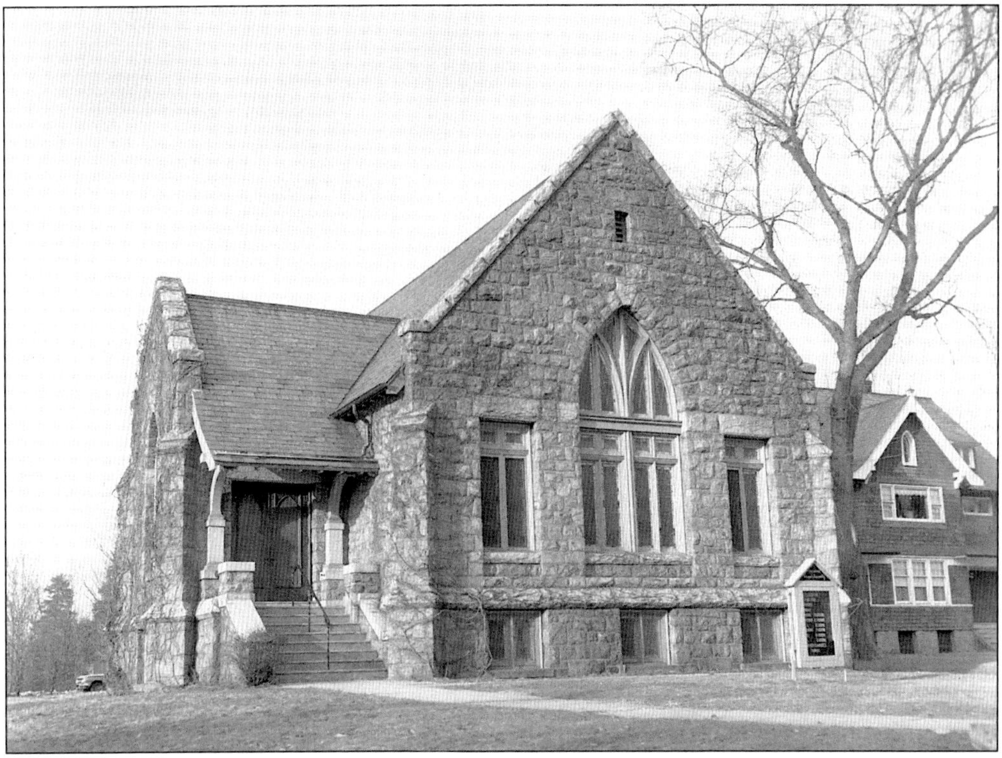

The Ossining Gospel Assembly Church, located on Croton Avenue, was constructed in 1914. The property was donated by the family of Sumner Stone, a New York banker whose summer residence was located on adjoining land. Stone Avenue is named after the family.

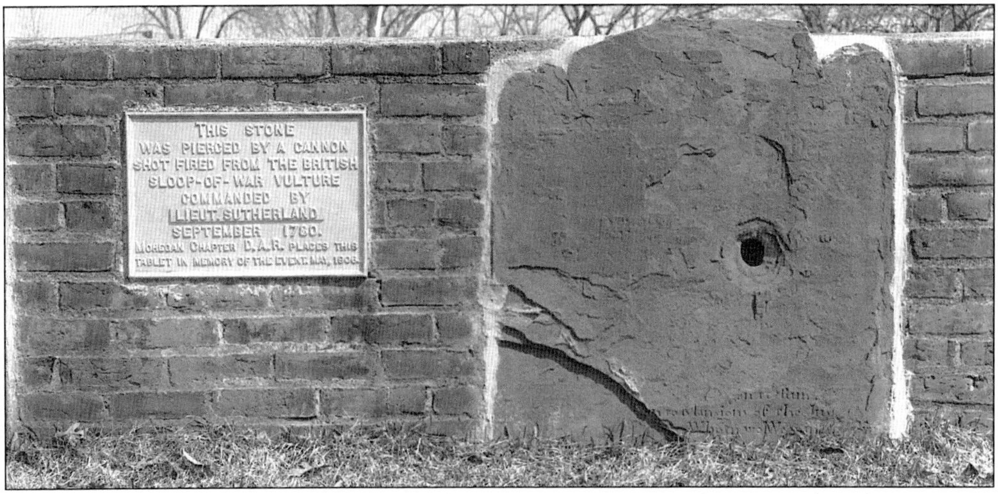

Sparta Cemetery, on Revolutionary Road, is a unique spot to observe Colonial gravestone carving as an art form, especially the red sandstone that was quarried across the Hudson River and Connecticut in the 18th century. The first church in the hamlet of Sing Sing opened in 1768. The church was Presbyterian, and its 3 acres were donated by the Phillipse family, Lords of the Manor. Next to the church was the Sparta Burying Ground. After the Revolutionary War, the state legislature passed an act granting the land forever to the Presbyterian church. The Ossining Historical Society assumed ownership in 1984.

Six

Up the River— The Big House

On May 14, 1825, Elam Lynds, former Warden of Auburn Prison in upstate New York, arrived at the Village of Sing Sing with 100 inmates from Auburn "without a place to receive the inmates or a wall to enclose them."

Sing Sing Prison rose to national notoriety during the 1920s, largely due to the efforts of Warden Lewis E. Lawes. Warden Lawes was the author of many books dealing with prison life and reform. He was also a popular media figure of the day, who appeared on many radio shows. His work, *20,000 Years in Sing Sing*, was developed into a radio drama. During Warden Lawes's tenure, the expression "Going up the river" meant a stay at Sing Sing for a convicted criminal. Sing Sing Prison is probably best known for its electric chair. Since its installation in 1891, 614 men and women have been put to death for various crimes against society. Some of the electrocutions were well publicized, such as Julius and Ethel Rosenberg and Louis "Lepke" Buchalter, while others are totally forgotten today. The first prisoners to be put to death at Sing Sing were Harris A. Smiler, James Slocum, Joseph Wood, and Schihick Judigo on July 7, 1891. The last prisoner to be electrocuted was Eddie Lee Mays on August 15, 1963. The largest group to be executed in one night was seven on August 12, 1912. No death penalties were performed during the years 1906, 1945, and 1962. In 1965, the State of New York curtailed the use of the electric chair for a number of capital crimes. Electrocution could be applied in cases of a police officer being killed or a convict (already serving a life sentence) killing someone while being incarcerated. In 1971, the electric chair was moved to Greenhaven Correctional Facility in upstate New York. Execution by lethal injection has been in effect since the restoration of the death penalty in 1995. Greenhaven, not Sing Sing Correctional Facility (as it is now called), has been outfitted to carry out any future executions.

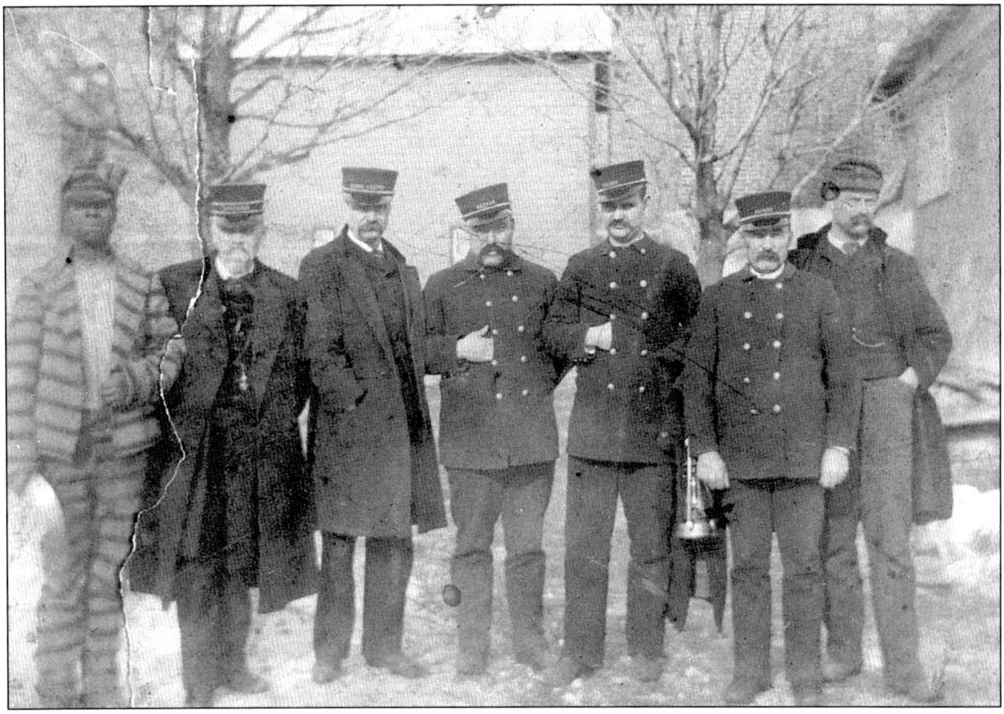

An inmate is shown here with prison personnel. In the early days, there were keepers and guards. Keepers had custodial charge of contractor's shops and maintenance groups and performed cell, hall, and gate duty. Guards were stationed around the grounds and did strictly guard duty, having no control over inmates.

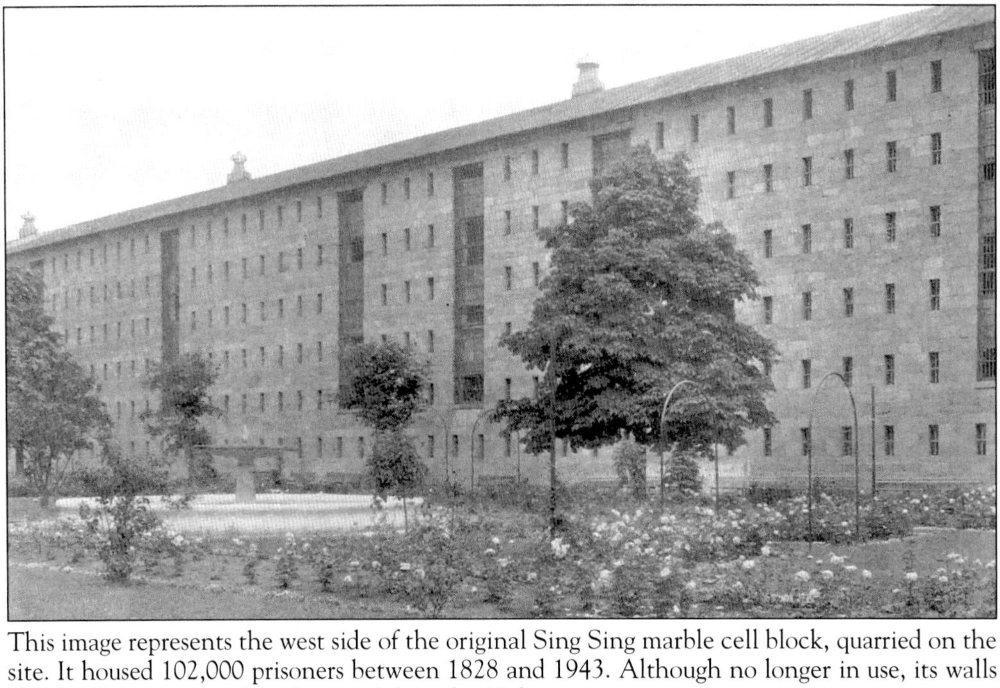

This image represents the west side of the original Sing Sing marble cell block, quarried on the site. It housed 102,000 prisoners between 1828 and 1943. Although no longer in use, its walls stand today as a reminder of prison life in the 19th century.

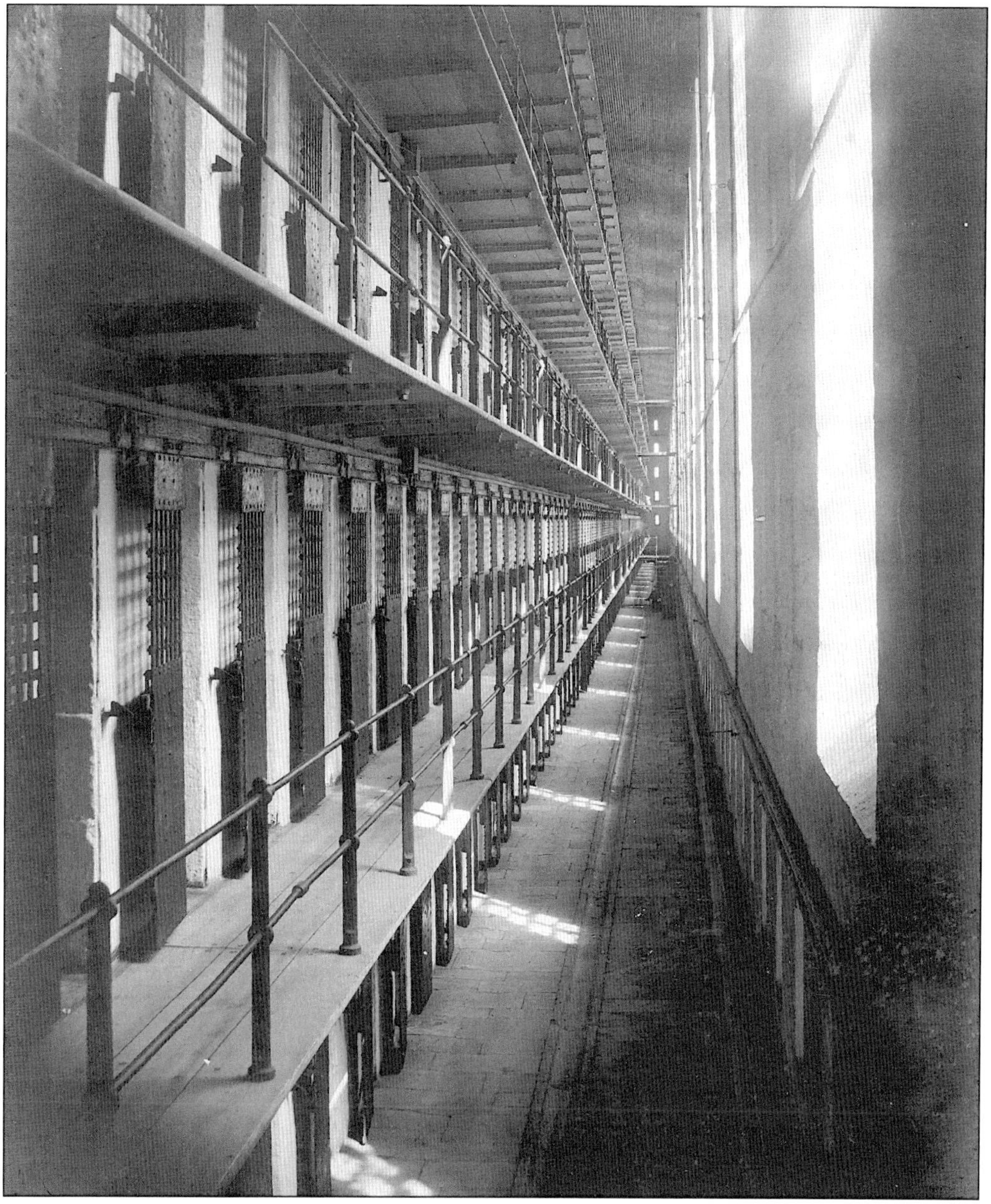

The specifications for the original cell block was 476 feet long, 44 feet wide, and 4 tiers high with each cell being 7 feet deep, 3 feet 3 inches wide, and 6 feet 7 inches high. The building was finished in 1828. In 1831, an addition removed the roof, constructed another tier of cells and re-enclosed the roof to add 200 cells. Around 1860, another roof raising was needed to bring the cell capacity to 1,200. In 1902, large windows were cut into the wall 31 feet high by 5 1/2 feet wide. In 1943, the last inmates were removed from the old cell block. Inside, demolition began at the top tier, which was removed by the end of the year. Stone from the building was used at the waterfront while iron doors and the locking systems were sold to aid the drive for scrap metal during the war years. In 1945, the bottom panes of the windows were bricked in to prevent escape attempts. By 1946, stone removed from the old cell block had provided approximately one-half acre of new waterfront at the northwest corner of the prison property.

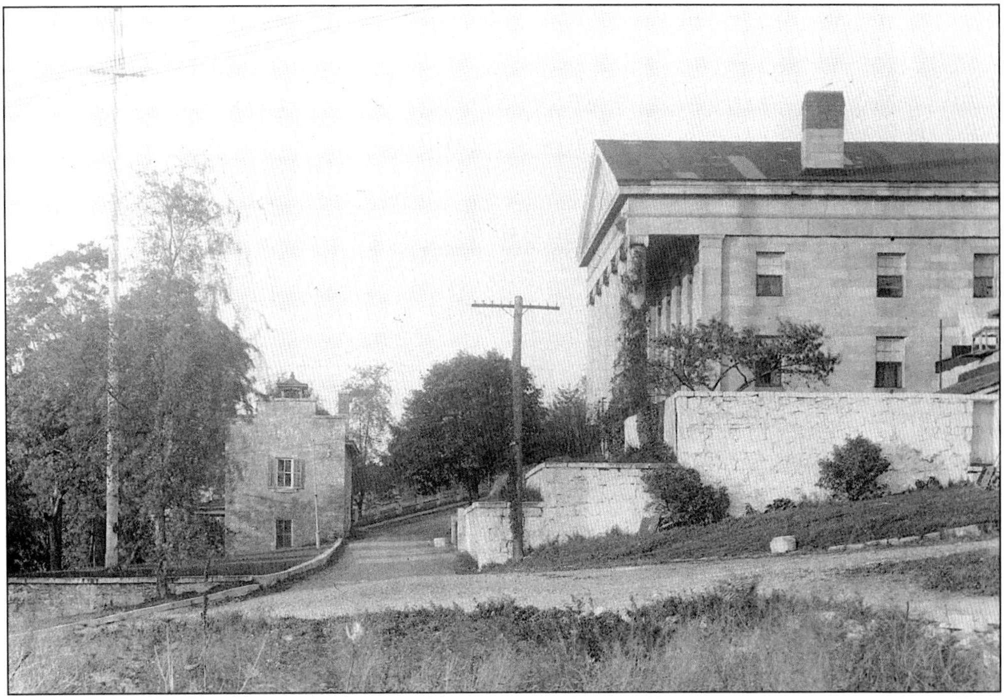

The Women's Prison at Sing Sing was completed in 1839, in the Greek Revival style, also using local marble. The number of female prisoners seldom amounted to more than 200. In 1877, the women were moved from Sing Sing to Crow Hill Penitentiary in Brooklyn and later housed at a separate facility at Auburn Prison in upstate New York. In 1927, this building was demolished and the stone was used to build a small 4-foot-high wall along state property on Spring Street.

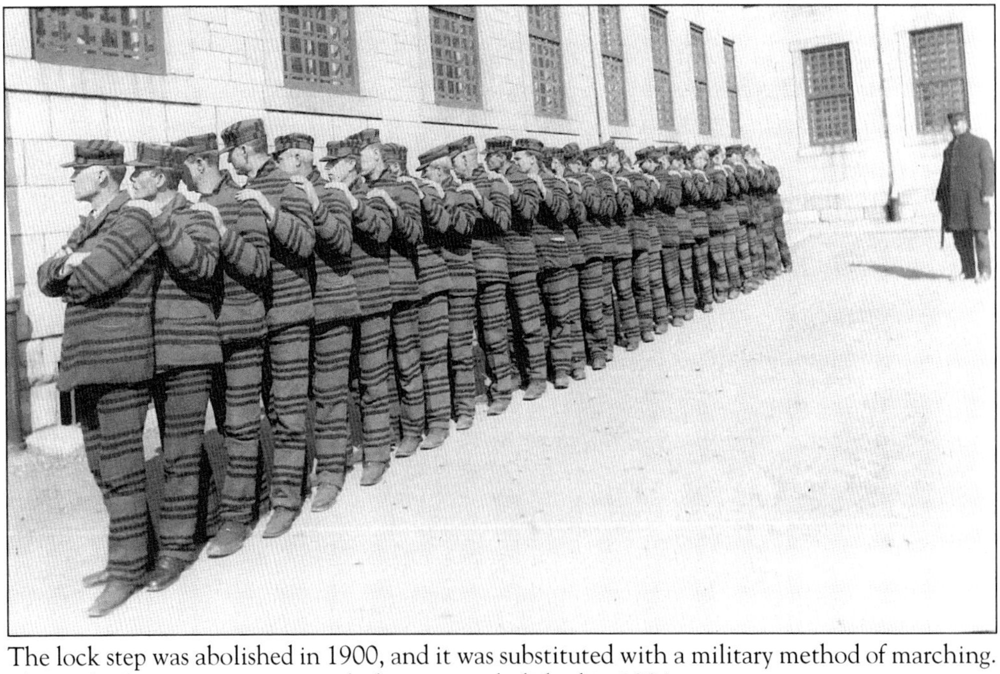

The lock step was abolished in 1900, and it was substituted with a military method of marching. The multiple stripes on inmate clothing were abolished in 1904.

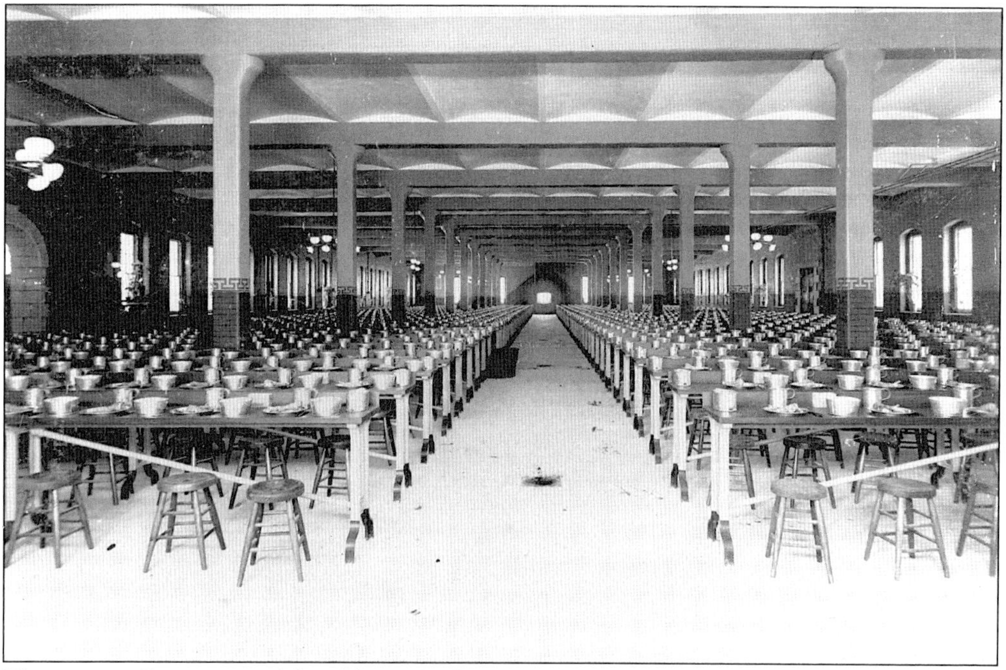

This image offers a view of the old mess hall at Sing Sing Prison. In 1912, the first Sunday meal was served in this facility.

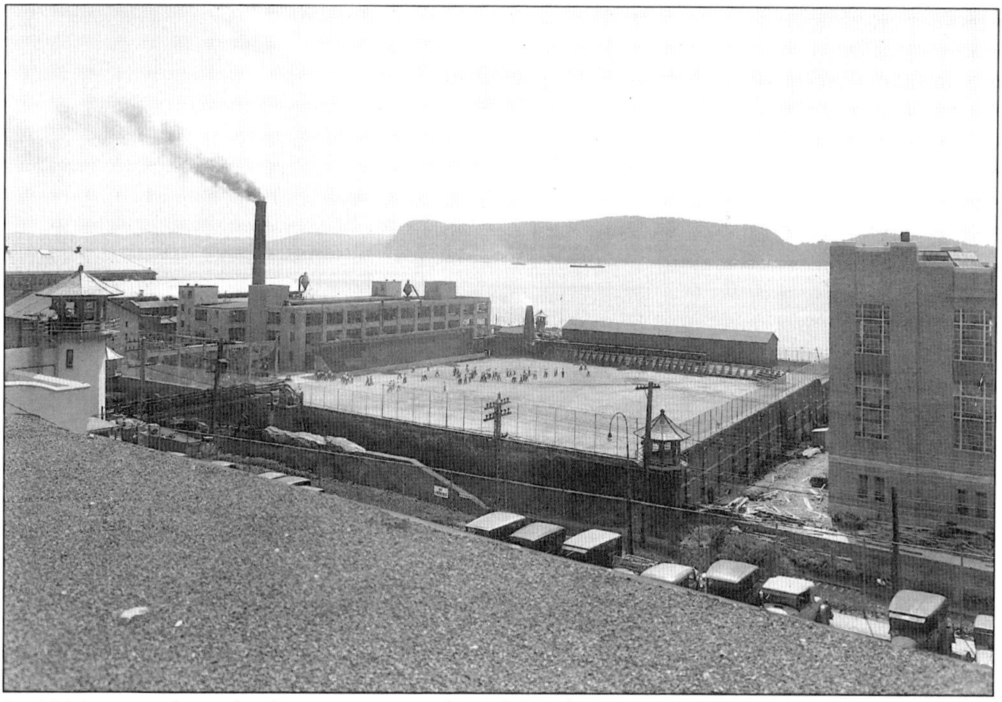

In 1914, ground inside the prison was cleared for the construction of a baseball diamond. Numerous professional teams like the New York Yankees and Giants played exhibition games here against the inmate squad. This photograph shows prisoners taking recreation on the field and was shot from the roof of the Administration Building on Hunter Street.

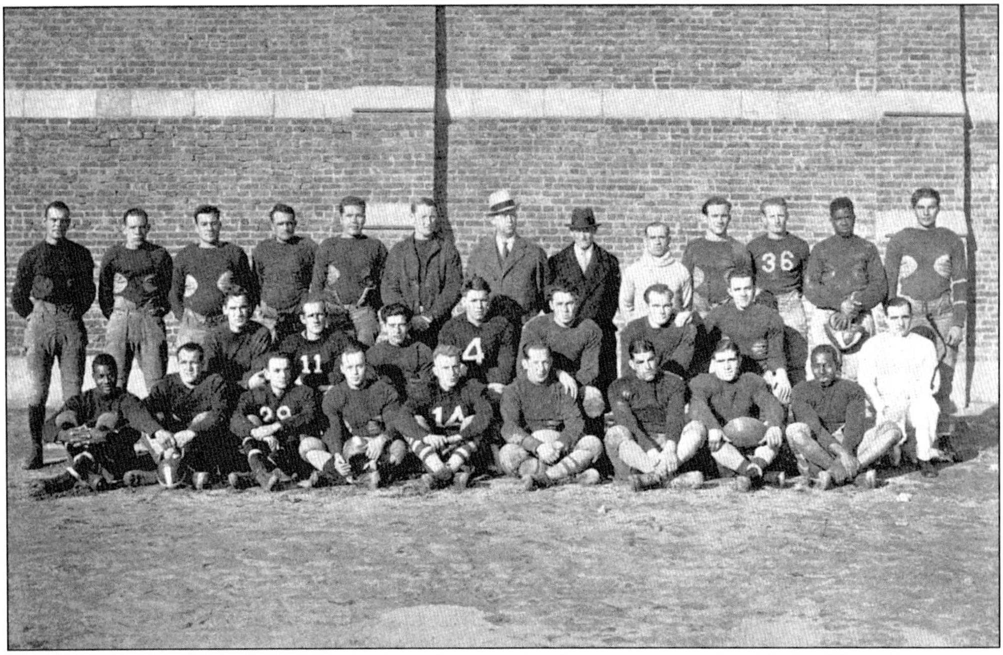

The prison authorities set up a number of teams for the inmates in the 1930s. This photograph depicts their football team. Men with long "bits," or sentences, were encouraged to play on the various squads.

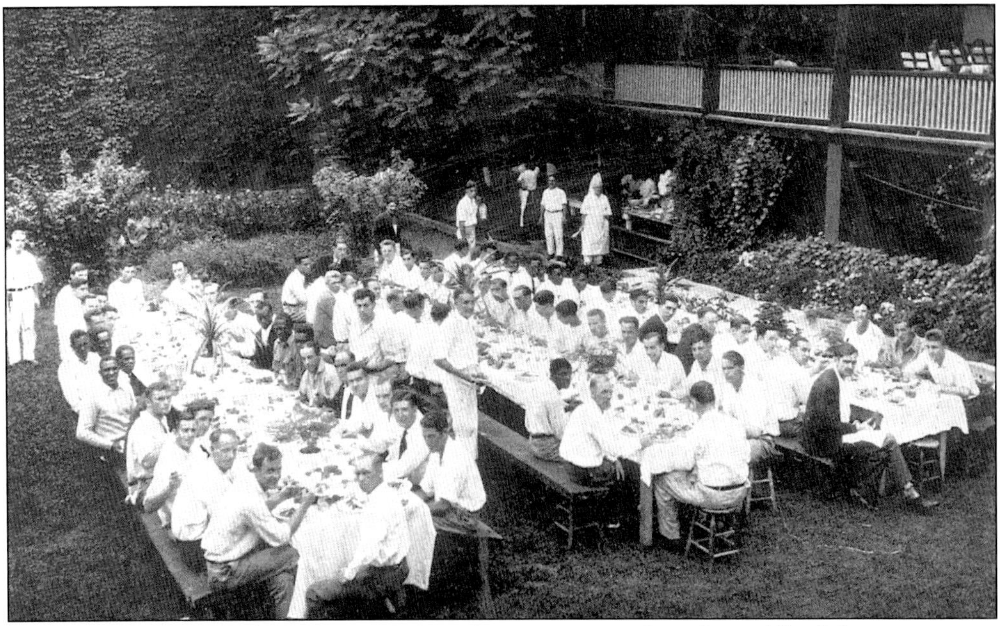

An annual Labor Day dinner was given to the prisoners at Sing Sing. All of the participants were winners of various athletic events. This photograph was taken in 1930.

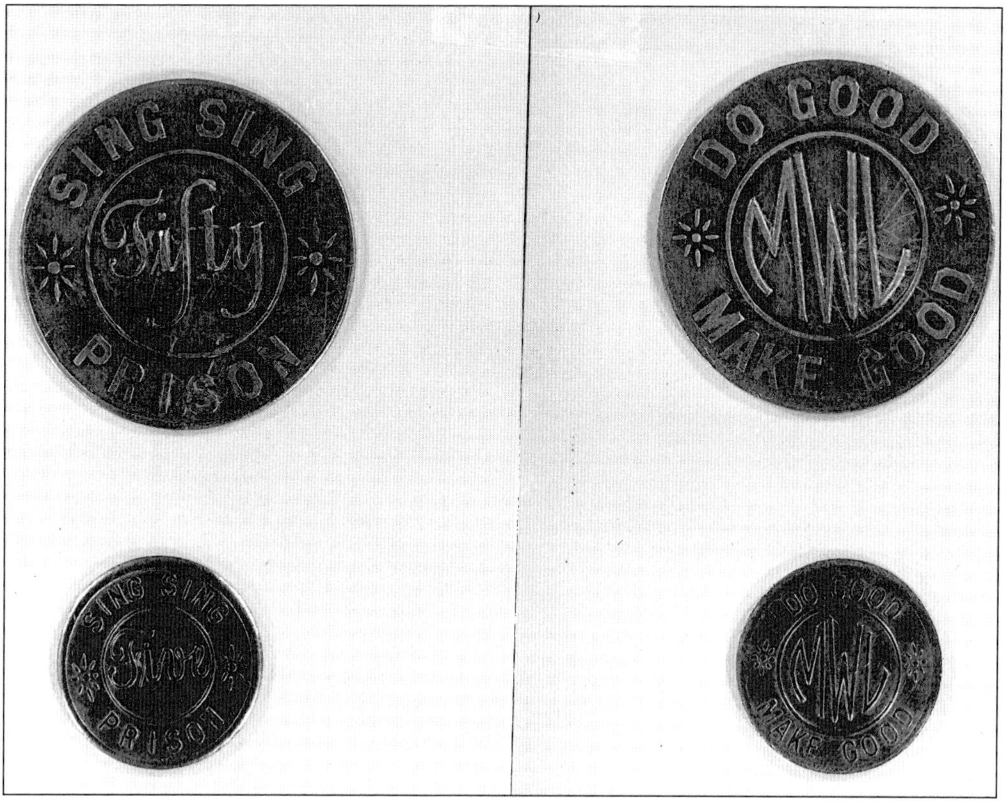

In 1914, the Mutual Welfare League was formed as an instrument of inmate government. They sponsored prison shows, athletics, and other activities. In 1919, they opened two stores at Sing Sing using both League coin and paper money. One store sold candy, clothing, tobacco, and cigarettes with a $3 maximum purchase. The other sold groceries, but not to exceed $6. In 1937, a ruling suspended all activities involving paid admissions on New York State premises. Mutual Welfare League coins appear in this photograph.

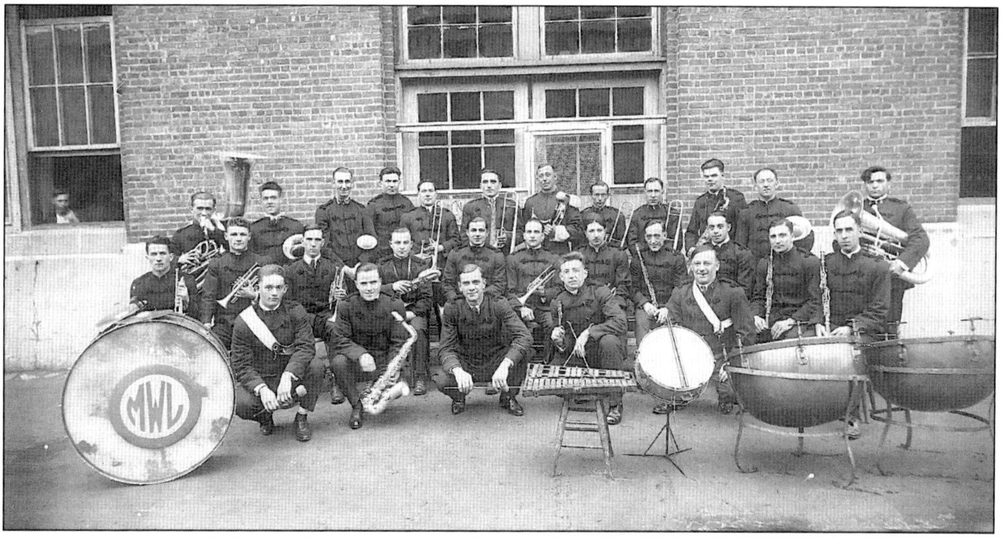

The inmate Mutual Welfare League band is shown here as it appeared in 1927.

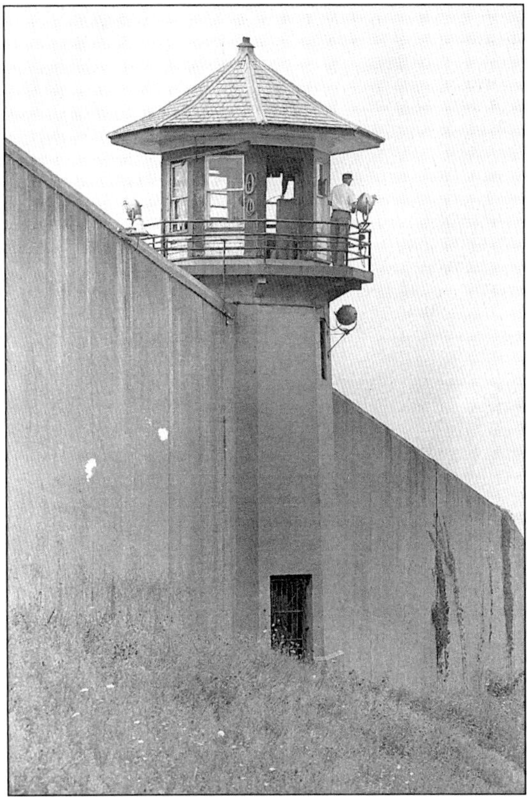

This photograph represents Wall Post Number 14 at Sing Sing Prison. In 1922, the foundation for the wall around the new prison was completed. In 1927, the structure "up the hill" towards State Street was finished.

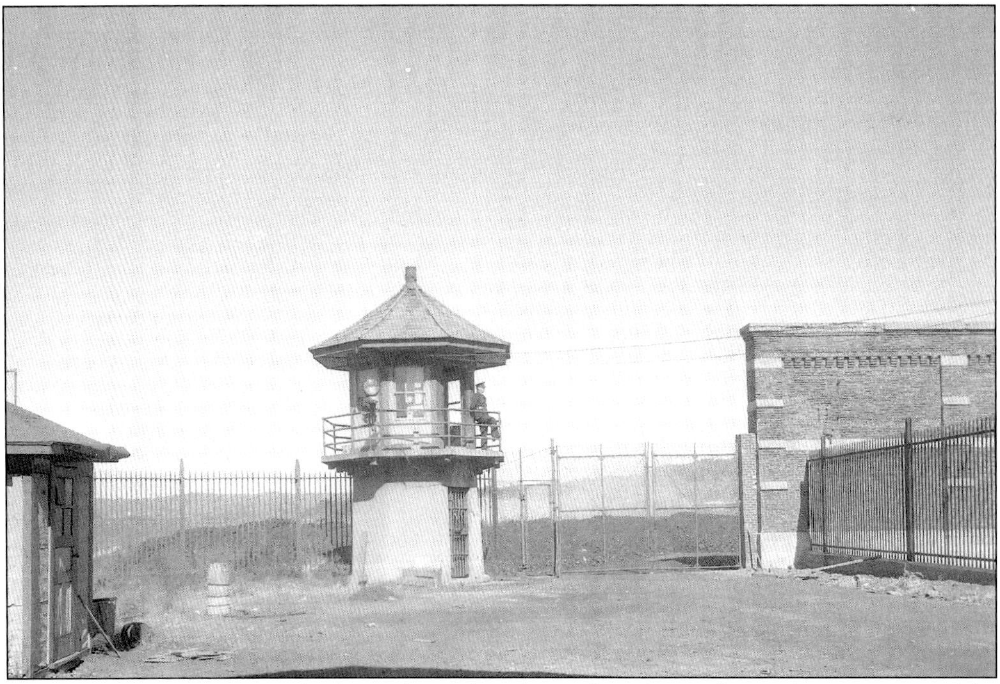

This is Tower Number 10, which was located at the coal yard near the Hudson River. Coal for electric power and heat was delivered by train, unloaded, and stockpiled by inmates.

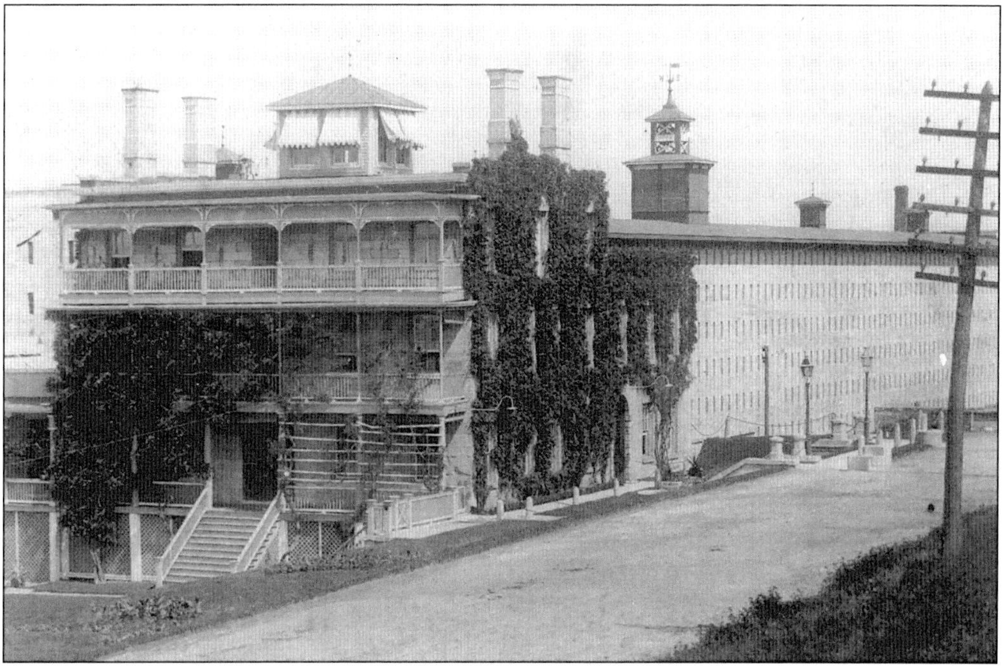

This shows the old warden's residence and east side of the original prison cell block. The residence was inside the walls of the institution, and 2,000 inmates passed it six times per day. In 1929, it was decided to construct a new home for the warden outside the grounds.

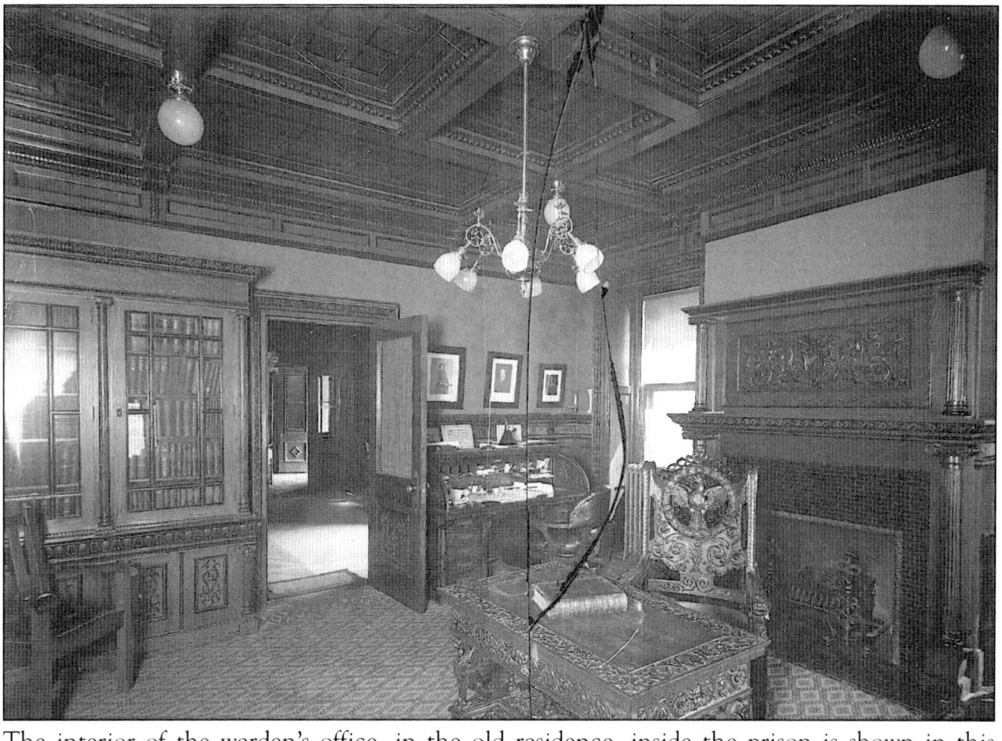

The interior of the warden's office, in the old residence, inside the prison is shown in this photograph.

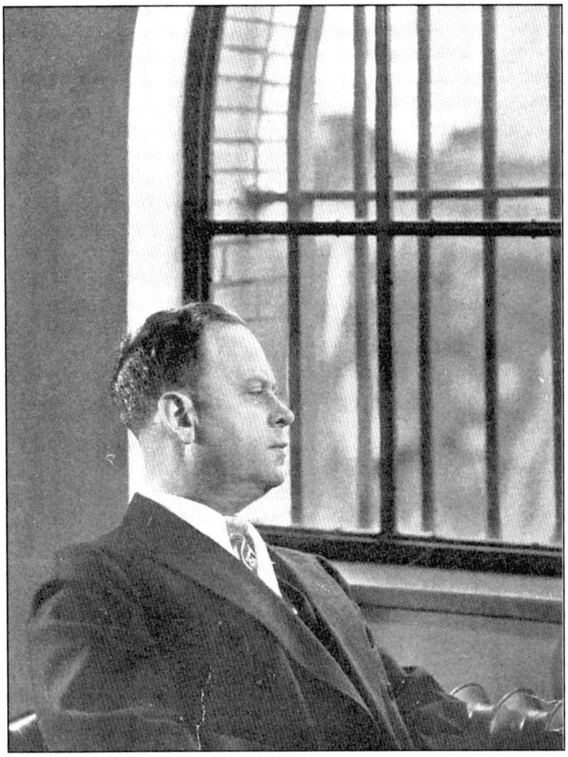

Warden Lewis E. Lawes, who was in charge of Sing Sing Prison from 1920 until 1941, is shown at left.

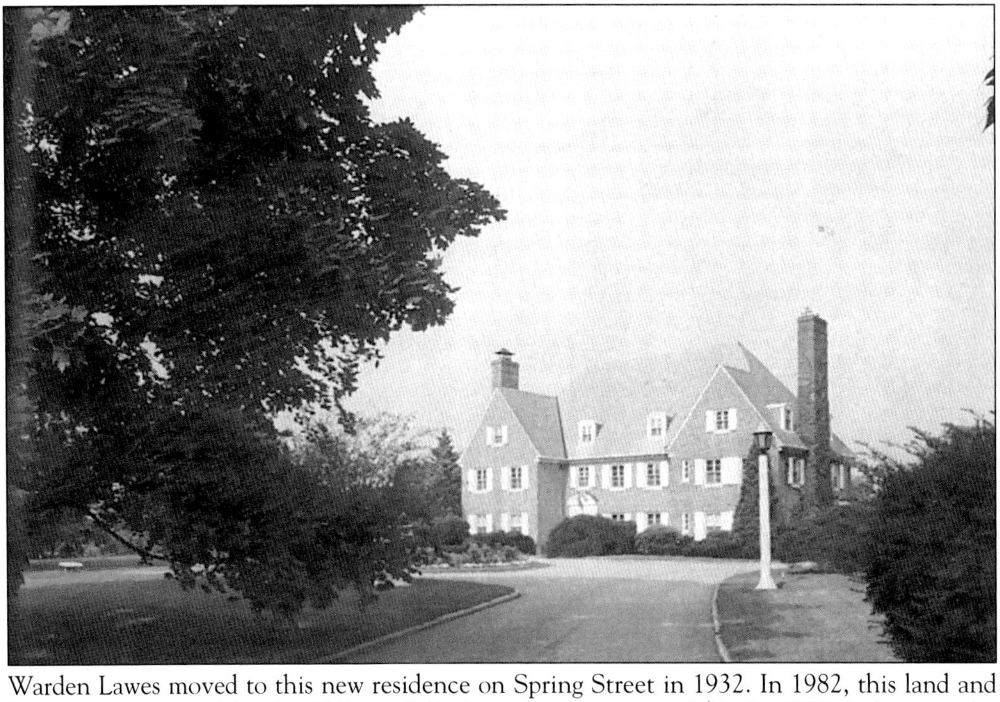

Warden Lawes moved to this new residence on Spring Street in 1932. In 1982, this land and house were acquired by the Village of Ossining for the price of $1. In 1987, it became the property of Hudson Point Condominiums. The warden's home was restored and used as a clubhouse for the condominiums.

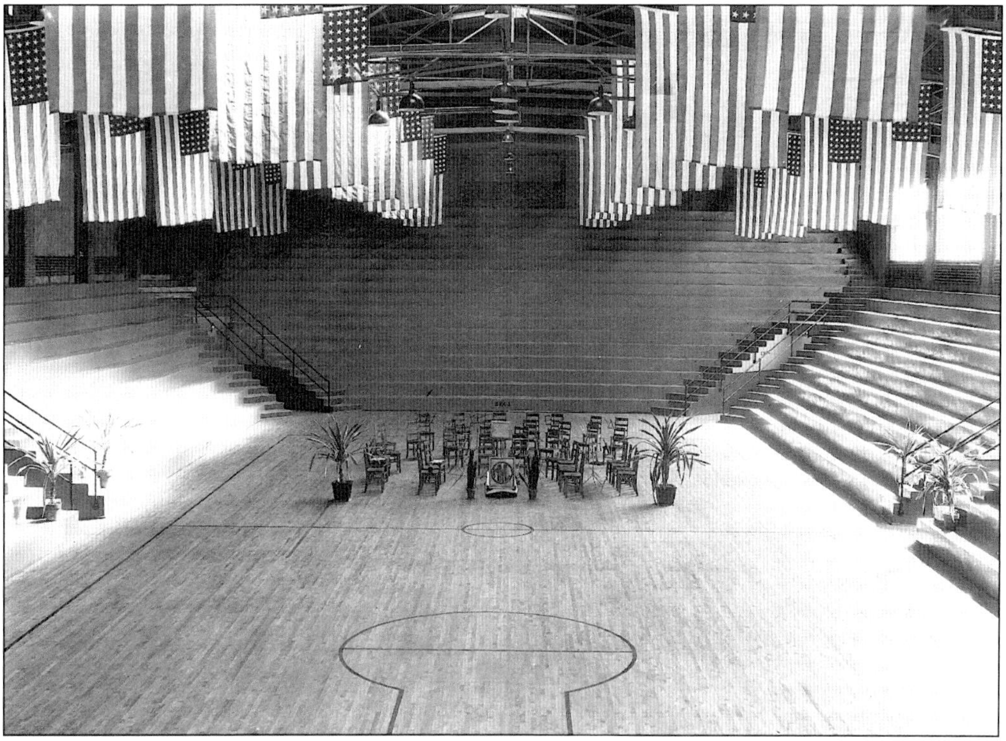

In 1934, the Warner Gymnasium was built by Warner Brothers Studio thanking Sing Sing Prison for allowing a series of gangster movies to be filmed there on location in the 1930s.

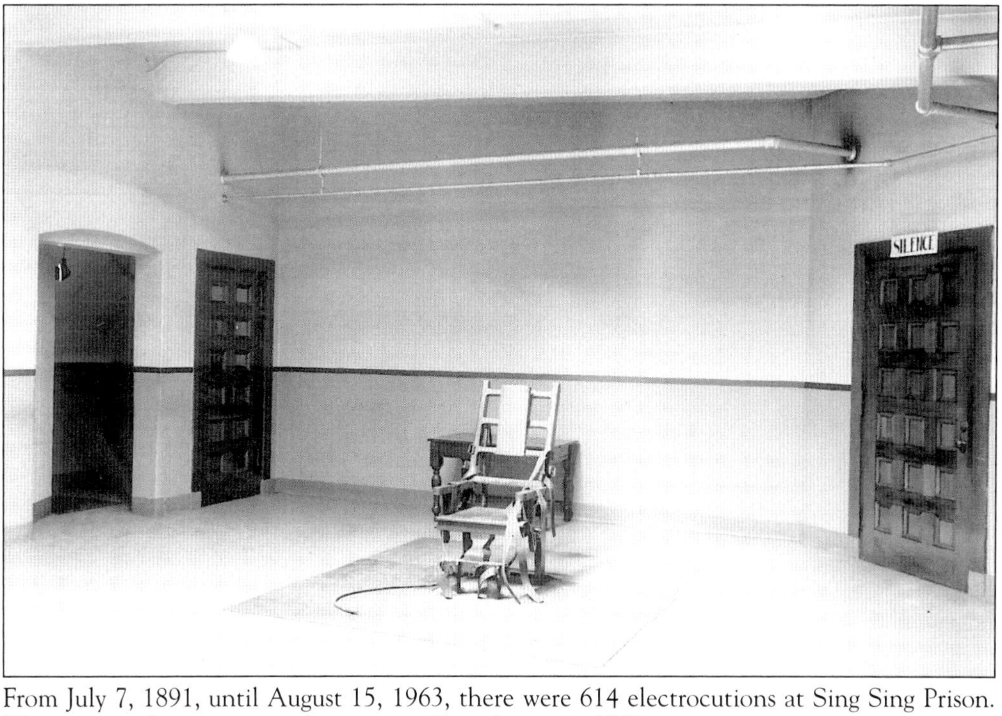

From July 7, 1891, until August 15, 1963, there were 614 electrocutions at Sing Sing Prison. The electric chair was moved upstate to Greenhaven in 1971.

Sing Sing Prison Historical Timeline

1825—A 130-acre site was selected in the Village of Sing Sing at a cost of $20,100.
1825—Captain Elam Lynds, the warden, arrived in the village with 100 inmates from upstate.
1826—A 60-cell prison was completed.
1828—A cell block constructed of local marble was finished.
1830—A wharf was built along Hudson River waterfront.
1831—French philosopher Alexis de Tocqueville visited Sing Sing to study prison reform and the "Auburn System."
1840—A library was established by the Chaplain Reverend John Luckey.
1846—Family visitations were permitted twice a year.
1847—Legislation was approved for two part-time teachers.
1859—The "double celling" of inmates was started.
1862—A law was passed providing inmates time off for good behavior.
1877—A wall around old prison, between railroad tracks and riverfront, was completed.
1880—Prisoners were granted the right to write one letter per month.
1884—Inmate contract labor was abolished by the state.
1897—The classification of prisoners began.
1897—New York State industries started.
1901—The first Parole System was established.
1903—A fingerprinting department starts, along with the "Bertillon Department," or statistics department.
1903—An inside paper, *The Star of Hope* was first printed.
1904—Department of Education initiates its work with the prison system.
1912—Columbus Day was the first holiday inmates spent out of their cells.
1913—The first time prisoners were allowed out of their cells for Sunday recreation.
1914—The "double celling" of inmates was abolished.
1917—Construction started for the "new Sing Sing" on the hill.
1922—Foundations for a wall around the new prison was completed.
1922—A new facility for the condemned finished, and inmates in old the "Death House" were transferred. The new "Death House" had cells for 36 males and 3 females.
1938—A position for Institutional Director of Education was created.
1943—The inmate Soraci was transported to Sing Sing from Clinton (upstate) in order to begin stained glass windows for new Chapel.
1947—Stained glass windows were completed in Catholic Chapel, and plans were underway to put the same type of glass windows in the Protestant Chapel.

(Compiled by Brant L. Kehn, Bob Matuszewski, and Eileen Osis)

Seven

The Hudson River Waterfront

THE RIVERFRONT WAS OUR COASTLINE, THE RIVER OUR SEA. The beaches and docks, in the area from Sparta on the south to Crawbuckie on the north, provided our access to the Hudson. The property adjacent to Sing Sing, just to the north, belonged to Joe Meister. It was a large, overgrown lot of land that once housed a chicken hatchery that jutted out to its own dock from which one could easily view the prison towers and even inmates working outside. At the beginning of that lot was Joe Meister's beach, later known as the P.A.L. Beach (when the Police Athletic League took over). It was here that many of Ossining's inhabitants from the south side of town swam. Typical of all the swimming areas along the rim of town, there was not much of a beach at high tide, and what was there was more pebbly than sandy. The tracks of the New York Central Railroad were within shouting distance of the rocky edge of the river (the southbound portion of the tracks being right alongside the path to the beach).

A couple of hundred yards north of Joe Meister's beach was the brown clapboard Ossining Boat and Canoe Club, one of two boat clubs overhanging the waters. Beyond that point, continuing north, was the Maue Oil Company, whose storage tanks received their supply from "the spiles," or spigots visible from the shores. This is where oil was pumped in from ships that brought the fuel into town. At low tide, the pipelines were visible midway out from the land's edge.

Next was the dock at which the *Sarah Jenks*, Ossining's excursion boat that took the populace to the ocean on summer Sundays, was moored. The tiny beach north of the *Sarah Jenks* was Holden's beach, a fishing spot. Beyond Holden's beach, separated by the Kill Brook that ran through town and emptied into the Hudson, was the Public Dock (at the end of Quimby Street) next to Rand McNally's, which was one of the town's most important employers. When in season, the edge of the dock was lined with people fishing and crabbing. A dock at the end of a boatyard, for a time, boasted a seaplane base, which was located just before the territory of the second (and more prestigious) boat club, the Shattemuc.

Two small areas, Flat Rock and Red Barn, were the last swimming places (used mainly by kids), before the final beach, Crawbuckie, which was frequented mostly by those who lived at the north end of town.

The street running parallel to the first portion of the riverfront, from the railroad station to Shattemuc (with a ramp traversing the tracks at those two places), was Westerly Road, also known as Railroad Avenue. The entire area, from the New York Central lines to the water, was known as "the other side of the tracks." Several important industries were situated here, but for much of the populace it was mainly where one went swimming.

Besides the two ramps mentioned, one at the base of Secor Road (leading to the railroad station), and one at the base of Broadway (pointing toward the Shattemuc), there were two high wooden footbridges. One of these footbridges was located at the bottom of Main Street, pointing toward the *Sarah Jenks*, and one at the base of Central Avenue, connecting with Quimby Street and Rand McNally. Rand McNally were the printers of world maps and atlases, as well as railroad time tables and tickets. Near Rand McNally was Collett-Week-Nibeker, Inc., producer of products like cod liver oil. The employees of the factories on "the other side of the tracks" used the footbridges to get to and from work, before everyone used cars.

Beyond the Broadway footbridge was the extensive property of Brandreth All-Purpose Pills, home also of Manicare personal products, Allcock's Porous Plasters, and Havahart Traps, all of whose wares were known and used throughout the world. The Hudson Wire Mill occupied an entire block of Water Street, paralleling the railroad tracks on the inland side. Impressive edifices and rambling lawns marked the area.

The depot plaza was a vibrant hub, since Ossining was a prime commuter station. One could take an express train to and from Grand Central Station, bypassing all 18 stations in between. Between seven and eight o'clock in the morning and six and seven o'clock in the evening, cars and buses filled the busy area. The line at the counter of the restaurant in Depot Square Hotel was five people deep, all waiting for the morning coffee.

As kids from the south side of town proudly called themselves "Southsiders," those from the waterfront area boastfully called themselves "Dockrats." Games played in the streets like One-Two-Three-One, Kick the Can, Hit the Curb, and Cor-Cor Ringalevio seemed straight out of *Dead End* and were a way of life. Anyone arriving by train for the first time got their impression from the waterfront, the industries, the depot plaza, and the vibrancy of kids at play.

Ossining, from the Indian phrase meaning "stone upon stone," describes the lay of the land that runs from the river up to the hills beyond it. Sing Sing, the original name of the town, was named for the Sint Sinck Indians, and its location was linked to the Sing Sing marble quarries not far from the water's edge.

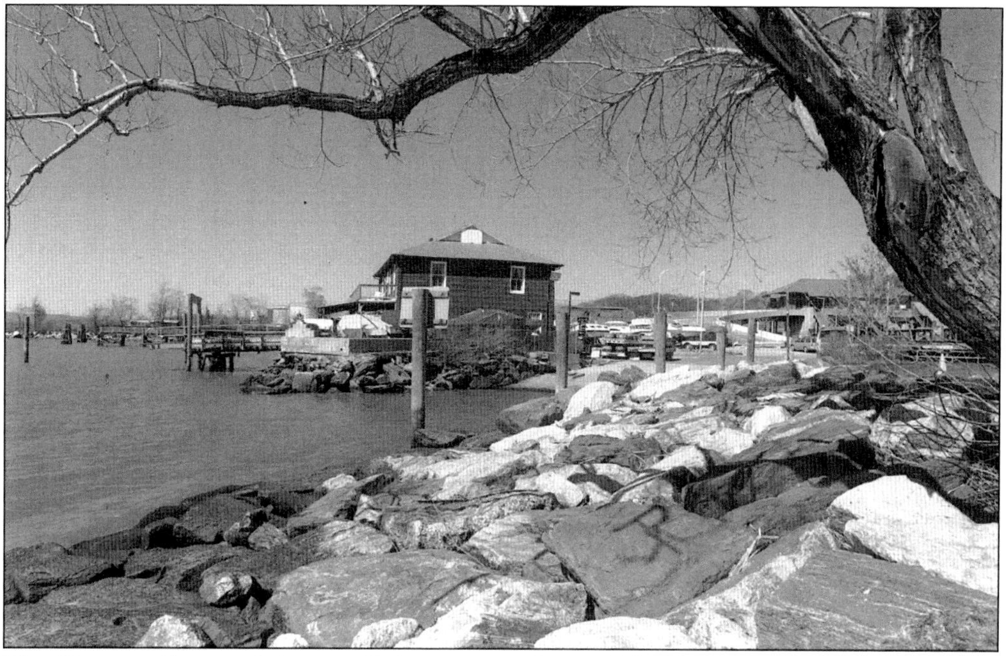

The Ossining Boat and Canoe Club was started in 1905, when a group of local boating enthusiasts began meeting in an old ice house near the Shattemuc Yacht Club. They were officially organized in 1921, and this club house building opened to the membership in 1922. The building is located on Westerly Road across from the railroad station.

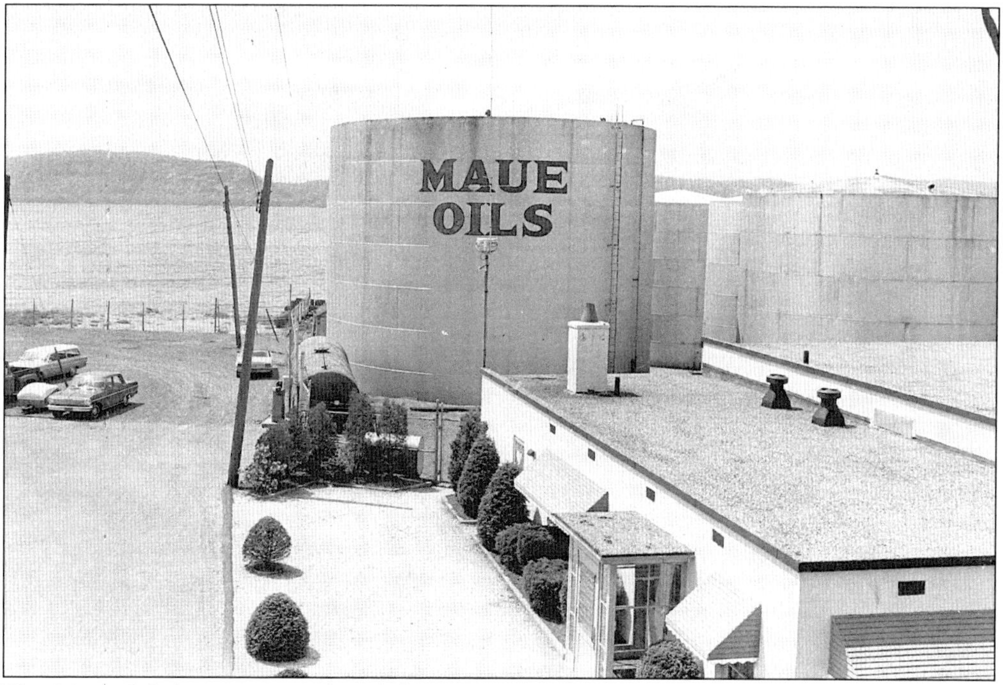

The Maue Oil Company was founded in 1922 by W. Gregory Maue. The firm originally had plants in Rye and Briarcliff Manor. After consolidating them, the company moved to Westerly Road around 1930. The area is now being developed into a commercial and residential complex.

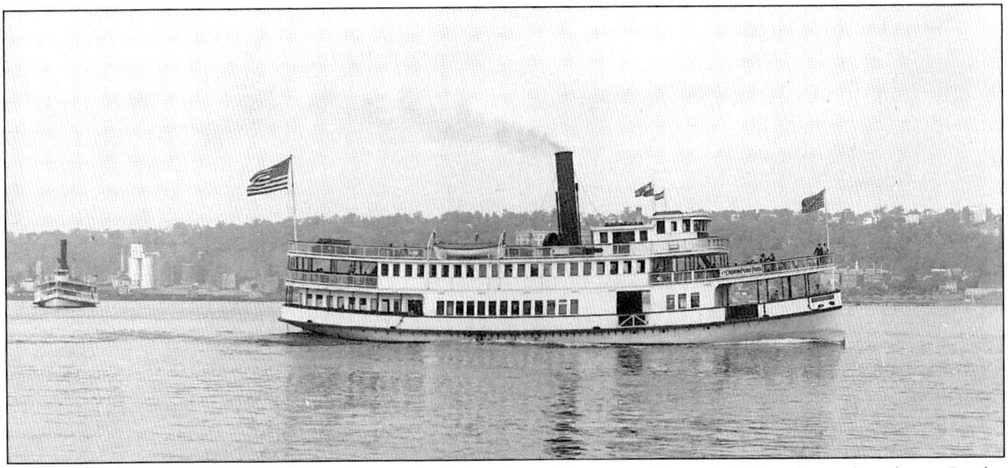

The *Sarah A. Jenks*, known locally as the "Sarah A.," was built in 1885, when the three Jenks brothers, who owned a fleet of river steamboats, named their new vessel after their mother. The vessel was used to haul freight and passengers between New York City and Ossining. A one-way ticket cost 25¢, and the trip, according to tides, took about two and a half hours. A typical day's cargo consisted of pickles, cotton gins, cider, files, iron pipes, pills, porous plasters, shoes, stoves, apples, and people. The punctuality of its departure was a legend. At 7 a.m., a warning signal of three long blasts sounded, and exactly 15 minutes later (so punctual that townspeople set their watches by it), three short blasts were sounded and the ship was underway.

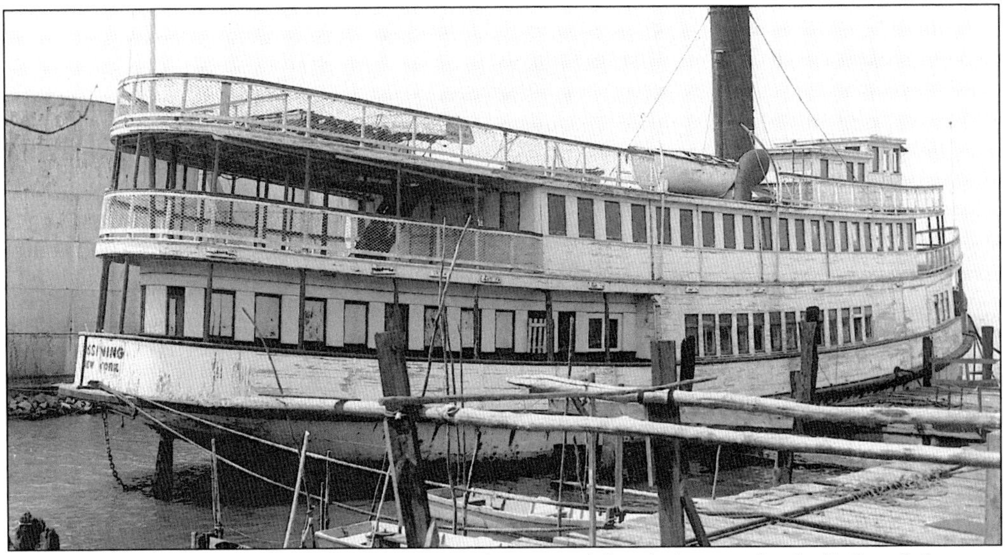

In 1913, a fire razed the decks of the "Sarah A." and leveled it to the hull. Local firemen contained the blaze and it was rebuilt in Hoboken, New Jersey, and renamed the *Ossining*. During WW I, the boat was used by the government to carry troops, wounded soldiers, and the remains of those killed in action within New York harbor. After the war in 1918, the *Ossining* resumed freight runs. With the coming of trucks to haul goods, the freight business collapsed. Thereafter, the vessel was used for excursions including a year's service on the Statue of Liberty run from Battery Park. The *Ossining* is seen here docked on the waterfront next to the Maue Oil Company. In 1949, as it was being towed down the Hudson to Jersey City to be converted into a commercial fishing vessel, another fire broke out opposite the village of Tarrytown, and it burned to the waterline.

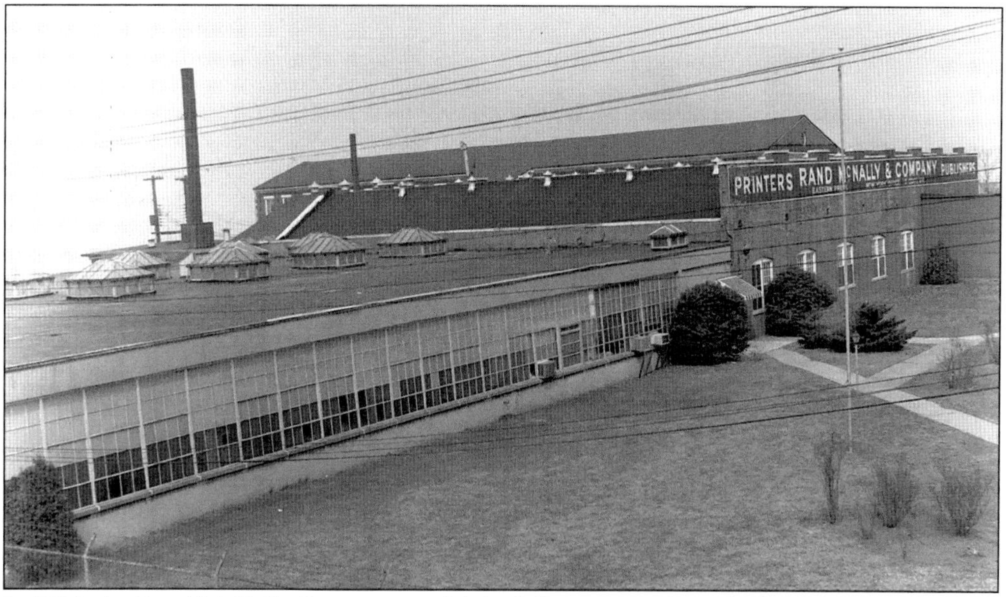

In 1910, the Rand McNally Company established their eastern branch plant in Ossining. Their first effort was the western portion of the company located in Chicago, Illinois. The company specialized in printing varied items including textbooks, maps, catalogs, and tickets for many events, and it was located on the corner of Westerly Road and Quimby Street.

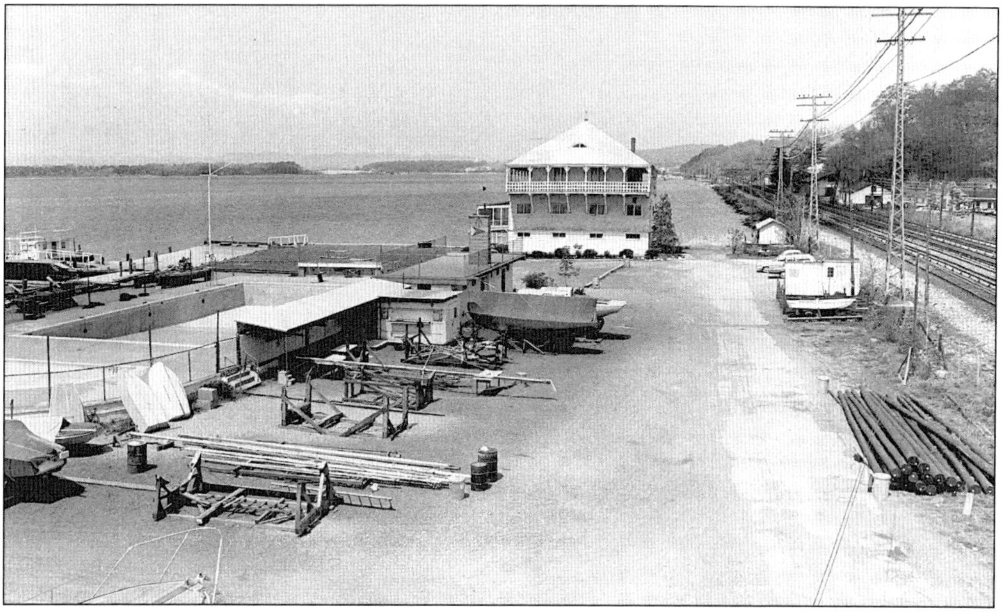

The Shattemuc Yacht and Canoe Club was organized in 1887. It began with 35 members and 3 small cat-boats. Sailboats were added within a few years, and the club merged into the Ossining Yacht Club. Two clubhouses on the riverfront were erected. The clubhouse shown here was the third on the same site. The group also had a clubroom on Main Street where billiards and pool were available during the winter months. When the name of the village changed from Sing Sing to Ossining, the club changed its title to include Canoe, as a number of canoeists were among the new members. This structure was destroyed by fire in 1973.

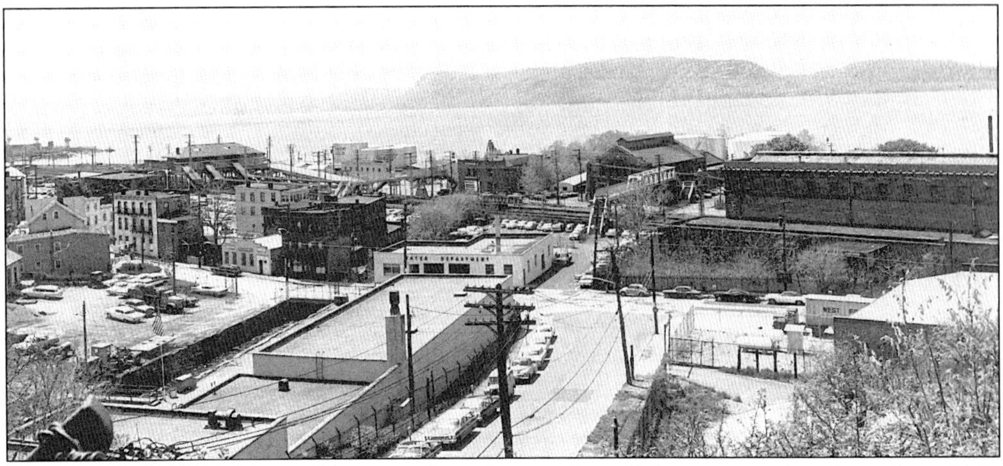

This c. 1950s birds-eye view of the waterfront depicts Central Avenue running down the middle of the photograph. Note the two pedestrian bridges crossing the railroad tracks to the riverfront and the Ossining Train Station to the left.

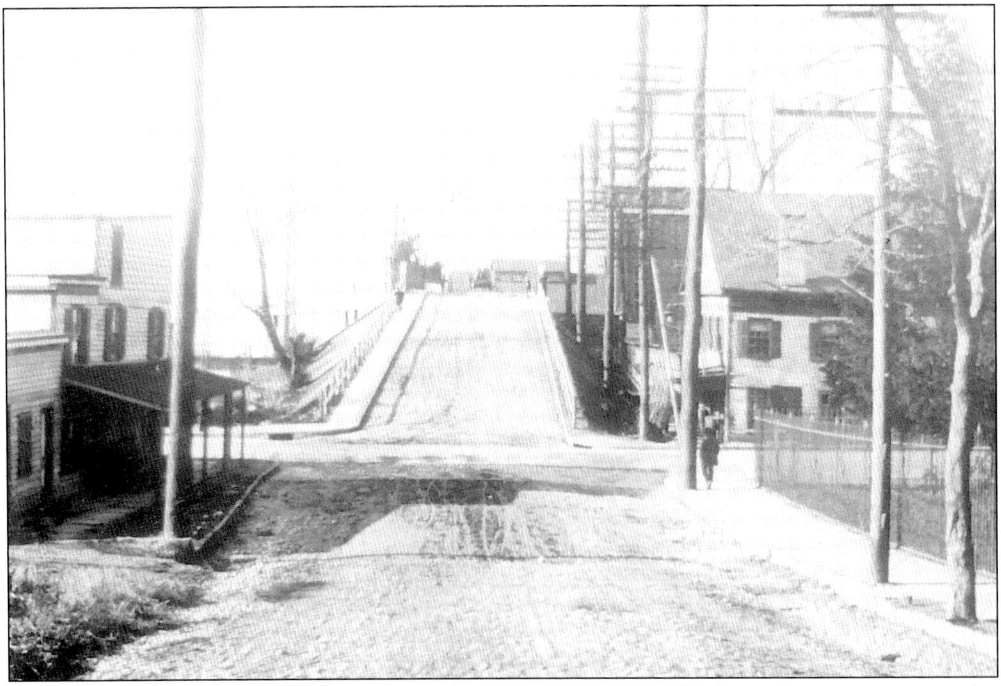

This image presents a view looking west from Broadway towards the wide ramp crossing the Hudson River Railroad tracks. South Water Street is seen here running from left to right.

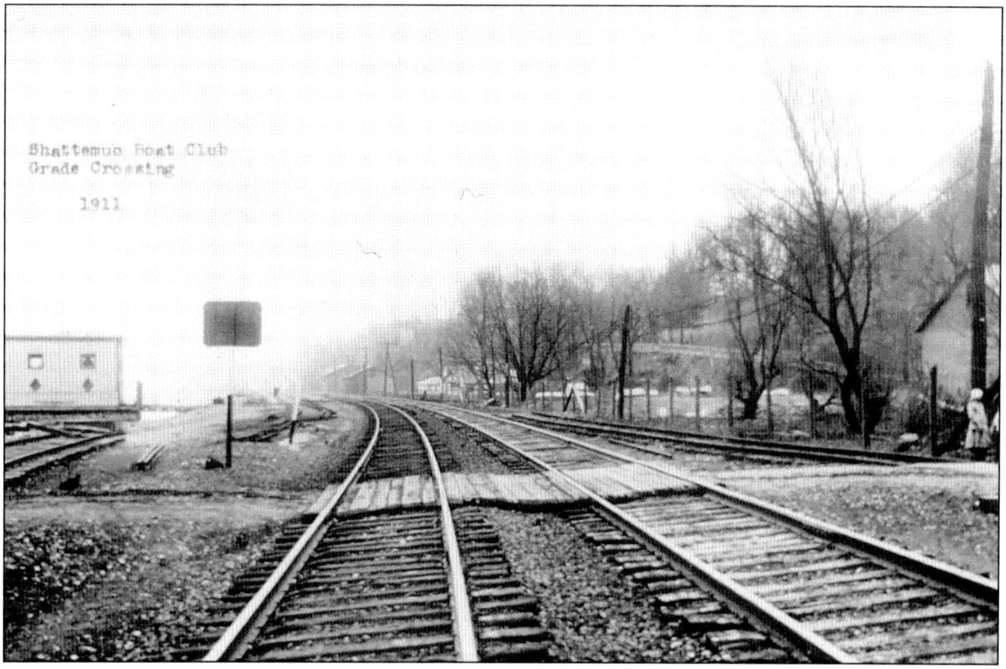

The tracks of the New York Central Railroad are represented here looking north towards Croton-Harmon in 1914. The Shattemuc Yacht Club is to the left of the image, and a wooden pedestrian crossing over the tracks (as well as Brandreth Park) is to the right.

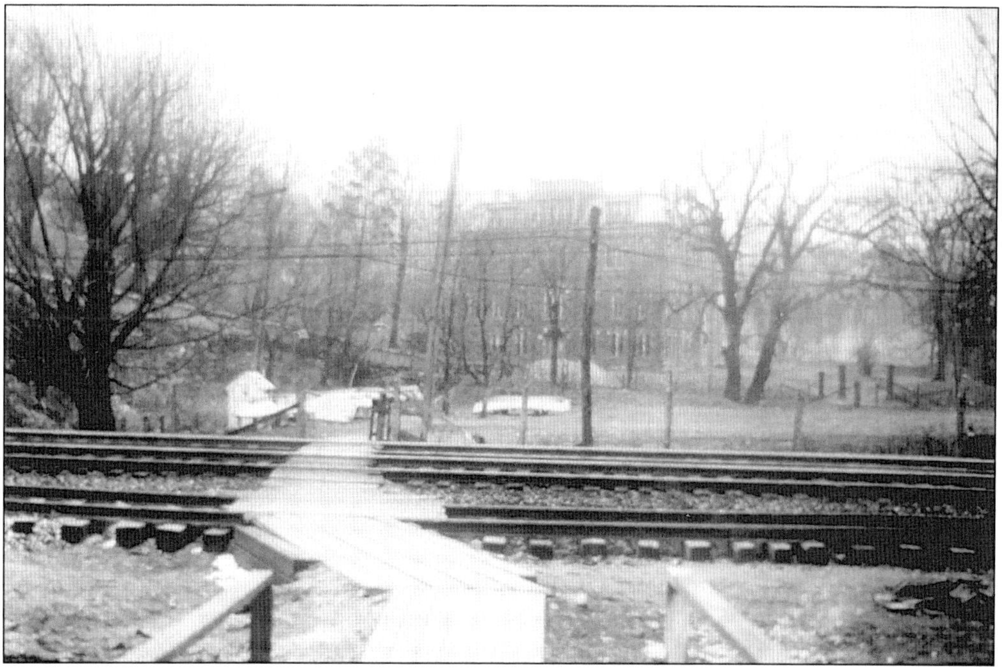

A zigzag railroad crossing is shown here looking east from the Hudson River towards the Vireun School, on lower Snowden Avenue. Later, this was the site of the Sterizol Manufacturing Company, producer of antiseptic powders and salve.

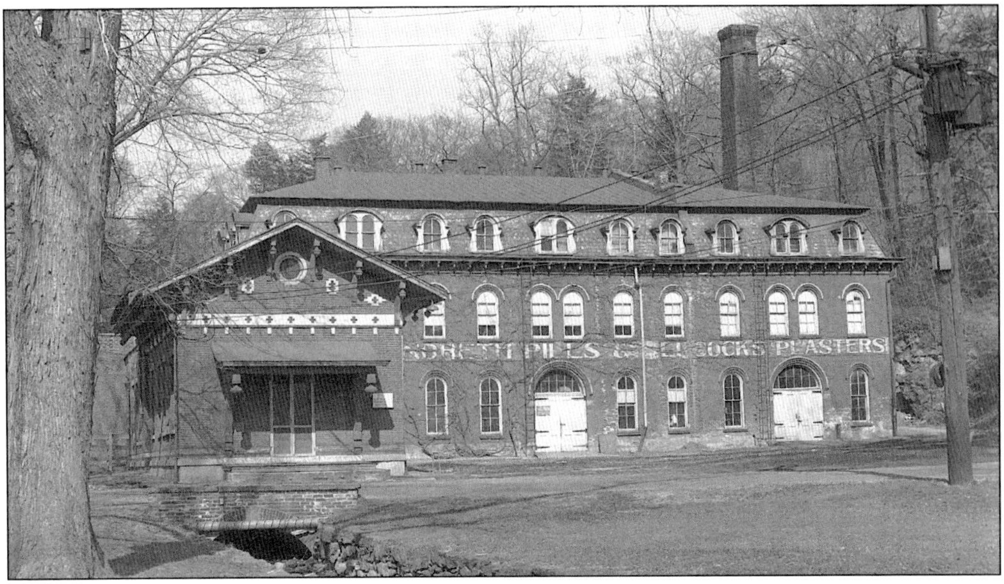

The Brandreth Pill Factory was one of the most successful companies in Westchester County. The factory, located on North Water Street, manufactured Brandreth's All-Purpose Pills, Allcock's Porous Plasters, and Havahart Traps. Constructed around 1850, the factory included a towering brick chimney overlooking the roof on one side and graced by a water wheel on the other. It is done in the Italianate Revival style, with a Second French Empire mansard roof, and is listed on the National Register of Historic Places.

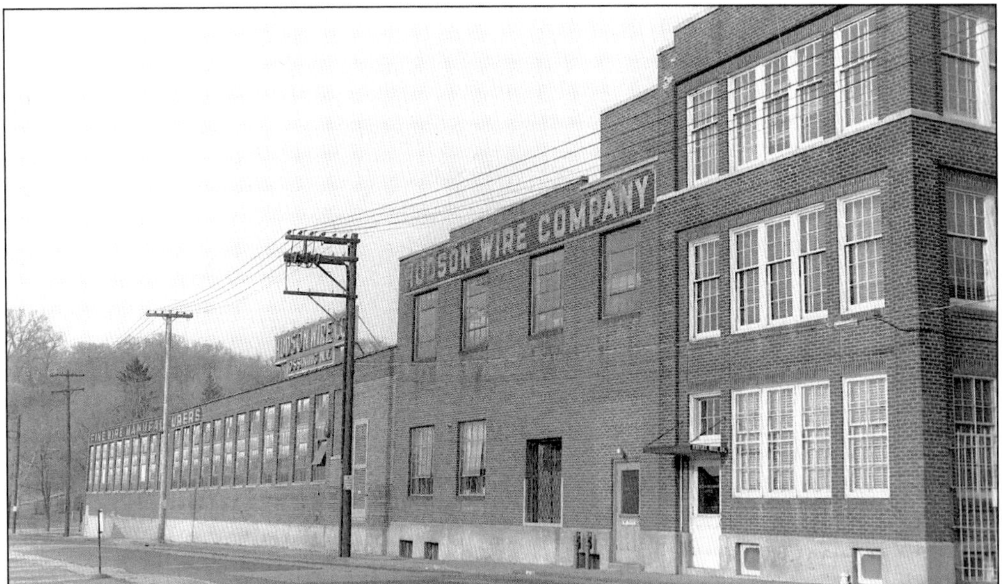

The Hudson Wire Company was founded in 1902, under the name of Royle and Akin, and started business in Newark, New Jersey. With rapidly increasing demands for wire, the enterprise moved to this larger plant in Ossining in 1904. The company pioneered many wire machines and processes that are in general use throughout the industry today. Services included plating wire, drawing and stranding facilities, and magnet wire, which was started in 1931. The complex was located on Water Street between Central Avenue and Broadway.

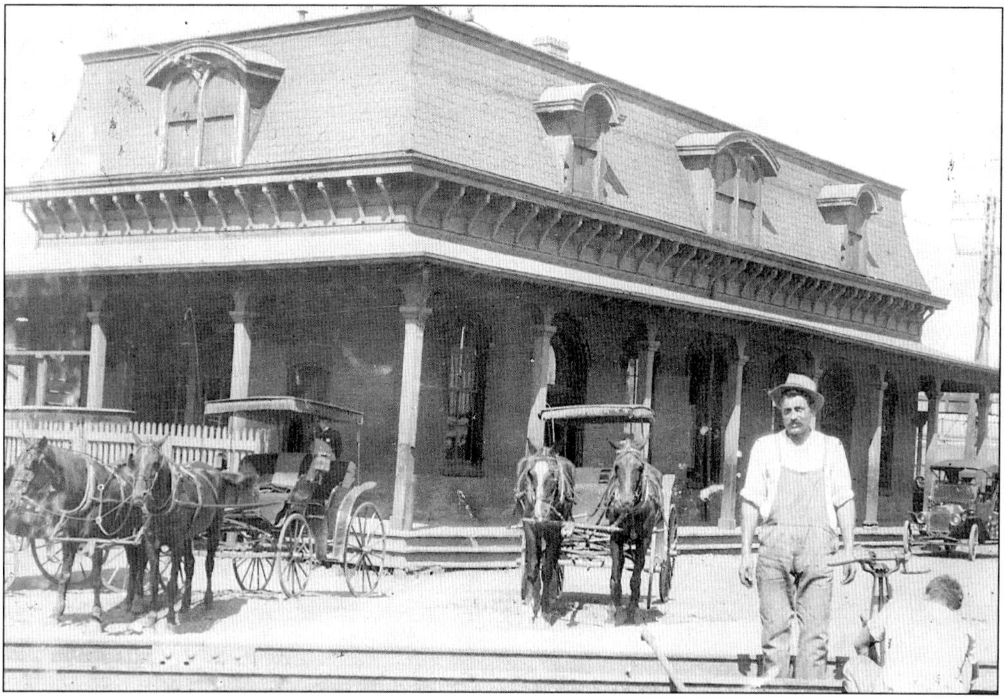

The first New York Central and Hudson River Railroad station in Sing Sing, seen here in 1914, was located in the plaza on the east side of the tracks. Built in the late 1800s, the station featured a Second French Empire concave mansard roof, wooden gingerbread trim, slate fish-scale shingles, and arched dormer windows. Horse drawn taxis stand in front of the station. Workmen are repairing rails for the Hudson River and Eastern Traction Company, Ossining's last trolley that went out of business in 1924, as the first bus company arrived in town. The railroad came through the village in 1851, built largely by Irish immigrants who had earlier completed the Croton Aqueduct. The telegraph came with the railroad and was located inside the building.

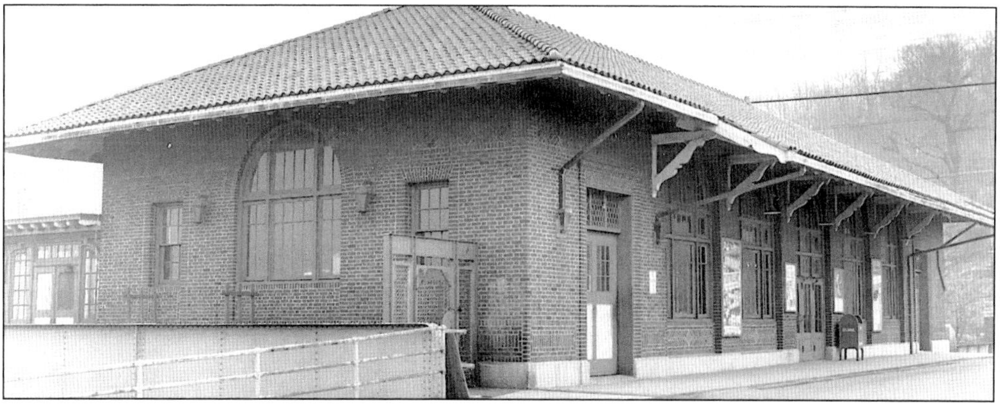

Constructed in 1914, the new railroad station was designed in the Classical style, as were stations in Yonkers, Ludlow, Glenwood, and Hastings. Rather than being characterized by stone, like those in Dobbs Ferry, Irvington, Tarrytown, and Greystone, Ossining's building featured red bricks and a hipped roof sheathed in clay tiles. It was sited so as to be one full story above the level of the tracks and span them east to west. The ramp and overpass allowed pedestrians to pass safely.

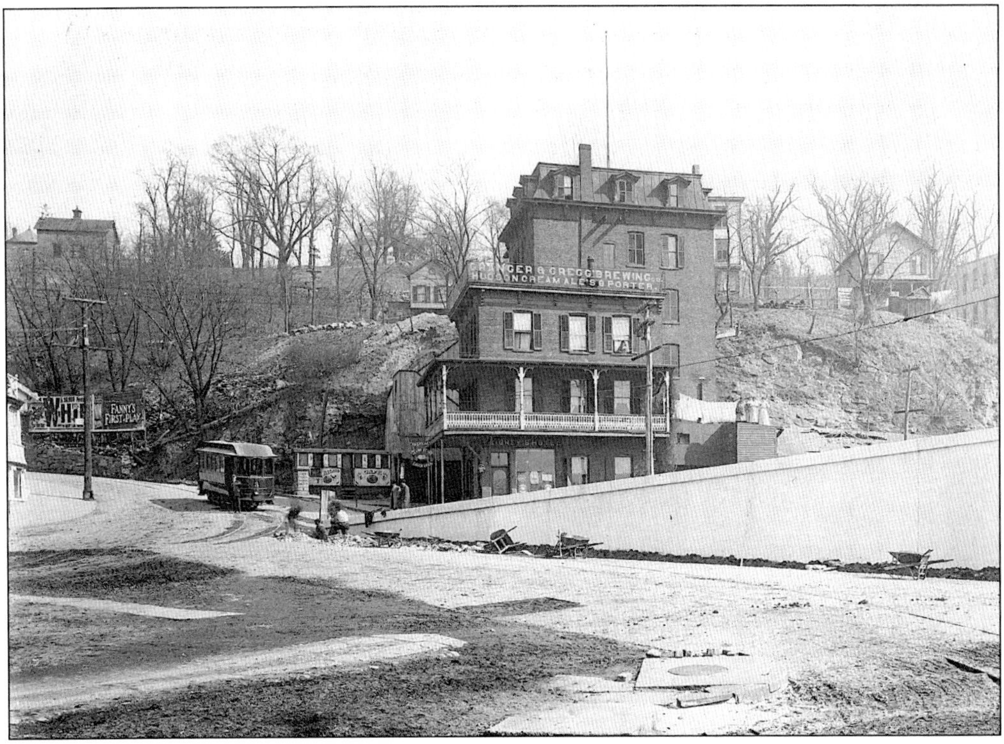

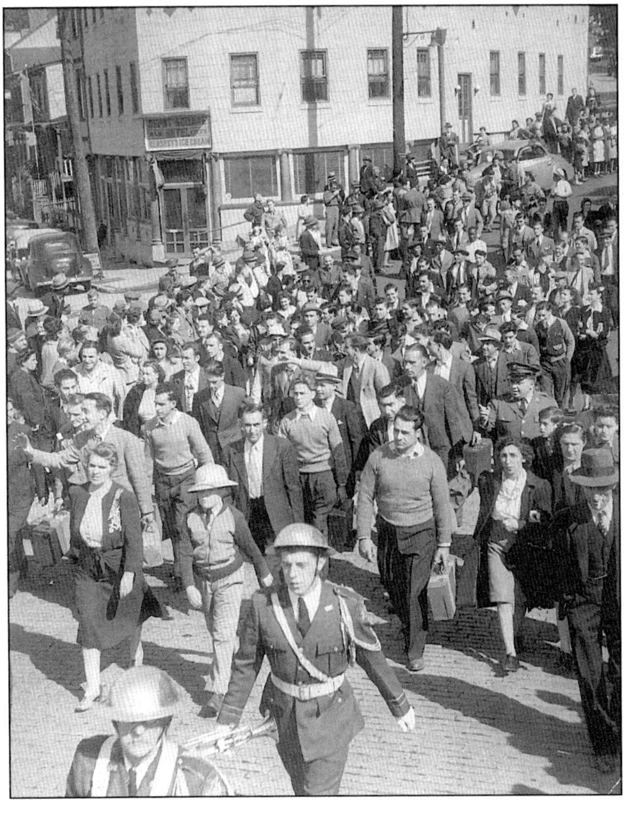

This *c.* 1914 photograph of the Railroad Station Plaza shows the trolley at the bottom of Secor Road and the newly constructed concrete ramp leading up to the station, across to the west side of the tracks. The five story Rigney Hotel is to the right of the photograph with Hunter Street at the top.

Shown here is another contingent of Ossining residents leaving for induction into the armed forces in 1942. They are seen at the bottom of Secor Road with the Depot Square Hotel in the background. The first few lines are approaching the ramp leading up to the railroad station.

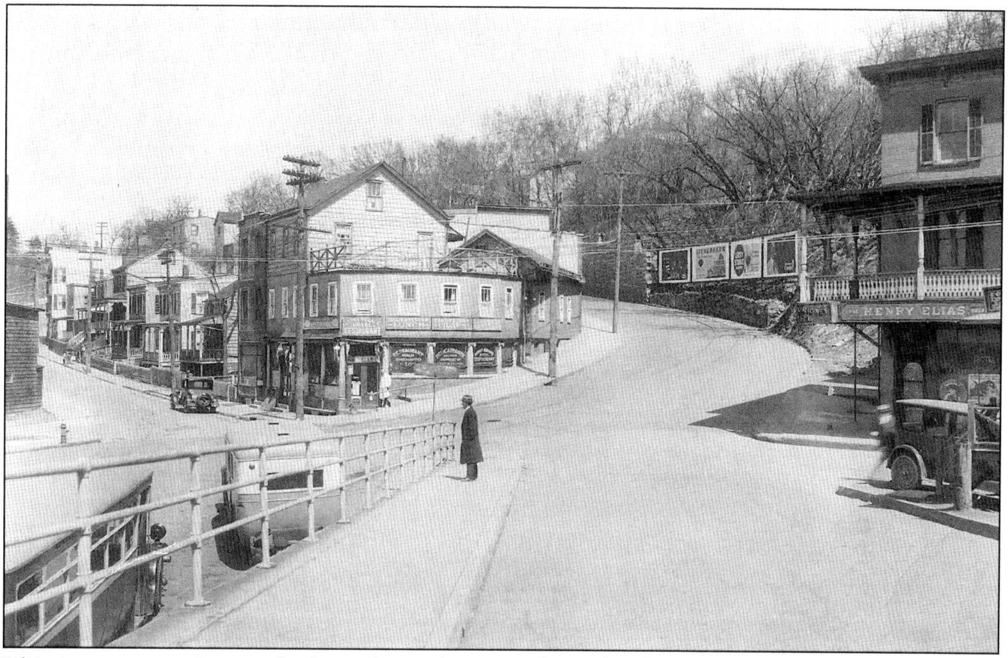

This is a panoramic view looking down the ramp from the Ossining Railroad Station towards Secor Road leading uptown to the village. The Rigney Hotel is on the right corner, Depot Square Hotel is in the center, and Water Street is off to the left of the image.

For anyone arriving in Ossining by train, there was no missing Depot Square Hotel, which stood as a sentinel at the base of the railroad ramp and Secor Road that led up to the town itself. As a one-of-a-kind restaurant, bar and grill, and small hotel, it stood directly opposite the Ossining Railroad Station, resembling a kind of fortress, with its crenelated right wall on Secor Road, and a workshoe, because of its higher left side on Water Street.

Although there were rooms for transients, the small hotel housed mainly year-round tenants who took their meals in the restaurant downstairs. The restaurant was a hub for breakfast for commuters in the morning and lunches for the many workers in the area. During the day, wives and mothers of Sing Sing inmates stopped in for refreshment before and after their visits. Visiting dignitaries and movie stars often stopped by the colorful place. The restaurant supplied the food for the casts of many movies made at and about the world famous prison, notably *Castle on the Hudson* and *Kiss of Death*. Edward G. Robinson, Ann Sheridan, John Garfield, Rudy Vallee, and Alice Faye were some actors who ate there. The families of "Murder Inc.," a group of famous New York City gangsters, ate there each week.

In 1934, an out-of-town bus filled with tourists roared down Secor Road, up the railroad station ramp, crashed through the guard rail, and hurled to the ground 35 feet below as the bus burst into flames, killing 19 people and injuring 26. Following the famous bus crash and fire, the survivors were moved into Depot Square, where they were given emergency treatment. At the time of the "Murder Inc." electrocution at Sing Sing in 1944, reporters from every newspaper in New York City made the place their center of operations, regularly calling in the latest information as the governor's word was awaited. During a political demonstration concerning the noted Rosenburg trial in 1952, Depot Square was used as headquarters for the police and FBI.

Bill and Bess Globerman owned and operated Depot Square Hotel from 1921 to 1956. During this time, the establishment underwent many physical changes that transformed what had been a second floor beer garden into hotel rooms and created the crenelated concrete structure from the earlier wooden one. When a fire damaged the 100-year-old building in 1977, the headlines and story of the event filled the front page of local newspapers.

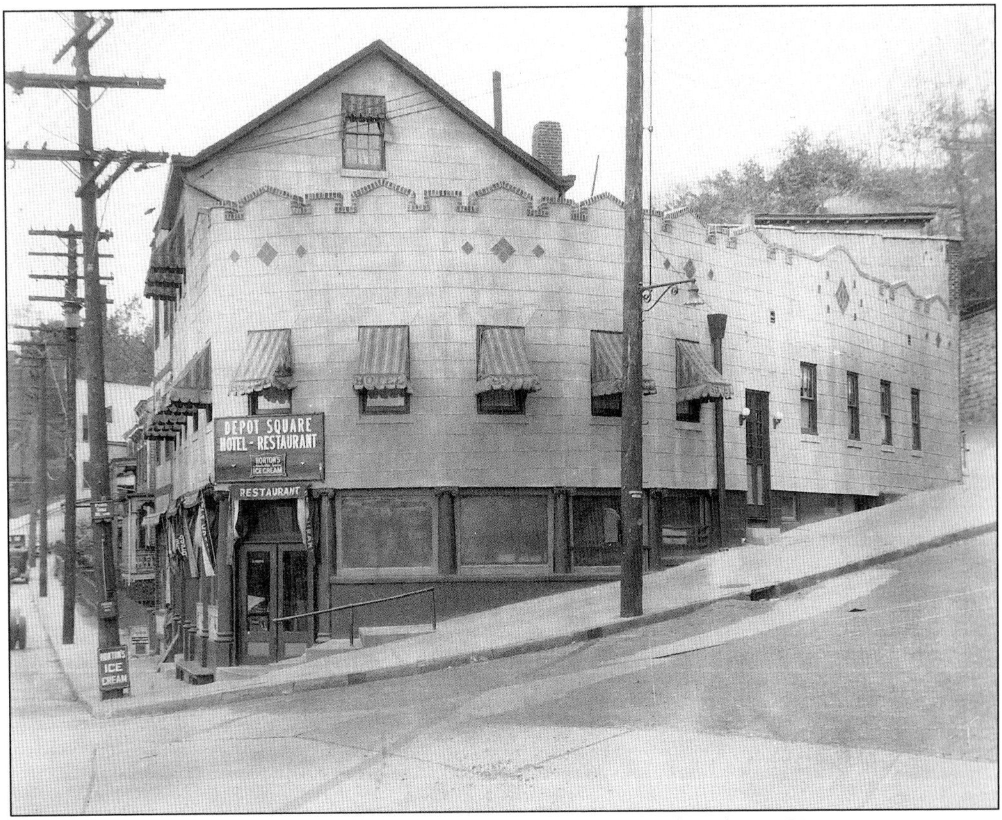

Depot Square Hotel and Restaurant is shown here as it appeared in the 1930s.